AF386402

THE ODYSSEY

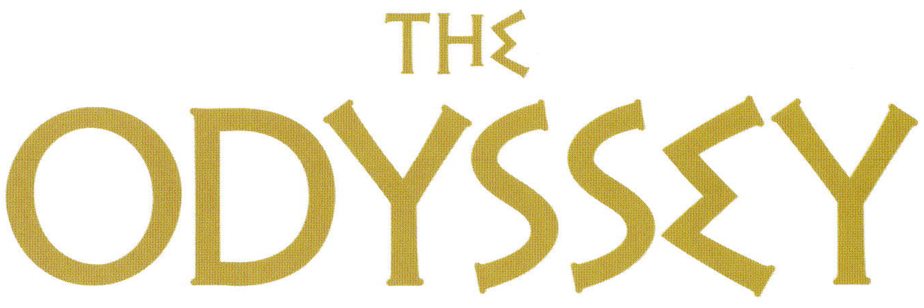

AN ILLUSTRATED GUIDE

A CHARACTER-BY-CHARACTER GUIDE TO THE STORY OF ODYSSEUS

DOUG METZGER, PhD

Host of the *Literature and History* Podcast

ILLUSTRATED BY

CHARLI VINCE

ADAMS MEDIA

NEW YORK   AMSTERDAM/ANTWERP   LONDON   TORONTO
SYDNEY/MELBOURNE   NEW DELHI

Adams Media
An Imprint of Simon & Schuster, LLC
100 Technology Center Drive
Stoughton, MA 02072

First Adams Media hardcover edition June 2026

Interior design by Kellie Emery
Illustrations by Charli Vince
Interior images © Adobe Stock/ayaidu, Lupascoroman, Konstantin; 123RF/Peterhermesfurian

Manufactured in the United States of America

1 2026

Library of Congress Cataloging-in-Publication Data has been applied for.

ISBN 978-1-5072-2645-2
ISBN 978-1-5072-2646-9 (ebook)

Let's stay in touch!
Scan here to get book recommendations, exclusive offers, and more delivered to your inbox.

CONTENTS

INTRODUCTION

For 2,700 years, across continents and cultures, the *Odyssey* has been a story for everyone. The ancient Greek epic tells the celebrated tale of a swashbuckling hero and his adventures on the deep blue sea—a saga about monsters and gods, a son finding his father, and a king coming home to take back his kingdom. But like many great stories, the *Odyssey* isn't as straightforward as it first seems. Odysseus is a strange, complicated man. He is not a white knight, out to help those in need. By the epic's end, the main character has worn so many disguises and told so many lies and half-truths that it's hard to tell whether even Odysseus himself knows exactly who he is.

The Odyssey: An Illustrated Guide is a voyage through the heroes, gods, nymphs, monsters, and commoners of the *Odyssey*. We'll meet them in roughly the order in which they appear in Homer's original story. Like Odysseus himself, the characters who surround the epic's central hero have many dimensions. The good guys, very often, aren't so good. The villains, just as often, aren't wicked through and through. From major characters, like Odysseus and Penelope, down to figures with smaller roles, like the Cyclops, Circe, Nausicaa, and Helen of Troy, the *Odyssey*'s sprawling cast has fascinated readers for thousands of years. Whether you studied the epic in school or only know bits of the story, this companion book will introduce you to all of them.

We'll meet the Homeric gods Zeus and Athena. We'll get to know scrappy young Telemachus, trying his best to find his father, Odysseus, in spite of the man's twenty-year absence. We'll learn about Penelope, the cornered queen, and the suitors trying to marry her. And as we come to know the *Odyssey*'s cast, we'll also explore the story of the *Odyssey* itself, a tale that twists and turns as its many characters encounter one another.

The Homeric gods are immortal, but really, all Homeric characters are immortal. In the millennia since the epic was written, this cast has lived on, appearing in poems, plays, statues, and paintings as later generations have revered ancient Greece's most beloved story.

Just as they did to readers centuries ago, the characters of the *Odyssey* still hold lessons for us today. Odysseus himself ultimately embodies the virtues of intelligence and resilience. Penelope remains dignified and noble, in spite of being mistreated by nearly everyone around her. Even minor figures, like energetic old Nestor, kind Nausicaa, and wise, weathered Menelaus, are admirable in their own timeless ways. And while we'll appreciate the ageless qualities of the *Odyssey*'s characters in this book, we'll also do the opposite, and explore what makes them ancient Greek. Immortal as the *Odyssey* is, it was also the product of a very specific age and culture, and the book's smallest details sometimes hold wondrous lessons about the ancient past.

BACKGROUND & HISTORICAL CONTEXT

In this section, you'll find a brief overview of the ancient Greek world the *Odyssey* arose from—and actually helped create. You'll also learn more about how the Homeric epics were performed orally ages ago, and why they've stood the test of time. In addition, you'll discover the ties between the *Odyssey* and its companion epic, the *Iliad*, and read through a clear synopsis of the *Odyssey*'s plot, timeline, and geography before you begin meeting its principal characters.

UNDERSTANDING THE TIME PERIOD

The *Odyssey* was first set down in its current form between about 725 and 625 BCE. If you're new to ancient Greek history, these dates don't mean much. What's important to understand for anyone interested in the Homeric epics is that they came along very *early* in ancient Greek history. Their appearance in written form coincides with the adoption of the phonetic alphabet in ancient Greece, which means that almost as soon as writing began to flourish in the Aegean world, it was used to record the story of Odysseus. The following timeline provides an overview of both when the events that inspired the *Odyssey* may have taken place and when the epic was actually written.

In a way, the Homeric epics *created* ancient Greece, just as much as they were created *by* ancient Greece. During the Classical period, when Socrates and Plato lived and the Parthenon was built and Athenian democracy reached its apex, the Homeric epics were already three hundred years old, and they'd been a part of the society of the ancient Aegean for a long time.

		Events
1800 BCE		
1700 BCE		
1600 BCE	**MYCENAEAN PERIOD**	
1500 BCE	(circa 1750–1200 BCE)	
1400 BCE		
1300 BCE		
1200 BCE		
1100 BCE	**BRONZE AGE COLLAPSE AND GREEK DARK AGE**	*Events of Homeric epics take place*
1000 BCE		
900 BCE	(circa 1200–800 BCE)	
800 BCE		
700 BCE	**ARCHAIC PERIOD**	*Phonetic alphabet usage grows in Greece*
600 BCE	(circa 800–480 BCE)	**725–625 BCE Homeric epics written**
500 BCE		
400 BCE	**CLASSICAL PERIOD**	*What most people think of when they think of "ancient Greece" (Plato, Socrates, etc.)*
300 BCE	(480–323 BCE)	
200 BCE	**HELLENISTIC PERIOD**	
100 BCE	(323–31 BCE)	
1 CE		

WHO WAS HOMER?

If you've heard of the *Odyssey*, you've probably heard it described as "Homer's *Odyssey*." Who was Homer, though?

For most of history, it has been accepted that a blind poet from the eastern Aegean island of Chios wrote both the *Odyssey* and its companion epic, the *Iliad*. Homer was a revered figure in the ancient Greek world, imagined as the genius who set in motion a great many subsequent stories, and thousands of years later, scholarship on the *Iliad* and *Odyssey* still calls them the "Homeric epics." Today, however, more often than not, the accepted theory is that both Homeric epics were ensemble productions that came together over a very long time frame. This theory has been around since 1795, when the German classicist Friedrich August Wolf published it in a book called *Prolegomena ad Homerum*.

Some people still argue for single Homeric authorship, while others believe he wrote one of the poems but not the other. From archaeology, to the careful study of Homeric language, to consideration of some of the objects described in the *Iliad* and *Odyssey*, a lot of work has gone into trying to figure out who wrote these epics. After a great deal of research, the general opinion today is that the *Iliad* and *Odyssey* are very old stories with roots way back in the 1100s BCE that, like metal on a blacksmith's anvil, were tempered and tempered over eons of performances until they reached their current written form between 725 and 625 BCE. Speaking of performances, let's discuss how we would have experienced the story of the *Odyssey* if we were ancient Greeks.

ANCIENT GREEK PERFORMANCE CULTURE

Although today people usually read the *Odyssey* in book form, the experience would have been very different in 600 or 500 BCE. Ancient Greek audiences most often encountered stories like the *Odyssey* during public performances, rather than reading them. In earlier centuries, the Greek alphabet was relatively new and unstandardized, and throughout all of antiquity, a box of papyrus scrolls that contained the entire poem would have been ridiculously expensive. The *Odyssey*, more than twelve thousand lines long, or five hundred pages, depending on the translation you're reading, had to be hand copied during ancient times. Additionally, reading the *Odyssey* wouldn't have made sense, anyway: The *Odyssey* was a song.

Here's how people actually encountered the *Odyssey* during the Archaic period. In the ancient Greek world, people got together to hang out. They socialized at house parties, in villages and town squares, and in shrines and temples built in picturesque places where fresh water and nice views drew people in, and wine, food, and good company kept them there. People celebrated seasonal occasions—planting, harvesting, the opening of the previous season's wine, and the departure of merchant ships when the seas grew calm in the spring. And at all of these gatherings, there was an entertainment industry.

The ancient Greek entertainment industry included musicians, singers, dancers, and storytellers, and, among them, a cast of professional narrators whom we call "bards." These bards, wielding simple harp-family instruments called "lyres" and "kitharas," sang songs and narrative poems to audiences. Bards collaborated with musicians and dancers, and these entertainers were compensated for their work in various fashions, including tips from audiences. As a bard, the better you were, the more money you made, and so there was an incentive for virtuoso retellings, and for making existing poems better and better.

We know from what survives of the earliest Greek poetry that bards sang all sorts of songs. They sang tunes about ancient Greek heroes. They performed numbers that bragged about how great they were, or how stupid their rivals were. They offered ditties that were written for specific occasions, congratulating athletes on victories, spouses on weddings, or party guests on birthdays. They sang graphic songs with adult themes. But of all the many songs ancient Greek bards performed, perhaps the most famous today are the Homeric epics themselves.

Since stories like the *Odyssey* are so long, bards did not perform them all the way through. (A staging of the *Odyssey*, according to one recent scholar, would have taken 20–25 hours.) Instead, a bard might perform a *scene* from the *Odyssey*, singing, for instance, about Odysseus getting past the Sirens, or Odysseus meeting his old dog. These excerpts would be mixed in with other poetry, in variety shows that also included other performers. Such multimedia stage performances were beloved by all of antiquity, and their great popularity is why a precious handful of stories like the Homeric epics were passed down and still exist today.

THE STRUCTURE AND RHYTHM OF THE *ODYSSEY*

Today, the *Odyssey* is broken down into twenty-four books, with "books" essentially meaning "chapters" rather than printed volumes sitting on shelves. It's a work of verse (in other words, lines of poetry), and though each line has a specific meter, the *Odyssey*'s language has no rhymes. In ancient Greece and Rome, fictional stories were, up until the Common Era, generally told in verse, while nonfictional works, like philosophy and history, were written in prose.

The greatest value that poetry had over prose in antiquity was that poetry was easier to memorize. Today, we think of rhyme and meter (and poetry more generally) as flowery and ornamental. In oral cultures like Homer's, however, poetry was a database used for preserving information, and rhyme and meter were the mnemonic technologies that powered that database. Ancient Greek poets were masters of using the rhythms and sounds implicit in language to write poetry that *sounded* beautiful, but that *also* contained interior patterns that helped make it easier to memorize.

THE METER USED IN THE *ODYSSEY*

The specific meter used in the *Odyssey* is called "dactylic hexameter." A dactyl is a metrical foot with one long syllable followed by two short syllables, like "OD-yss-ey," "IL-i-ad," "FI-re-fly," or "AL-li-son." "Hexameter" means that there are six dactyls in the line. The Homeric epics, from end to end, are written in highly structured language like this.

1	2	3	4	5	6
HERE is one,	THIS is a	LINE in which	EACH foot is	US ually	DACTYL.

The *Odyssey* is made up of twelve thousand of these units, though ancient Greeks substituted dactyls for another kind of metrical foot called spondees in the middles and ends of lines, depending on context (in the earlier example, the final foot is a spondee, rather than a dactyl, which was an ordinary part of Archaic Greek meter). Poetic jargon aside, the original language of the *Odyssey* has a strong rhythmic beat, and its rhythm was part of what drew ancient audiences in.

EPITHETS

Another central element of Homeric poetry is the epithet. (An epithet is a description added to someone's name, as in "Richard the Lionheart.") The *Odyssey* uses repeated epithets, like πολύτλας δῖος Ὀδυσσεύς (po-LYT-lass

DI-os o-DYSS-eus, or "much-suffering godlike Odysseus"), and ποδάρκης δῖος Ἀχιλλεὺς (po-DAR-kes DI-os a-KELL-eus, or "swift-footed godlike Achilles"). These epithets, repeated dozens of times throughout Homer's stories and constructed with carefully metered language, helped poets remember long sequences of lines, and just as importantly, helped audience members recall who was who in Homer's large casts of characters.

Besides meter and epithets, Homeric poetry is sometimes built of larger modular blocks. When characters offer sacrifices to the gods, for instance, the *Iliad* and *Odyssey* reuse identical selections of text, or nearly identical ones. The same is the case with sequences involving heroes armoring, and characters bathing, praying, sailing, or sharing meals. If you were a Homeric bard who needed to describe a hero armoring, you could simply deploy a prefabricated slab of lines, and audiences may have even enjoyed these repetitious aspects of ancient Greek narrative poetry.

In summation, the language of Homer's *Odyssey* was carefully structured, and this structuring was crucial to helping performers keep hours and hours of narrative poetry memorized. Today, we might have the lyrics to a few songs memorized, but in 700 BCE, ancient Greek bards were brilliant products of a literary tradition built on memorization and oral delivery, and with training, simple musical instruments, and the modest handful of tools we've just discussed, they could entertain crowds for hours.

TIMELESS ELEMENTS OF HOMERIC POETRY

Today, while we don't get to hear lyres, or see ancient Greek dancers when we read Homer's *Odyssey*, we still get to enjoy a lot of the same magic that the poem's original audiences did. Like a modern novel or movie, the *Odyssey* engages its reader by changing scenes. Here, we are atop Mount Olympus, listening to a conference of the gods; there, we survey what has happened on the island of Ithaca during Odysseus's long absence; here, we observe brave young Telemachus, trying to pinpoint his father's trail; there, we join Odysseus as he paddles away from the island of Calypso over the dangerous, wild sea, and thus, the story begins! Homer's narrative technique is varied, rich, and cinematic. The *Odyssey* might be 2,700 years old, but the ways that the epic sets scenes, introduces characters, develops narrative tension, and leverages timeless tools like foreshadowing and dramatic irony are as enchanting today as they were eons ago.

While Homer's plotting and scene changes are as enthralling as they were in antiquity, his language is just as breathtaking too. The *Odyssey* shimmers with descriptions of rosy dawn over the morning ocean; crystalline springs, vines, and cormorants on woodsy islands; decorative blue enamel paint on polished palace walls; and, at a climactic moment, a bowstring, plucked with the warm and mellow sound of a swallow's song. The beauty of the *Odyssey*'s language is prismatic, and it befits Homer's world. In the *Iliad* and *Odyssey*, humanity is a vulnerable thing, pressed beneath the vastly more powerful forces of gods and nature, but nonetheless, within our fragility and transience, there is an intense beauty. The *Odyssey* is a story about a man coming home, but it is also a sequence of vividly narrated scenes, in which even brief descriptions of waves, or looming headlands, or shy smiles together remind us that human life on earth is a long sequence of precious and irrecoverable moments.

THE ANCIENT GREEK MCU

We've discussed the *Odyssey*'s historical background and explored how its language worked, in the past and present. Let's learn about what we might call the "Ancient Greek MCU." To modern audiences, the MCU (or "Marvel Cinematic Universe") is shorthand for the fictional world of Iron Man, Captain America, Wolverine, and (appropriately for Homer) Cyclops. These characters have been mainstays of cinematic entertainment for a generation. A different actor might play Spider-Man in different films, but he's always going to shoot webs out of his hands and do acrobatics among skyscrapers. Hulk might have different motivations for getting involved in a conflict in each new movie, but when he does, he's going to turn green and smash things, because that's what he does.

The ancient Greeks had a mythological universe as well, and it worked in much the same way. Odysseus is the hero of the *Odyssey*. He also shows up in the *Iliad*. He's a character in Sophocles's *Ajax* and *Philoctetes*, and Euripides's *Iphigenia at Aulis*, *Hecuba*, *Rhesus*, and *Cyclops*. The later Roman authors Virgil and Ovid, who loved ancient Greek literature, put Odysseus in their most famous works, the *Aeneid* and *Metamorphoses*, respectively. Odysseus, like Iron Man, was a franchise, but he wasn't copyrighted. Anyone who wanted to get theater seats filled, or to perk up ears at a poetic performance, might mention his name, and in doing so enjoy ready-made audience expectations. Odysseus was the wily guy. You might not know the *exact* story that was going to unfold about him, but you knew he was going to be a trickster who outsmarted everyone else.

While every culture has its web of archetypal characters, trying to understand a *different* culture's "cinematic universe" is challenging. The Odysseus of the *Iliad* is a decent enough guy, defending friends and trying to keep everyone on the team together. The Odysseus of Sophocles's *Ajax* is a selfish blowhard who realizes too late that he's caused the suicide of his friend. In other ancient Greek stories, Odysseus plays a hero, a villain, and everything in between. This is the case with many Homeric characters. Iphigenia dies in one version of her story. In another one, she lives. Homer's Helen of Troy goes to Troy. Euripides's Helen of Troy never does. Dionysus is the fun-loving god of wine, isn't he? Or is he the genocidal maniac at the heart of Nonnus's epic the *Dionysiaca*, an ancient forty-eight-book-long Greek poem written *a thousand years after the Odyssey*?

When we first come to the Greek myths, it is often with the mistaken sense that they are narratives that remained relatively static from century to century. They did not. Ancient Greek myths survive in uncountable versions, and in archaeological objects like cups and statues that suggest even more versions, still. The ancient Greek MCU endured for more than ten centuries, and one century's Odysseus was generally a bit different than the previous century's, even if some core elements of his character stayed the same.

Still, if all of this sounds intimidating, there's some good news. Literature ages differently than films do. And words, unlike even the most majestic statues and tympanums, are indestructible. For newcomers to the endlessly tangled thicket of Greek myths, there is no better starting place than the Homeric epics.

THE CONNECTION BETWEEN THE *ILIAD* AND THE *ODYSSEY*

If we picture ancient Greek literature as a river, the *Iliad* and the *Odyssey* are its headwaters. Many of the stories that were told downstream in history in the ancient Mediterranean world, first by Greeks and later by Romans, concerned characters from Homer's two epics. The *Iliad* tells the story of the Trojan War, while the *Odyssey* tells the story of how Odysseus made it home from this war. For a thousand years, these two epic poems sired new story cycles, including poems, plays, and new epics.

	ILIAD	*ODYSSEY*
Main Topic	The tenth year of the Trojan War	Odysseus's return from the Trojan War
Length	24 books; 15,700 lines	24 books; 12,000 lines
Setting	In and around Troy (probably northwest of modern-day Turkey)	All over the ancient Aegean, but the second half is on the island of Ithaca
Named After	*Ilium*, the Greek word for the city of Troy	The main character, Odysseus
Written Form First Appears	Between about 725 and 625 BCE	Between about 725 and 625 BCE

Once, thousands of years ago, the *Iliad* and the *Odyssey* were part of an even *longer* saga. The two Homeric epics were originally the second and seventh installments of an eight-story sequence that today's scholars call the "Epic Cycle."

COMPONENTS OF THE EPIC CYCLE

NAME OF WORK	**NUMBER OF BOOKS**	**MAIN TOPICS**
Cypria	11 books	Judgment of Paris; abduction of Helen; start of Trojan War
Iliad*	24 books	Year ten of the Trojan War; death of Hector
Aethiopis	5 books	Arrival of Trojan allies; death of Achilles
Little Iliad	4 books	Death of Paris; construction of Trojan Horse

continued

Name of Work	Number of Books	Main Topics
Iliou Persis	2 books	Sack of Troy; rampage of Achilles' son; death of Priam
Nostoi	5 books	Return of Menelaus and Agamemnon from Troy
*Odyssey**	24 books	Return of Odysseus from Troy
Telegony	2 books	Subsequent adventures of Odysseus and his sons

*Still survives today. The rest have been lost. (Source: Proclus's *Chrestomathia*)

Our sources on the Epic Cycle are minimal, and from much later on in history than the century that gave rise to the *Iliad* and *Odyssey*. While the outline shown here is probably not altogether accurate, we definitely know that *something* like this existed when the Homeric poems came together. Homer's epics are enormous, but they don't contain the entire story of the Trojan War by a long shot.

The scene of Odysseus coming up with the Trojan Horse, and the Greeks building it? Not in the Homeric epics. The abduction of Helen of Troy, and the launching of a thousand ships? Nope. Paris shooting Achilles in the heel? Not in Homer. The end of the war? Also, not in Homer. In short, the Homeric epics are a sprawling mass of text, but they don't contain everything we might expect.

The sections of the Epic Cycle that pleased audiences best evolved into increasingly refined and standardized poetry. The rest, though it remained a part of general cultural memory, was staged less and less, and slowly faded away.

Beginning at the Beginning: The *Iliad*

The *Iliad* tells the story of the Trojan War—whose aftermath we find in the *Odyssey*. The ten-year-long Trojan War was the defining event of an entire generation of mythological characters central to ancient Greek literature. Odysseus fought on the Greek side of this conflict, which, at a very simple level, pitted the Greeks and their king, Agamemnon, against the Trojans and their king, Priam.

The Trojan War began when the beautiful Greek woman Helen left her husband and married the Trojan prince Paris. Helen was the woman with "the face that launched a thousand ships" from Greece to Troy. The war ended when the Greek tactician Odysseus built a hollow horse to hide Greek soldiers, and the Trojans wheeled it inside their city. Then, out came the Greeks, who were finally able to get Troy's defenses down and conquer the city.

Homer's *Iliad* doesn't tell these stories of the Trojan War's beginning, nor its ending. It is an epic about the final year of the war, when nine years of carnage and loss have already affected everyone involved. In the *Iliad*'s opening pages, tempers are getting short. The Greeks want to go home. The Greek king is barely holding everything together, and ugly disagreements seethe in the ranks of the invaders. As for the Trojans, besieged for nearly a decade at the epic's outset, the years have taken their toll on them as well.

A series of whipsawing battles are the main action of the *Iliad*. Desperate to finally end the war, and putting everything on the table, the Greeks charge up from their beach camp to attack the city of Troy. The Trojans fend them off, however, and soon strike back, such that the defenders are suddenly attacking the Greek earthworks, in a shocking turn of the tides. And so it goes, book after book, in a series of jaw-droppingly violent and action-packed chapters in which warriors are compared to eagles, lions, and fire itself, their blood-splattered bronze armor blazing in the Mediterranean sun.

There are hundreds of named warriors on each side, but two stand out as most important. The Trojan champion, Hector, is depicted as a family man and recent father, exhausted by the fighting. He's a defender who would prefer peace. The Greek champion, Achilles, is also a very human, three-dimensional character. He is the greatest warrior of his generation, but, in the *Iliad*, Achilles is tired of war and thinking about heading home. When Achilles' dear companion Patroclus is killed, though, Achilles goes into a furious rampage so overwhelming that he defeats the Trojan champion Hector and turns the tide of the war.

The victory of Achilles at the end of the *Iliad* is as unsettling as it is exhilarating. The *Iliad* depicts war as a spectacular test of mortal endurance, but also as something horrifying. When Achilles wins, we know that Troy's days are numbered, although the city never falls in Homer's poem. The *Iliad* isn't about the beginnings or endings of wars, after all, but instead their long, grinding, awful middles. Its last line doesn't promise any peace or resolution. Hector is dead, Homer writes, and so the Trojans bury him. That's it. The war will continue. The warriors, many mangled and dispirited, will keep fighting, including Odysseus.

That's the story of the first Homeric poem, the *Iliad.* If you heard the second Homeric poem—the *Odyssey*—being performed in ancient Greece, you would know this prehistory. You'd sit down to hear a bard sing about Odysseus's homeward adventures, and you'd understand that he was coming home from something transformative, searing, and traumatizing. The Trojan War, in Homer's poetic world, has scarred an entire generation, and Odysseus is no exception.

An Overview of the *Odyssey*'s Plot

As long and complex as the *Odyssey* is, there's a pretty simple way to understand the epic's twenty-four books. That is to understand it as essentially a three-act play. In the first act, Odysseus's son is trying to find his father, who's been gone for twenty years. The second act recounts how Odysseus gets home. And the third act is a revenge story, revealing what happens when Odysseus makes it back to his kingdom. Here's how those three acts proceed and eventually weave together.

Act 1: Telemachus

Act 1 of the *Odyssey* is a detective story about an underdog youngster, Odysseus's son Telemachus, and the beginning of a long coming-of-age narrative that's one of the main plotlines of the entire *Odyssey.* When we meet Odysseus Junior, he's about nineteen years old. Young men in ancient Greece, especially highborn ones like Telemachus, underwent physical and military training to get them ready for the vigorous demands of adult life, under the guidance of older male role models. Telemachus, though, has no such role model. The youth, at the *Odyssey*'s opening, has been swept under the rug. More than a hundred men, assuming that Odysseus is dead, have made themselves at home in the Ithacan palace. Almost all of them are trying to marry Telemachus's mother, Penelope, and none of them show the poor teenage prince any respect.

These hundred or so men are called "the suitors." The suitors, literature's most notorious couch surfers, are a weird bunch. They seem unconcerned that only one of them can actually marry the queen. Though they're from prominent families, they appear as little more than blissfully unemployed braggarts in Homer's story. There's an absurdity to the suitors, but they're cruel as well. They don't care what Queen Penelope wants. They don't care what Telemachus wants. And so, short on options and prompted by Athena, off Telemachus goes to the east to look for Odysseus, in the direction of Troy, where his dad vanished almost two decades before.

First, Telemachus visits a gabby graybeard named Nestor, an old-timer who's still alive and kicking even though he was already quite elderly during the time of the Trojan War. Next, Telemachus meets with other heroes who knew his father, Menelaus and Helen, but they can't help him out much either. By the end of the first act of the *Odyssey* (which concludes with the close of Book 4), Telemachus heads back to Ithaca, planning to try and do what he can there, since he's turned up no leads.

Many readers hurry through the "Telemachus" books in search of the blockbuster scenes of Odysseus wrestling monsters and braving the briny depths. Act 1 of the *Odyssey*, though, still tells a very touching tale. Telemachus grows considerably over the beginning of the story, conducting himself well in foreign courts and with the deity Athena alike. He may not have the gravitas of his father, but he's a decent person, and this would have counted for a lot to the story's original readers, just as it still does to us today.

ACT 2: MONSTERS AND ADVENTURES

That's Act 1 of the *Odyssey*. What we can think of as Act 2 of the *Odyssey*, or Books 5–12, is the most famous portion of the epic. Before *The Legend of Zelda*, The Lord of the Rings, the Arthurian legends, and Virgil's *Aeneid*, there was Homer's archetypal tale of a guy on a boat. Odysseus is a prisoner when we meet him, held captive on the plush penitentiary of a nymph named Calypso, suffering a fate that is simultaneously sumptuous and degrading. He's been there for seven years. When Athena shows up and tells the lusty Calypso to let Odysseus go, the nymph sends him on his way. What ensues is a surprisingly confusing series of chronological jumps and stories within stories that together see Odysseus leapfrogging all over the place and barely staying alive.

From Calypso's island, Odysseus undertakes a very arduous twenty-two-day journey, alone, across part of the eastern Mediterranean. He washes up on the shore of a land called Phaeacia. The Phaeacians are friendly folks. Odysseus is friendly in return. He gets to talking with the Phaeacian king and queen one night, and then, in a four-book-long story within a story, he tells them all about what happened before he ended up stuck on Calypso's island. Thus begins the sequence of island-hopping adventures most of us associate with the *Odyssey*.

The adventures include the island of the Lotus-Eaters, the Cyclops, the wind god Aeolus, the Laestrygonians, a yearlong hookup with the witch Circe, a visit to Hades, a trip back to Circe, a paddle past the Sirens, a voyage between the monster Scylla and the whirlpool Charybdis, the island of Helios, and the shipwreck that led him to wash up on Calypso's island. Odysseus's long narrative is spellbinding and marvelous. Each episode is a self-contained story; each story has an archetypal theme universal to human folklore. An inhospitable Cyclops pays for his rudeness. Men are tempted by what is forbidden. The seductress Circe is seduced. A hero must make an impossible choice. There's a good reason that the epic's central portion is especially famous. After Odysseus tells his tale, the friendly Phaeacians get Odysseus to his homeland of Ithaca in relatively short order.

ACT 3: REVENGE

The entire second half of the *Odyssey* is a revenge story. The epic's final act, Books 13–24 (precisely half of the book), first tells of Odysseus, after partnering with Athena, sneaking around Ithaca and trying to find out who's been naughty and who's been nice.

Once he has some preliminary contacts, the hero, divinely disguised as an old beggar, starts snooping around his palace. The suitors and their flunkies, by this time, have generally been portrayed as unlikable scumbags, and they ridicule and batter the incognito hero. As the plot thickens, foreshadowing and dramatic irony tell us that the return of the king is not going to be a peaceful event.

The tension builds. Odysseus meets his son for the first time, and Telemachus helps his father scheme. In book after book, the suitors fail to give either of the island's rightful rulers an iota of respect, and Odysseus remembers all of it. He notes which servants have been loyal to him. He conspires with Athena. He tests his wife, Penelope, to see if she can still be trusted. And then, when the time comes, he attacks.

The carnage that ends the epic is shocking. The *Odyssey* shows us peaceful palaces, warm moments of diplomacy, gift giving, and considerate conversations over shared meals. But in the end, it descends into the ultra-violent hurricane of the *Iliad*. Odysseus, Telemachus, and two other men butcher the suitors, even as many of their victims beg for their lives. They kill and torture disloyal domestics who served the suitors. Blood slicks the floor of the Ithacan feasting hall, where so many of the epic's central scenes have happened.

There's a coda. Odysseus and Penelope finally get back together. Odysseus reunites with his father. But then, the Ithacans of Odysseus's kingdom come for revenge. The fathers and families of the suitors Odysseus has killed no longer want to be ruled by a mass-murdering monarch who's been gone for decades. Ithaca is about to explode into factional violence, perhaps starting a new Trojan War and spinning the Ouroboros serpent of revenge for a new generation. But Athena shows up and stops it. And that's the end.

That, then, is the tale of the *Odyssey* in three acts. Act 1: underdog coming-of-age story. Act 2: monsters and adventures. Act 3: revenge. All of them are magnificent and thematically interwoven with one another, their tight plotting and interconnectedness making the *Odyssey* perhaps the best-known story from the ancient world, the Bible excepted.

NOW YOU KNOW

A central dilemma in the Homeric epics is the choice between κλέος (*kleos*), or "battle glory," and νόστος (*nostos*), or "homecoming." Characters who opt for *kleos* go all in on war, seeking to distinguish themselves in battle at all costs, no matter whether or not they survive. Those who opt for *nostos* take a different path. They choose to go home and, in doing so, relinquish the glory of war in order to live happy, unassuming lives. (The modern noun "nostalgia" comes from the ancient Greek word *nostos*.) The *Odyssey* is essentially a story about a hero going from *kleos* to *nostos*. Although the Trojan War is over, Odysseus still bears its scars, both mentally and physically, and his journey back to peacetime civilization is a psychological one as well as a voyage across the sea.

The *Odyssey*'s Confusing Chronology and Geography

Both of Homer's epics have complicated time frames. The Trojan War lasted ten years, and Odysseus's journey home, when the *Odyssey* begins, has already taken him an additional nine years. From a big picture, the chronology of the Homeric epics looks like this.

Year Number	Age of Key Characters	What's Happening
1	Odysseus: 25 years old; Penelope: 20 years old	Helen leaves her husband, and the Trojan War begins.
2		
3		
4		
5		Trojan War is fought.
6		
7		
8		
9		
10		Events of the *Iliad* take place.
11	Odysseus: 35 years old; Penelope: 30 years old; Telemachus: 10 years old	
12		
13		
14		Odysseus's voyage home begins.
15		
16		
17		
18		
19		
20	Odysseus: 45 years old; Penelope: 40 years old; Telemachus: 20 years old	Most events of the *Odyssey* take place.

Though the characters' ages in this illustration are mostly guesswork, they should roughly capture how old each main character is at the different junctures of Homer's stories. Put simply, the *Iliad* takes place toward the end of the Trojan War, and the *Odyssey* takes place toward the end of Odysseus's long journey home.

Though it's ultimately just the tale of how Odysseus came home, the *Odyssey* itself has some confusing chronological jumps. A lot of the epic is a story within a story, with Odysseus narrating adventures that have already taken place. So while Odysseus's voyage to Phaeacia and the events on Ithaca take place in the *Odyssey*'s "present day," many of the more famous tales (for example, those about the Lotus-Eaters, the Cyclops, Circe, and the Sirens) are told as flashbacks.

While more than half of the *Odyssey* takes place on the small island of Ithaca, the main character has put a lot of miles on his odometer by the time he gets there. But where, exactly, does Odysseus go, over the course of his many adventures? That's a tough question to answer.

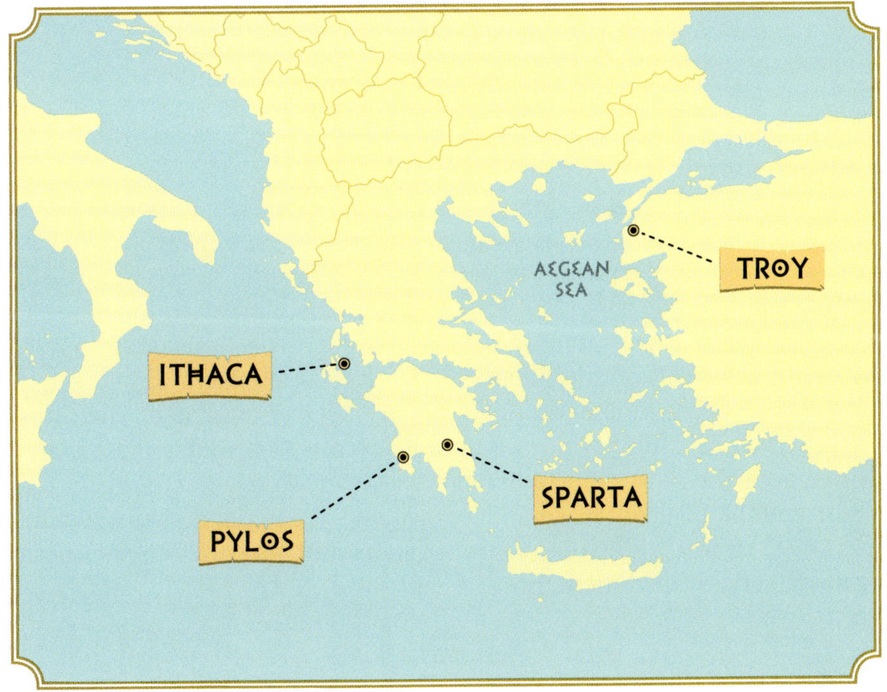

Ancient "Greece" was a maritime civilization that encompassed a number of modern-day countries. Wherever there were navigable harbors and places where some subsistence and cash crops could grow in the eastern Mediterranean, Greek-speaking settlements flourished. Around 725–625 BCE, when scholars believe the *Odyssey* was completed, Greek civilization encompassed the Aegean basin and parts of the Adriatic and Ionian Seas, and it was growing quickly too.

Various readers, over the ages, have speculated where Odysseus went when he traveled to, for instance, Circe's island, the land of the Sirens, and even the entrance to Hades! As an example, the Strait of Messina between Italy and Sicily has often been imagined as the setting that inspired the story of Scylla and Charybdis. Some readers have conjectured that Homer's Phaeacia was the island of Corfu. This kind of guesswork is fun, and it's great for Greek tourism. But the *Odyssey* is also a fairy tale, and the ancient Mediterranean was full of dangerous straits and peaceful islands. By the time Homer came along, centuries of bards had created an entire imaginary world full of storied locations. Ithaca is still the same Ithaca it's been since the Iron Age, and so are Pylos and Sparta. But as for other locations of the *Odyssey*, trying to pinpoint them on a map is a bit like looking for Wakanda or Gotham City.

The 700s and 600s BCE were periods of rapid population growth and migration for Greek-speaking populations. As Archaic period Greeks switched from herding to stationary agriculture, villages grew into cities, and entrepreneurs looked for opportunities to expand. New settlements in the eastern and central Mediterranean rim promised fertile soil and grazing lands. While some Greeks put down roots in western Anatolia and along the Black Sea, even more built colonies in Sicily and southern Italy. As the pace of colonization accelerated, Greek colonizers developed an increasingly keen eye for resource-rich stretches of coastland. The *Odyssey* is a product of this period of waterborne pioneering and homesteading. Throughout the story, Odysseus and his crewmen disembark again and again, and the poem's early audiences would have understood just what it was like to step off a ship onto a strange shore and not know whether harm or hospitality awaited them there.

How to Use This Book

Now that you've learned a bit about the Homeric epics and their historical background, it's time to dive into the *Odyssey*. The rest of this book will introduce you to the epic's characters roughly in the order in which they appear in the story and, in doing so, offer a full retelling of ancient Greece's most famous story.

A Note on Translations

As you make your way through each character profile, you'll see many quotes from the *Odyssey*. These quotes come from modern renderings of the poem done by different translators with somewhat different styles. Emily Wilson's *Odyssey*, for instance, is economic, metrical, and done in more modern English than has sometimes been customary in Homeric translations. Robert Fagles's is denser and more literal, working to render some of the stranger features of the *Odyssey* into English. E.V. Rieu's translation is in prose (in other words, paragraphs, rather than lines of poetry), which some readers prefer. Other translations used in this volume have other excellent qualities, and if you're interested in reading the poem yourself, there's a section at the end of this book titled Further Resources that will direct you to recommended versions.

Meeting the *Odyssey's* Characters

In the following pages, you'll meet the central characters of the *Odyssey*. And even if you've never read the epic, you'll feel like you know them already. Goodly old Eurycleia, brave young Telemachus, blabbing Nestor, randy Calypso—these characters are archetypes who had many descendants. Each character's profile covers their role in the Homeric epics and facts about their legacy in later literature and cultural history. Each entry wraps up with a small section that delves deeper into the history of the Homeric world, considers Odysseus's story in its original context, and helps you understand the *Odyssey* as ancient Greeks would have understood it. So turn the page, imagine the songs of lyres and the warm Aegean sun all around you, and get to know the cast of Homer's *Odyssey*. Ancient as they are, they're among the most important characters in all literature, and they can still delight and surprise us, just as they did 2,700 years ago.

THE GODS

THE HOTHEADED, HORNY DEITIES IN CHARGE OF THE COSMOS IN ANCIENT GREEK EPICS.

LIKE: Sex, Violence, Machinations

DISLIKE: Hubris, Boredom, Each Other

SPECIAL POWERS: Explosions, Vengeance, Magnificence

NARRATIVE ROLE: Puppeteering the action of the Homeric epics.

The *Odyssey*'s opening scene takes place in the palace of Olympus. The first two figures onstage are Zeus, patriarch of the gods, and Athena, his daughter. Zeus was lost in thought, pondering the relationships between gods and men. Athena saw an opening to make a plea on behalf of her favorite mortal. The human hero Odysseus, Athena told Zeus, still hadn't made it home from the Trojan War. The unfortunate mortal was being held captive on a remote island in the Aegean. His palace had been invaded by suitors who were trying to marry his wife. The gods had to help him!

Athena then hit her father Zeus with what we might call a "dad pun," asking him why he has hated (ὠδύσαο, or *odusao*) Odysseus (Ὀδυσσεύς, or *Odysseos*). This got Zeus's attention. Zeus, recollecting that Odysseus was quite an impressive fellow, for a mortal, rumbled that indeed they ought to help the pitiable castaway get back home. Zeus resolved to dispatch Hermes, the messenger god, to help Odysseus. Athena set her sights on Ithaca, flying down to the small island west of the Greek mainland to help Odysseus's son Telemachus.

Narratively, the epic's opening is a tour de force. In about three pages, we learn who the main players are. We learn what's going on. We learn that Odysseus is going to be the hero, that Telemachus is going to be the junior hero, that the suitors are going to be the bad guys, and that the mighty fists of Athena are going to be around if anything goes sideways. We know that Homer is going to get Odysseus home, but that it's going to be a long trip.

The epic's first couple of pages also introduce us to the Homeric gods, and how they operate. In the *Iliad* and the *Odyssey*, the gods treat human life on earth like a large, and sometimes very bloody, chessboard. Some deities favor certain mortals, in the way that Athena likes Odysseus. Some deities detest certain mortals. Later in the *Odyssey*, we'll learn that Poseidon despises Odysseus, and why this is the case. The Homeric epics are, in a nutshell, stories about gods favoring and disfavoring humans, and gods using humans to fight their proxy wars. In Homer's stories, the gods are neither beneficent nor malevolent. They are flawed beings, capable of clunky reasoning and laughable blunders, more often demonstrating supernatural strength and libidos than divine wisdom or clemency.

Although the Homeric epics are the primary means by which stories about Zeus and his family come down to many of us today, we should remember that *the gods in Homeric poetry* don't really represent the *gods that the ancient Greeks actually worshipped.*

The ancient Greeks were polytheists. Most obviously, this means they believed in numerous gods. Of the Olympians, the first generation is commonly understood as Hestia, Demeter, Hera, Hades, Poseidon, and Zeus. After these six comes the younger generation, including Athena, Artemis, Apollo, Ares, Hephaestus, Hermes, and Dionysus. This is already a long list of names, and it excludes Aphrodite, who has a separate birth story, and elder generations of divine beings, like Zeus's parents, Kronos and Rhea, and his grandparents Gaia and Ouranos. There are other ancient Greek gods besides these, not to mention titans (giants who came before the gods), nymphs (nature spirits), and an endless list of semidivine heroes and heroines (the children of gods and humans), like Heracles.

Some parts of the ancient Greek pantheon remained pretty consistent over the centuries: Zeus was always married to Hera, and the marriage was always a trainwreck. But there were evolutions within the ancient Greek pantheon too. In the Homeric epics, Zeus is a gorgeous idiot, as bumbling and imperceptive as he is the king of the gods. By contrast, four hundred years after Homer lived, right around 300 BCE, the Stoic philosopher Cleanthes wrote a hymn to Zeus in which Zeus sounds pretty much like the God of Christianity and Islam—omniscient, omnipresent, and in control of all the movement of the cosmos.

What happened to Zeus in ancient history happened to *all* of the Greek gods. Different generations imagined them a little bit differently. As people moved around in the ancient Mediterranean, new gods joined old pantheons, and hybrid deities emerged as well. If you had a river god named Billy, and the town over in the next valley had one named Joe, you could simply call the river god Billy-Joe, and everyone could shake hands. If your town, like the ancient city of Thebes did, revered Dionysus, you could start assigning more and more roles and responsibilities to him, so that he wasn't just the wine god anymore. Before widespread literacy and organized clergies, religion was more flexible. Without any institution enforcing orthodoxy, the ancient Greek gods grew and changed along with the civilizations that revered them.

Homer's gods, then, have often served as the archetypal portrait of the beings that ancient Greek people worshipped and revered. And to be clear, as we can see from corroded Bronze Age figurines to glossy Roman marble copies of Greek originals, the gods whom we meet in Homer's works were venerated for more than a thousand years. At the same time, at the moments when Homer's deities seem more like a mosh pit, or a madhouse, it's important to remember that we shouldn't confuse ancient Greek *literature* with ancient Greek *religion*. The latter is an obscurer subject, and the domain of archaeologists as much as it is that of readers of poetry.

Kooky as they are from time to time, the Homeric gods are narrative gasoline. They make plots move along, and they make things explode. They aren't particularly likable figures, neither by our standards nor those of ancient Greece. But when they show up on Homer's stage and start howling commandments, issuing covenants, scowling, swaggering, playing favorites, and sparkling magnificently in the Aegean sun, we know that stuff is about to go down. That's their role in Homer's stories today, just as it has been for almost three thousand years.

NOW YOU KNOW

The poet Homer had an ancient Greek contemporary named Hesiod. Like Homer, Hesiod left behind two major works. One of them was the *Theogony*. The *Theogony* is a long narrative poem that tells the story of the beginning of the universe. Starting with a period of primeval chaos before creation, Hesiod tells the tales of the first generations of titans and gods. It's a rollicking saga of gods and monsters fit for any generation.

ATHENA

SMART. SHREWD. ODYSSEUS'S DIVINE COUNTERPART.

LIKES: Subterfuge, Odysseus, Complexity
DISLIKES: Being Straightforward, Romantic Relationships
SPECIAL POWERS: Knowing Just What to Say, Transforming Into Birds
NARRATIVE ROLE: Odysseus's fairy godmother.

Athena is one of the most celebrated figures in ancient Greek mythology, and her most famous appearance of all is in Homer's *Odyssey*. Homer often calls her γλαυκῶπις Ἀθήνη (*glaukopis Athene*), an epithet that is most simply translated as "bright eyed" but can also be translated as "owl eyed." Like every Homeric god, Athena is neither good nor evil, but instead, an independent agent, pursuing her own interests and vendettas. Many of us know her today as a goddess of wisdom, associated with owls and the city of Athens. But before Athens rose to prominence in the 400s BCE, and even before the Homeric epics are thought to have come together in the late 700s BCE, Athena had already been around for a long time.

ATHENA'S LONG HISTORY

The ancient world had numerous warrior goddesses who, like Athena, served other functions as well. Back in the 2000s BCE, Inanna was ancient Sumer's goddess of war and sex. The city of Ugarit, on the coast of modern-day Syria, worshipped a warrior goddess named Anat. Ancient Egyptians revered a deity called Neith, who, like Athena, was associated with weaving, in addition to war. Out of this very ancient lineage of multifaceted war goddesses, sometime before 1000 BCE, Athena arose in the

Aegean world. Although we meet her in the *Odyssey* as the main character's helpful chum, ancient Greeks knew that Athena had a deep, dark past.

This past is epitomized by a statue from the late Archaic period (around 525 BCE) that you can still see today in the Acropolis Museum in Athens. The statue displays Athena, fierce and wild, wearing a himation (or outer robe) embroidered with living serpents, and standing triumphantly over a fallen titan while gripping a spear. Hair snaking down over her shoulder, her eyes serenely murderous, the Athena of the Gigantomachy Pediment, as she's known, looks like something from a heavy metal album cover. The statue shows a ferocious and destructive side of Athena—a side that even her father Zeus feared.

Why would Athena make the very powerful Zeus feel apprehensive, though? Here's the answer. While Zeus was still young, he married the goddess of wisdom, Metis. Metis became pregnant. Zeus learned from a prophecy that Metis would give birth to a daughter equal to her father, and a son who would one day rule over the gods. To avoid having children as powerful as him, Zeus ate Metis. Though the unborn son remained an ominous legend, the daughter, Athena, was born. Another ancient Greek poet, Hesiod, wrote in the *Theogony* that "From [Zeus's] own head he gave birth to owl-eyed Athena, / The awesome, battle-rousing, army-leading, untiring / Lady, whose pleasure is fighting and the metallic din of war" (Lombardo translation, 929–31). The story of Athena's birth from Zeus's head is well known today. (One might say that she made him more open-minded.) But what's not so well known is *why* Athena was born this way. Mighty, cunning, and insuppressible, Athena was born from Zeus's head because he attempted to devour her and her mother.

THE HOMERIC ATHENA

These very early stories are important for an understanding of the Homeric Athena. Odysseus's collaborator in the *Odyssey* is calm, calculated, and confident. She is not, like Zeus or Aphrodite, tarnished by a long legacy of blunders and sexual indiscretions. Nor, like Hera, is Athena perpetually huffing and puffing about being cheated on by a lusty spouse. More farsighted and dignified than some of her family members, Athena helps

Odysseus because she feels kinship with the wily hero, and not because she's pursuing some quarrel out of wounded pride.

Nonetheless, the Homeric Athena is still an Olympian god, which means she is extremely dangerous. Athena, after all, was partially responsible for the Trojan War, which got started due to a feud between Aphrodite, Hera, and Athena over which goddess was the fairest. In spite of Athena's wisdom and composure, like the rest of her family, she still sometimes threw herself into feuds with the other gods that caused enormous human suffering, and placed little stock in the sanctity of human life. Another Homeric epithet for her, Τριτογένεια (*Tritogeneia*), may mean something like "head born" or "third born," perhaps alluding to the circumstances of her emergence from Zeus's head. Whatever the name meant, it invites us to remember that Odysseus's main helper is the daughter of a jealous and greedy god who tried to kill her, a centuries-old enigma, and a guardian demon as much as she is a guardian angel.

As morally ambiguous as Athena is in the greater world of ancient Greek mythology, from the beginning to the end of the *Odyssey*, she's the hero's benefactor. Athena gets the second spoken line in the epic (after Zeus), telling her father and the other Olympians, "It is for Odysseus that my heart is wrung, the wise and unlucky Odysseus, who has been parted so long from all his friends and is pining on a lonely island far away in the middle of the seas" (Rieu translation, 1.47–51). Athena's perspective becomes the reader's perspective, and throughout much of the rest of the epic, the proverbial camera follows her from region to region as she does her best to get her protégé back home to Ithaca.

ATHENA IN THE *ODYSSEY*

We first meet Athena atop Mount Olympus in Book 1 of the *Odyssey*. Athena urged Zeus and the other gods to give Odysseus a break and let her get him back home from Calypso's island. There was a problem, though. Poseidon was very angry at Odysseus. Athena, however, was undaunted. With suitable pomp, she buckled on gleaming golden sandals and sped over land and water to Ithaca, where she disguised herself as an old man named Mentes and began investigating what was happening on the ground in Ithaca.

What happens next sets the stage for Athena's role in the remainder of the epic. Her participation in human events is sporadic. For example, Athena took note when the greedy suitors didn't offer her hospitality, but didn't say anything. She urged Telemachus into action and helped him on his way to the mainland to track down Odysseus, but she didn't actually tell him where his father was, or even that Odysseus was alive. In their dealings with humans, Homeric gods are often unassertive and indirect in just this fashion, giving clues and foreshadowings but not clear answers; probing and testing mortals but being oddly restrained when it comes to actually helping. Athena flew down from Olympus to the island of Ithaca gripping her giant bronze spear like she meant business, but upon arriving, she skulked around, told Telemachus to toughen up and get to the mainland, and left everything up in the air.

From a narrative perspective, Athena's passive-aggressive participation in the story's events makes sense. After all, if she showed up, pummeled the suitors, and whisked Odysseus home in a puff of smoke, the *Odyssey* would be a short, boring story. Still, her erratic involvement in much of the epic's central action is occasionally puzzling. If she likes Odysseus so much, can't the juggernaut genius of the gods figure out a more expedient way to get him home?

One answer is that Athena, like Odysseus, enjoys playing games. One of the most unique elements of the entire *Odyssey* is the complex relationship between this goddess and mortal. It's not a romantic relationship. Athena is a fighter, not a lover, in Greek mythology. Odysseus, notwithstanding his liaisons with Calypso and Circe, is trying to get back to Penelope. Their relationship is one between kindred spirits. At an amusing moment in the epic, both Odysseus and Athena are lying to one another, and she breaks disguise and exclaims:

You wily bastard,

You cunning, elusive, habitual liar!

Even in your own land you weren't about

To give up the stories and sly deceits

That are so much a part of you. . . . Here we are,

Athena and Odysseus share a capacity to move, deceive, adapt, and get things done. Both of them are capable of lying and making up colorful stories to suit any occasion at hand. At various points, we see Athena pretending to be a trader, a shepherd boy, a little girl carrying a pitcher, and a bird, all the while nudging humans around like miniatures in a diorama. Although her disguises and falsehoods suit many occasions in the story, she clearly enjoys duping others and spinning tall tales.

At the very end of the story, after twenty-four books of puppeteering the central action of the *Odyssey*, Athena takes on her final role: a peacemaker. Following the climactic confrontation between Odysseus and the suitors, all was not well on the small island of Ithaca. The families and acquaintances of the suitors, shocked at the violence that unfolded in Odysseus's palace, were out for revenge. In the book's final pages, Athena watched as the fathers of all of Penelope's suitors planned a bloody coup against the returned king. Just paragraphs before the epic ends, the *Odyssey* careens toward disaster. Grieving Ithacan families confronted Odysseus. The hero, flanked by his father and son, prepared to defend himself, and a battle began.

But just as Ithaca seemed about to collapse into violent insurgency, Athena did something she hadn't done before in the *Odyssey*. She got directly involved. She screamed the word "ITHACANS!" And she told everyone, including Odysseus, to put down their weapons. The last line of the epic is "The goddess made both sides swear binding oaths— / Pallas Athena, daughter of the Storm Cloud" (Lombardo translation, 24.570–1). That's it. The goddess of war demanded peace, and, presumably, the mortals obeyed.

It's a jarring ending. Athena has been putzing around for thousands of lines in the epic, and in the story's last sixty seconds she suddenly puts her foot down and the curtains close. Later in ancient Greek history, the term ἀπὸ μηχανῆς θεός (*apo mekhanes theos*), or "god from the machine," arose to describe theatrical endings in which deities abruptly appeared and ended the action onstage. The word μηχανή (*mekhane*) means "machine" and, in this context, "crane," because on ancient Greek theatrical stages, the μηχανή was a contraption that hoisted Greek gods high above the stage, where they shouted climactic proclamations that ended various plays. While the *Odyssey* is an epic, rather than a theater play, the term "god from the machine," or its Latin translation *deus ex machina*, still applies to its closing lines. The island of Ithaca seems like it's about to degenerate into violence and tribalism. Athena shows up and stops the fighting.

In the story, she is not always an agent of justice for all, however. She plays favorites, lies for fun, and draws things out. Humanity is a horse race for her, rather than a world of vulnerable people with hopes and dreams, and to ancient Greeks, this was precisely the point. Homer's gods were not the benevolent and omniscient beings of our modern religions. They were emblems of the great impersonal forces of the universe, and in all cases, their ruthlessness, strangeness, and unpredictability helped explain the ups and downs of human life on earth.

NOW YOU KNOW

Athena's second-most-famous appearance in literature is in the *Oresteia*, a trilogy of plays written by the tragedian Aeschylus, which were staged in Athens in 458 BCE. Just as Athena takes on the role of peacemaker at the very end of the *Odyssey*, she does the same thing at the climax of Classical Athens's only surviving theatrical trilogy. Ancient Greeks understood her as a deity who could end wars as well as start them.

TELEMACHUS

A LIKABLE YOUNG MAN LOOKING FOR HIS LONG-LOST DAD.

PRONUNCIATION: tell-EH-muh-kus

LIKES: Ithaca, His Mother, Being Treated with Basic Decency

DISLIKES: Bullies, Moochers, Loudmouths

SPECIAL POWERS: Patience, Respect, Staying Hopeful

NARRATIVE ROLE: Odysseus's son, the epic's secondary hero.

Sometimes, in an epic full of earthshaking gods, heroes swigging protein shakes, predatory vixens, and ravenous monsters, you need someone who's just a normal dude. At the *Odyssey*'s opening, the normal dude in question is Telemachus, the epic's number two hero, a young man who has never punched a Hydra, nor fought in an epic war, nor spent a sultry night with a nymph. In spite of Telemachus's modest credentials at the epic's outset, though, there's a lot to like about him.

The first passage in the *Odyssey* that involves Telemachus tells us most of what we need to know about the nineteen-year-old prince of Ithaca. Athena beamed herself down to Odysseus's palace, disguising herself as an old man. And Homer writes, "The first to see her was Telemachus . . . who was sitting disconsolate among the Suitors, imagining how his noble father might come back out of the blue, drive the Suitors headlong from the house, and so regain his royal honours, and reign over his own once more" (Rieu translation, 1.113–18). And there we have Telemachus, a kid who, throughout the *Odyssey*'s opening four books, is courageous, assertive, timid, and scared all at the same time, just like the rest of us. He doesn't have the chest hair and death stare of an epic hero yet, but really, that's part of his appeal.

Homer always describes his characters best, as is the case with Telemachus. He is periodically called πεπνυμένος (*pepnumenos*), meaning "heedful" or "thoughtful." He's called σαόφρων (*saophron*), meaning "prudent" or "of sound mind." Trapped between adolescence and adulthood, Telemachus doesn't quite know whether it's time to act, or to just keep his head down. The palace where he grew up has been invaded by more than a hundred lusty jocks, any one of whom would be happy to marry his mother and kick him out of Ithaca. Neither brave enough to challenge dozens of bullies nor complacent enough to just shut up and take it, Telemachus is a dark horse in Homer's story, and yet like all protagonists in underdog stories, Telemachus has enough grit and fiber that we know he's going to eventually get some justice.

That justice comes to him slowly and modestly at the epic's beginning. Here's the story that some scholars call the "Telemachy," or the portion of the *Odyssey* having to do with Telemachus.

THE STORY OF THE "TELEMACHY"

Athena knew that Telemachus was going to be important to the future of Ithaca. And so rather than parachuting down to help Odysseus directly, Athena went to help his son. Telemachus did not disappoint the goddess when the two met for the first time. He honored the disguised Athena, showing her hospitality even as all the suitors ignored her. He also made it clear, when the goddess suggested it, that he was willing and ready to embark on a quest to find his father. Later, Telemachus impressed Athena again. The young hero told the suitors, in a speech that was brave, emotional, raw, and honest, that what they were doing to his family was wrong. The suitors guffawed and ignored him. He still had no idea, at this point in the narrative, that Athena had come to help him. Telemachus, scolding the suitors and hopping on a boat with his fingers crossed, was a kid who felt largely alone in an unjust world, leaving his home and banking on the ghost of a chance that Odysseus was out there somewhere.

Telemachus had some good luck at the outset. Not far from Ithaca was the palace of an elderly monarch named Nestor. There, Telemachus befriended the king, who was his father's old comrade from the Trojan War. Telemachus's next stop was Sparta, where he got to know more of his father's former acquaintances, Menelaus and Helen. In conversations with old family friends like Nestor, Menelaus, and Helen, Telemachus began to blossom. As it turned out, when he wasn't being insulted and browbeaten, he could really handle himself. When treated with courtesy, Telemachus was gracious in return. When others actually listened to him, he listened back. And gradually, over the course of the *Odyssey*'s beginning, we get the sense that although Telemachus grew up with no father figure, in a house increasingly invaded by rude layabouts, he's astute, perceptive, and smart enough to be a decent king, whether or not his dad ever makes it home.

If you read the two Homeric epics in order, in fact, the "Telemachy" is a high point. The *Iliad*'s grisly war story shows scene after scene of gods lashing mortals into fierce combat. Heroes make marvelously eloquent speeches but, often, only as preludes to killing each other. By contrast, the *Odyssey*'s opening books show what Homer calls ἔπεα πτερόεντα (*epea pteroenta*) or "winged words" at work during regular old civilian life. Telemachus might not have a big beard yet, but he's great at expressing himself. As he meets some of his father's dearest friends, and they talk and tell stories about bygone days over long meals, the young man starts to feel like a prince, instead of a chump whom nobody takes seriously. In the *Iliad*, Homer shows us war burning out of control. In the opening of the *Odyssey*, though, Homer shows us that through diplomacy, consideration, and a small shimmer of eloquence, peace can spread just as quickly.

By the end of the "Telemachy" in Book 4, Odysseus Junior has some wind in his sails. He's built connections with local kingdoms. He's made a new friend, a guy about his own age named Peisistratus, the youngest son of old King Nestor. He's progressed from being a nonentity in the corner of his father's dining hall in Book 1 to a prince with confidence and regional alliances by the end of Book 4. The *Odyssey*, if it had never involved Odysseus, might have been a story about young Telemachus making his way in the world.

Instead, Odysseus shows up in Book 5, and Telemachus sits things out for ten books. When we meet him again, for the rest of the story, Telemachus is in the sidecar while Odysseus drives the motorcycle. And Odysseus makes clear pretty quickly, upon meeting his son, that it's going to be a violent ride. Although Telemachus has wanted to meet his father all his life, when Odysseus lumbers in and tells his son that they're going to butcher more than a hundred suitors together, the younger man is understandably concerned.

Telemachus, who always does his best to be sensible and moderate in a world ruled by strong personalities and deranged gods, does what his father tells him to do. After Telemachus reunites with Odysseus, he's generally a respectful Robin to Odysseus's berserk Batman. Telemachus certainly has no love for the suitors. And yet it's a little sad, having watched the courteous, eloquent youth find his own way in Books 1–4, to see Telemachus devolve into a mere sidekick at the story's end. Had Telemachus been in the driver's seat at the *Odyssey*'s climax, there likely would have been less dismemberment and more talking things out. But instead, about halfway through the epic, Telemachus gets swept up into Odysseus's homicidal tornado, and as the curtains close, he's a different person from the despondent goth kid we first saw sitting alone in the feasting hall, who befriended Athena without knowing who she was.

NOW YOU KNOW

The opening four books of Homer's *Odyssey*, which concern themselves with Telemachus, are often thought to have been produced at a later date than the central portion of the poem. The "Telemachy," appearing as it now does at the epic's beginning, helps us understand why Odysseus needs to hurry home to Ithaca.

In ancient Greek, Telemachus's name is Τηλέμαχος (*Telemakhos*), meaning something like "far battler." The name might have meant that Telemachus was a long-range fighter, using bows and thrown spears, or perhaps that while Odysseus was fighting in Troy, Telemachus, far away, had his own battle to fight with the suitors. The ancient Greek word τηλέ (*tele*), or "far," is where we get the words "telephone" and "telegraph."

THE SUITORS

MORE THAN A HUNDRED DUDES, ALL TRYING TO MARRY THE SAME WOMAN.

LIKE: Sloth, Wine, Saturated Fat

DISLIKE: Rightful Monarchs, Paying for Things

SPECIAL POWERS: Callousness, Gluttony

NARRATIVE ROLE: The central antagonists of the epic.

The suitors, antiquity's most notorious sausage party, are the villains of the *Odyssey*. Their role in the story is as simple as it is staggeringly ridiculous. Odysseus has been gone for almost twenty years. In his absence, precisely 108 suitors, together with a few lackeys, have dogpiled into his palace, and every single one of them is trying to marry his wife, Penelope. A number of them are named characters, and some are drawn with nuance and specificity. Overall, though, they play guffawing Goliaths to Telemachus's downtrodden David, having turned his ancestral palace into a frat house, complete with all the requisite machismo, chest bumps, and binge drinking.

Their first scene in the *Odyssey* perfectly represents their peculiar role in the story. When Homer initially describes them, they are more absurd than threatening, although they are both as the epic proceeds. Here's the first appearance of the suitors, just a few pages into the *Odyssey*:

> Athena . . . took the spear,
>
> Bronze-tipped and massive . . .
>
> And her eyes rested on the arrogant suitors.
>
> They were playing dice in the courtyard,
>
> *continued*

This opening shot contrasts the knuckle-cracking, spear-thwacking war goddess Athena with what appears to be a bunch of slackers playing grab-ass and eating themselves into food comas. The suitors, from the epic's opening minutes, just don't look like they stand a chance next to steely-jawed Athena and brilliant, bustling Odysseus. They're not *doing* anything. In the Homeric universe, where warriors pursue war, farmers farm, herders herd, and sailors sail, the suitors initially strike us as little more than horny, alcoholic locusts.

And yet as the story proceeds, we learn that, by virtue of their sheer numbers and shamelessness, they're quite dangerous. They have ruined Telemachus's life. They have made Penelope a prisoner in her own home. They're not actually vagrants; they're noblemen from the aristocracies of Ithaca and its adjacent islands. Some of them are skilled in warcraft. And though they have spent an unspecified quantity of time freeloading at Odysseus's palace, their ultimate purpose is a coup and regime change. For Homer's original audience, who knew of Odysseus's harrowing and extraordinary deeds during the Trojan War, the invasion of the suitors would have appeared as a cowardly flank attack, as unwise as it was ultimately doomed.

From nearly their first appearance in the *Odyssey*, the suitors break all the rules of the important ancient Greek principle of ξενία (*xenia*), or "hospitality," also known as "guest-friendship." Most obviously, they are uninvited guests in the household of an absent king. They take without asking. They are entitled, raucous, and rude. And when *other* guests appear at Odysseus's palace, the suitors are either indifferent or outright cruel to *them*. The disguised Athena hardly gets the time of day from the suitors. Later, Odysseus, disguised as a beggar, endures physical and verbal abuse from them. In sharp contrast, Telemachus and Odysseus are both model guests in lengthy scenes in the *Odyssey*, showing tact and geniality and making excellent impressions on the people whom they meet.

It's no coincidence that Homer's good guys are exemplars of *xenia*. Hospitality is a paramount virtue in ancient Greek literature. Within Homer's moral framework, a warrior could kill enemies left and right and enslave women and children whenever he wanted. But only absolute slimeballs would demand, refuse, or take advantage of hospitality or the guest-friendships established by hosting and then being hosted in return (the Greek word ξένος [*xenos*] meant both "host" and "guest," though it's often translated as "stranger" as well, as in the words "xenophobia" and "xenophilia").

Here's an extreme example of how important hosting and hospitality are considered in the Homeric epics. At one point in the *Iliad*, a Greek hero named Diomedes was wrapping up a very productive, murderous day on the battlefield. Diomedes then met a fighter on the opposing side—a Trojan named Glaucus. The two warriors, who had never met one another, eyed each other from their bloody chariots and prepared to fight. As they approach one another, we expect that only one of the two warriors will survive the meeting. Instead, a weirdly touching scene unfolds. Mighty Diomedes asked the other fellow who he was. Glaucus, in a nearly one-hundred-line, three-page speech (6.170–250), told Diomedes all about his heritage. Diomedes listened carefully and then shook his head ruefully. Slamming his spear down in the ground, Diomedes stepped down from his chariot. Well, shucks, said Diomedes, *he* couldn't fight Glaucus. His grandfather had once *hosted* Glaucus's grandfather. The two seniors had been guest-friends and had exchanged gifts. Glaucus, also stepping down from his chariot, nodded in understanding, and soon the two warriors were high-fiving and trading gear with each other to seal their bonds of friendship. They shook hands and, parting company and exchanging professional courtesies, wished one another well with the rest of the day's butchery.

Clearly, real Homeric heroes, like brawny Diomedes and Glaucus in the *Iliad*, deeply valued the sacred bond established between guest and host, even down to the third generation. If someone put you up for the night, or if you had a lengthier stayover at their place, or the other way around, you began an inviolable relationship with them. And likewise, if someone came to you seeking hospitality, you had to offer it, because shipwrecks, robberies, and downturns in fortune made everyone need to seek lodgings from time to time.

The suitors have many unlikable qualities in the *Odyssey*, but to Homer's original audience, their foremost sin would have been breaking all the rules of hospitality. Some of them do have distinguishing characteristics. Antinous, Eurymachus, and Amphinomus, in particular, are fairly three-dimensional characters. And yet it is their abuse of Penelope's hospitality that makes them the bad guys, such that for most of the narrative, they're just bowling pins we know are eventually going to be knocked down.

NOW YOU KNOW

Homeric hospitality had a long history in ancient Greek narratives. In the Bible's New Testament Gospel of Matthew, Jesus imagines those who reject his teachings with a metaphor involving hospitality, saying, "I was a stranger (ξένος [*xenos*]) and you did not welcome me" (Matthew 25:43).

Beyond the *Odyssey*, the most well-known ancient Greek story involving hospitality is the myth of Baucis and Philemon. The pair were an elderly married couple without much money. One evening, two vagrants knocked at their door, seeking food and lodging. Baucis and Philemon welcomed them in and pulled out all the stops, feeding their guests with everything in the pantry. As it turned out, the guests were Zeus and Hermes, and the myth is a parable about the importance of *xenia*. The longest version of this myth appears in the *Metamorphoses* (8.611–724), completed by the Roman poet Ovid around 8 CE.

NESTOR

"BACK IN MY DAY, WE USED TO BENCH-PRESS CENTAURS BEFORE BREAKFAST."

PRONUNCIATION: NES-tor

LIKES: The Sound of His Own Voice, Staying Active

DISLIKES: Retirement, Being Underestimated

SPECIAL POWERS: Wisdom, Self-Aggrandizement

NARRATIVE ROLE: Helping Telemachus find his father.

Nestor was an elderly king from the southwest of the Peloponnese. He fought in the Trojan War with Odysseus, and during that great conflict, both Odysseus and Nestor offered wisdom and coolheadedness to their Greek comrades. Pylos, the kingdom that Nestor ruled, was pretty close to Odysseus's homeland of Ithaca. Thus, when young Telemachus hops aboard a ship to go and search for his dad at the beginning of the *Odyssey*, making Pylos his first stop is a very sensible decision. Here's the story of Nestor in the *Odyssey*.

Embodying that cherished ancient Greek virtue of hospitality, old Nestor rolled out the proverbial red carpet when young Telemachus arrived, even though the youth was, at that point, traveling in disguise for the purposes of safety. After Telemachus revealed his identity, Nestor was both delighted and melancholy—delighted to meet his dear friend's son but melancholy that Odysseus was still missing. Nestor, sadly, couldn't point Telemachus in Odysseus's direction. But Nestor still offered Telemachus some helpful information.

Nestor told Telemachus, in one of the *Odyssey*'s many flashback scenes, about what had happened after the Greeks had won the Trojan War. Ten years prior, said Nestor, after Odysseus's signature Trojan Horse enabled

the Greeks to finally sack the city of Troy, a new crisis had unfolded. The Greeks had begun fighting among themselves. Specifically, the foremost Greek kings, the brothers Agamemnon and Menelaus, began feuding with one another. As a result, some Greek forces left Troy, in the company of Menelaus. Nestor was among them, and Nestor explained that his own journey home to western Greece had been smooth sailing. Odysseus had remained in Troy with Agamemnon, however. Though Nestor knew that Agamemnon was dead—murdered by his wife and her lover—Nestor had no idea of Odysseus's whereabouts.

Although Nestor didn't know exactly where Odysseus was, Nestor's tale nonetheless left Telemachus with hope that his father might still be out there somewhere. And while Nestor's long story about the end of the Trojan War was little comfort to the young man, Nestor's warmth and hospitality were both quite heartening. So, too, was the advice that Telemachus received from Nestor, who told him to head east to Sparta and meet with King Menelaus to try and find Odysseus's elusive trail. Odysseus and Nestor stayed up late and talked for a long time, and the next morning, after a feast, Nestor sent Telemachus on his way. Nestor not only loaned Telemachus horses and chariots, but also sent his son Peisistratus along to Sparta, and the two young men soon became close friends.

And that's a summary of Nestor's appearance in the *Odyssey*. His cameo is sizable, but it's also confined to just Book 3. He's a friendly old helper character, perhaps a bit of a windbag, but with kindly intentions. A lot of the *Odyssey*'s readers, looking forward to hearing the maritime adventures of the protagonist, rush through the Nestor scenes in search of the epic's more iconic moments. But nonetheless, Nestor is a strange, fascinating Homeric character who can teach us a lot about ancient Greek society.

Nestor actually *almost* makes a second appearance in the *Odyssey*. In Book 15, Telemachus is hurrying back to Ithaca. He's about to pass through Nestor's kingdom of Pylos. However, Telemachus decides to just steer around the talkative graybeard's city. Telemachus's decision to avoid Nestor at this juncture is sensible, and also funny. We've all avoided visiting someone whose hospitality is so extensive that it's actually burdensome, and we've all felt socially tapped out, at some point. When

Telemachus sneaks around Pylos, these are perhaps precisely the feelings he's experiencing.

Homer's original audience likely would have remembered Nestor's more extensive appearances in the *Iliad*. In the earlier epic, Nestor is often a comic character, managing to be insightful and slightly ridiculous at the same time. At a tense moment when everything is up in the air for the Greeks, Nestor scrunches up his brow, thinks for a moment, and then announces, "I will tell you what seems best to me. / No one will offer a better plan than this" (Fagles translation, 9.122–3). These two lines epitomize Nestor in a nutshell. Throughout the *Iliad*, Nestor is *always* willing to step up and give advice (which is often prefaced by stories about how awesome he used to be) or tell stories about the amazing stuff he did when he was young. He has plenty to brag about. Nestor once participated in a legendary battle with centaurs, and he has many other heroic exploits under his belt. But Nestor's advice is a mixed bag, sometimes helpful and sometimes dicey, and as his counsel is peppered with boastful yarns about his past, Nestor sometimes tests his comrades' patience when he takes it upon himself to make a speech.

Homer emphasizes Nestor's advanced age at several junctures, explaining that even at the Trojan War's beginning, Nestor had lived through the lives of two generations of men, and gone onto a third. The phrasing is vague, but considering how Nestor is repeatedly described as old throughout the ten-year Trojan War, and the Trojan War has been over for *another decade* when the *Odyssey* starts, the king of Pylos is definitely the most senior of Homer's senior citizens.

In spite of the fact that Nestor can be a doddering loudmouth, he's quite a lovable character. In the *Iliad*, when things get ugly among the Greeks, he's there, willing to step up and say *something*, at least, even if it's not terribly relevant. In the *Odyssey*, Nestor is the first highborn Greek who treats Telemachus with courtesy and respect, before he even knows who Telemachus is, and the gesture means a lot to the younger man. And in both stories, Nestor is a paragon of old age well spent—active, gabby, revered, a little clumsy, but altogether well intentioned and indispensable. Though he's not a tent-pole Homeric character like Odysseus or Achilles, for 2,700 years, Nestor has reminded readers that you can still be an epic hero, even if you're as old as the hills.

NOW YOU KNOW

In the *Iliad*, Nestor offers medicine in a large cup to an injured Greek warrior. Homer describes the medicine as a κυκεών (*kykeon*), or a "mixture," in this case made of mixed wine, grated goat cheese, and barley. It's a strange-sounding drink, and invites us to remember that ancient Greeks commonly mixed wine with other things in various *kykeons*, or "mixtures."

A cup was discovered in Italy in 1954 that archaeologists call "Nestor's Cup" (not to be confused with the fictional cup mentioned previously). This cup, dated by archaeologists to around 730 BCE, has a three-line inscription (one of the earliest Greek inscriptions) on it announcing that it is the "cup of Nestor" (probably referring to the fictional person). The important artifact is a solid piece of evidence that stories from the Homeric epics were in existence by the late 700s BCE.

MENELAUS

ODYSSEUS'S OLD ARMY BUDDY, AND THE GOOD TIMES THEY SHARED AT TROY.

PRONUNCIATION: men-uh-LAY-us

LIKES: Helen, Sparta, Retirement, Shampoo

DISLIKES: Trojans, Adultery

SPECIAL POWERS: Loyalty, Dedication, Having Great Hair

NARRATIVE ROLE: Helping Telemachus find his father.

Menelaus, the king of Sparta, got cheated on. This has always been the foremost bullet point on the poor guy's proverbial resume. After his wife, Helen, left him for a Trojan playboy, King Menelaus and his brother, King Agamemnon of Argos, distributed enough military-recruitment posters to launch a thousand ships. Off went the Greeks, all the way across the Aegean, to fight a ten-year war—all because some guy got dumped.

Menelaus thus appears to us at first as a self-important cuckold, willing to instigate a mass-casualty event out of lovelorn jealousy. If he could have simply put on his big-boy pants and moved on, perhaps the Greeks and Trojans could have continued playing lyres, gazing wistfully out to the sea, and staying out of trouble. And yet even though Menelaus seems like a selfish blowhard based on the circumstances of the Trojan War and its aftermath, in the actual Homeric epics, he is a complex, self-conscious character who feels accountable for his actions. (Helen is, too, as we'll learn in the next entry, but let's stick with Menelaus for now.)

In the *Odyssey*, Menelaus's appearance is confined to Book 4. Here's the story of Menelaus in the *Odyssey*. Odysseus's son Telemachus showed up in Sparta. The city was in a festive state, because a double wedding was taking place. Menelaus and Helen's daughter Hermione was being

married, as was Menelaus's son Megapenthes, the offspring of Menelaus and one of his slaves. (Menelaus's infidelity, unlike Helen's, did not result in a catastrophic war.) Menelaus, though he didn't know who the newcomer was, welcomed Telemachus to the palace. Pleasantries were exchanged. Menelaus made sure Telemachus enjoyed some food. After years of being pushed around by the suitors, the youth was happy to receive such kind treatment from a kingly stranger. Before long, Menelaus was putting it all on the table, both in terms of hospitality as well as emotional honesty. Menelaus, looking around the glitz of his own palace, said he knew he had a nice home, but that he'd give the majority of it away to have his friends back. The Trojan War, Menelaus said, had been awful, and they couldn't have won without Odysseus. No one had fought harder than Odysseus, and no one had done more for the war efforts.

Hearing such praises of his father made Telemachus choke up, and it wasn't long before Menelaus's wife Helen (they had reunited) realized who Telemachus was. The couple offered the poor young prince their sincerest embraces thereafter. The night grew later and later, and Menelaus was crestfallen to learn that Odysseus was still missing. Menelaus again emphasized that Odysseus was an indispensable powerhouse during the war. Helen, too, told stories about Odysseus, and both husband and wife had only good things to say about Telemachus's father. It was just what the young man needed to hear. By dawn, they were all friends.

The next day, Telemachus and the Spartan king got to know each other more. As it turned out, Menelaus had had quite a tough time getting home from the Trojan War as well, though not as tough as Odysseus's. In a long flashback, Menelaus recollected how he came home, summarizing some of the events of the *Nostoi*, a lost saga that used to come before the *Odyssey* in the Epic Cycle. Menelaus explained how he ended up stranded in Egypt for a long time, and it took some wheeling and dealing with the gods and other semidivine beings for him to get back on the road to Sparta. The main thing that young Telemachus took away from Menelaus's reminiscences was that Odysseus had recently been reported to be alive and well and stuck on the island of Calypso.

Menelaus invited Telemachus to stay for a while, but the younger man politely declined. Enjoying Menelaus's hospitality, as wonderful as it was, was tempting, but Telemachus still had a houseful of suitors that needed to be dealt with. Menelaus, nothing if not gracious in the *Odyssey*, told the younger man that he certainly understood. The Menelaus whom we meet in the *Odyssey*, then, is a single-serving character who tells Telemachus some war stories and sends the youth on his way.

Yet like many characters who make cameos in Homer's *Odyssey*, Menelaus had a lot of history behind him. He was part of a lineage commonly called the "House of Atreus" by fans of ancient Greek literature. The House of Atreus, even by the standards of antiquity, had a gory, checkered history. This history involved madness, fratricide, patricide, filicide, matricide, and incest, and, most notoriously, Menelaus's father butchered Menelaus's cousins and served them to Menelaus's uncle in a stew. To put it mildly, Menelaus came from a dysfunctional family.

And yet in spite of the carnival of incest, murder, and cannibalism that produced Menelaus, and even though he did have a lot of blood on his kingly Spartan hands, the stories that ancient Greeks tended to tell about Menelaus were on the whole optimistic. The House of Atreus hit absolute moral rock bottom, but ancient Greek authors also wrote about things taking a turn for the better for Menelaus's family.

The Menelaus we meet in the *Odyssey* is doing fine. He's a little sad. The war has taken its toll on him, but he's also moved on. He and Helen have come to some kind of mutual understanding, and overall, they seem happy. And in other ancient Greek stories, Menelaus's extended family also ended on upswings. His niece Iphigenia, in Euripides's play *Iphigenia in Tauris* (412 BCE), helps her stranded brother, Orestes, get back home. In a different work of ancient Greek literature called the *Oresteia*, Orestes is instrumental to the establishment of a justice system in the city of Athens engineered to end the seesawing violence that plagued the House of Atreus and other families like it.

In short, then, to ancient Greek audiences, Menelaus was a multidimensional, appealing character who lived through a conflict to see a better future. They understood him, as we do, as the jealous husband behind the Trojan War. But they also understood him as a figurehead of forgiveness and second chances, who, after a war's end, could overcome his own pride and grudges for the sake of peace.

NOW YOU KNOW

Menelaus is from a land called Λακεδαίμων (*Lakedaimon*), the Homeric name for Sparta. The English adjective "laconic" (meaning "using very few words") comes from the word *Lakonia*, another, later, word for Sparta, because in antiquity, the Spartans were stereotypically very concise with their speech.

Homer often calls Menelaus ξανθὸς (*xanthos*), translated as "fair haired" or "auburn haired." The epithet occurs frequently in the *Iliad* and *Odyssey*, suggesting that Menelaus's auburn mane was one of his most distinguishing characteristics.

Speaking of hair, let it be known that Homer's *Iliad* contains history's first known reference to mullets. The poet writes of the Abantes, one of the many tribes that came to fight in the Trojan War: "The sprinting Abantes followed . . . / their forelocks cropped, hair grown long at the back" (Fagles translation, 2.632–3).

HELEN OF TROY

BEHIND THE FACE THAT LAUNCHED A THOUSAND SHIPS.

LIKES: Menelaus, the Trojan Royal Family

DISLIKES: Being Repeatedly Abducted and Fought Over

SPECIAL POWERS: Looking Great, Being a Decent Person

NARRATIVE ROLE: Helping Telemachus, offering Trojan War backstory.

If you know just one or two things about the Homeric epics, you probably know *something* about Helen of Troy. And that something is that Helen left her Spartan husband Menelaus and eloped with the Trojan pretty boy Paris to the other side of the Aegean and, in doing so, became the cause of the Trojan War.

Helen's English-language epithet is faintly degrading: "The face that launched a thousand ships" seems to describe someone whose external beauty is her only quality worth mentioning. And indeed, if all we know about Helen of Troy is that her act of adultery started ancient literature's most dire war, she doesn't seem like a very appealing person. Yet Helen is actually one of the most magnificent of all Homeric characters. Neither a floozy nor a carefree supermodel, Homer's Helen has gravitas, compassion, intelligence, and even a certain spark of dangerous magic.

HELEN'S YOUNGER YEARS

Let's get to know the real Helen of Troy, as the ancient Greeks would have known her. Helen was the daughter of Zeus and Leda, a Spartan queen. In one of ancient Greece's many bizarre tales of divine sexual violence, Zeus raped Leda when he was in the form of a swan to conceal his infidelity from

his wife Hera. In spite of the unfortunate circumstances of her birth, Helen grew up healthy and strong in the Spartan royal family, and she had some famous siblings. Two of these siblings helped her out of something very scary that happened to her when she was no more than ten years old. The Athenian hero Theseus kidnapped poor Helen, intending to marry her. Thankfully, her brothers Castor and Pollux sacked Athens to get her back home.

Helen enjoyed some happier years after this awful kidnapping. Later Latin authors imagined young Helen as a tomboy princess, sparring with other Spartan girls. Her teenage years were spent among family and friends who loved her. When the time came for Helen to wed, her union was arranged, and she married a brave, fair-minded king from the east named Menelaus. Helen's sister Clytemnestra (pronounced kly-tem-NESS-tra) married Menelaus's brother Agamemnon, and regardless of everything that happened later, the unlucky Spartan princess must have enjoyed a few decent years before and after being married. Then, regrettably, the gods began meddling with her life.

There was once an epic called the *Cypria* (the *Cypria* was the first volume of the eight-book Epic Cycle of which the *Odyssey* was once seventh). The *Cypria* offered its audiences the tale of a certain fruit commonly called the "Apple of Discord." What happened was that a who's who of ancient Greek gods and heroes had gathered for a wedding. An uninvited guest showed up. Her name was Eris, and she was the goddess of strife. Eris left a golden apple engraved with the words "For the Fairest" at the wedding feast. All the goddesses who fancied themselves attractive wanted it. They decided that the handsome mortal hero Paris would decide which goddess ought to receive it. Athena promised wisdom and martial skill if Paris chose her. Hera promised Paris kingship over a vast swath of the earth. And Aphrodite promised marriage to the most beautiful woman in the world—Helen of Sparta. Paris chose Aphrodite. And so poor Helen, though married already, was compelled by divine will into a union with Paris, a man from the other side of the ancient Greek world.

Helen in the *Iliad*

Different ancient sources have different takes on how Helen felt about all of this. Sappho, who lived not long after Homer, wrote that Helen happily and glibly abandoned her family for the sake of Paris. Other writers from ancient Greece, however, said that Paris kidnapped her, or that Aphrodite forced her to come to Troy. However it happened, by the time we meet her in the *Iliad*, Helen is a restrained, tragic figure. We first see her in the *Iliad* above one of the gates of Troy, watching her flamboyant husband Paris meet her burly ex-husband Menelaus in battle. Since Helen loved her new Trojan in-laws as well as her old Greek friends and family, the Trojan War was an unending nightmare for her:

If only death had pleased me then, grim death,

that day I followed [Paris] to Troy, forsaking

my marriage bed, my kinsmen and my child . . .

and the lovely comradeship of women my own age.

Death never came, so now I can only waste away in tears.

—Helen, on the walls of Troy, in the *Iliad*
(Fagles translation, 3.208–214)

Helen, then, in the pages of Homer's *Iliad*, has paid an awful price for her act of adultery, whether it was even voluntary to begin with. When we meet her in the *Odyssey*, fortunately, things are looking up for the cursed heroine. She's back together with Menelaus in Sparta. Overall, they appear happy, in spite of the war and Menelaus's long journey home afterward. She's a middle-aged woman, and the Trojan War has been over for ten years. And when Helen meets Odysseus's son Telemachus in the *Odyssey*, she tells the young man about some of his father's deeds.

HELEN IN THE *ODYSSEY*

Helen told Telemachus that she always knew what Odysseus was up to during the war. Although she was a Trojan princess, she was a Greek queen as well, and had strong sympathies with the Greek armies besieging Troy. Accordingly, one day when Helen recognized Odysseus disguised as a beggar and sneaking around Troy to gather information, she didn't say anything. At that point, she wanted the Greeks to win, and she knew that Odysseus could probably figure out how to make it happen. And at a second, much more memorable juncture at the twilight of the Trojan War, Helen also chose to remain silent.

In an unforgettable flashback scene in Book 4 of the *Odyssey*, we encounter a very different Helen than the one most people imagine. Helen had been right about Odysseus—he *had* hatched the plot that finally won the war. He'd come up with the idea of the Trojan Horse, that famous wooden sculpture that held dangerous Greek assailants inside. The Trojans, in a moment of curious gullibility, had wheeled the giant Trojan Horse into their city, thinking that it was a peace offering from their exhausted adversaries. Night had fallen. Before any of the Greeks had a chance to sneak out of the Trojan Horse, Helen had inspected it.

Menelaus told young Telemachus that in the Trojan War's most climactic moment, Helen had stalked around the Trojan Horse in the dark, brushing the wooden sculpture with her beautiful fingers. She circled it and circled it. She called out to the Greek warriors inside, mimicking the voices of their wives. The concealed Greeks, who missed their spouses desperately, nearly replied, but Odysseus himself forced them to keep silent. In the end, Helen had crept off into the night, allowing the Greeks to carry out their plan.

The epic's many readers, over the ages, have pondered this strange little grotto of the *Odyssey*. How did Helen know the Greeks were inside the horse, and not only that, but *which* Greeks? Why would she prowl around their hiding place and make it clear she knew they were there? Was she really trying to get them to reveal themselves? One answer—a very satisfying answer—is that Helen was reminding the Greeks that they were completely under her power. Odysseus and his men were quite literally at her mercy at that moment, stuffed into the Trojan Horse, because Helen could have alerted the city guard to their presence. But, as she called to them in the voices of wives they had not seen for a decade, Helen almost menacingly reminded the Greek heroes that they had all come across the Aegean Sea for her. She reminded them that all their homesickness and suffering had been for her, and even that they had abandoned their wives *for her*. It's an awesome moment of self-assertion for a character who has spent so much of her life powerless and downcast! And it's not the only time in ancient Greek literature that Helen appears as terrifying and formidable. In

Aeschylus's play *The Libation Bearers*, the chorus compares Helen to a lion cub, coddled and petted until it realizes its true nature and tears everyone around it to pieces.

Helen only makes a brief appearance in Homer's *Odyssey*, and she's also a fairly minor character in the *Iliad*. But in both cases, she's not what you might expect. The daughter of Zeus, and born into Spartan royalty with great beauty, Helen nonetheless spends much of her life luckless, miserable, and repentant, and in her sadness, there is a profound and moving humanity. And very occasionally, in ancient Greek literature, we see an even more unexpected Helen—a dark angel who knows full well the carnage she has caused. As the playwright Aeschylus puts it in the play *Agamemnon*, "She was war, / angel of war, angel of agony, lighting men to death" (Fagles translation, 1456–7).

NOW YOU KNOW

In an alternate version of Helen's story (made famous in Euripides's play *Helen*), Helen never went to Troy! Instead, her doppelgänger went there, married to Paris, while she stayed loyal to Menelaus, hiding in a cave in Egypt as the war dragged on.

In the *Odyssey*, Helen and Menelaus are an unusual example of a happy ending in ancient Greek literature. Classical Greek plays and ancient Mediterranean epics, including the *Odyssey* itself, did not conclude with happy marriages, and it wasn't until the theatrical works of the late 300s BCE and afterward that happy marriages started wrapping stories up. By the Common Era, ancient Greek novels like *Callirhoe* (first century CE), and *An Ephesian Tale* and *Leucippe and Clitophon* (second century CE) frequently ended with joyous romantic unions. Menelaus and Helen, then, were way ahead of their time!

PENELOPE: THE QUEEN

THE *ODYSSEY'S* MAIN HEROINE IS PRETTY QUIET AT FIRST.

PRONUNCIATION: pe-NELL-uh-pee

LIKES: Privacy, Weaving, Being Left Alone

DISLIKES: Uninvited Guests

SPECIAL POWERS: Putting Up with Arrogant Men, Delay Tactics

NARRATIVE ROLE: Waiting to be rescued by her husband and son, and possibly undertaking some scheming of her own.

Penelope, the wife of Odysseus, is a marvelous enigma. It is possible to read the *Odyssey* and see her as little more than a damsel in distress, passively awaiting the arrival of her rescuer. It is equally possible to read her as a female Odysseus—a disarmingly intelligent operator who can control situations even while seeming like she isn't. The closer we look at Penelope, the less clear she becomes. Ancient Romans praised Penelope as a model matron, heroic mostly in that she kept her bedroom door locked and stayed loyal to her husband. Modern readers, though, often see a more multidimensional Penelope, one who has a definite ὁμοφροσύνη (*homophrosyne*), or "like-mindedness," to her wily husband.

Though she doesn't get a great deal of camera time, Penelope's appearances in the *Odyssey* are often momentous. She is the reason, after all, that the suitors are all in the palace of Ithaca. Penelope is the magnet drawing Odysseus home. (Similarly, Helen was the cause of the events of the *Iliad*. Homer may have had a heroine addiction.) In her first scene in the epic, a bard has been singing a song about the aftermath of the Trojan War. Penelope appears on a staircase overlooking the area where the suitors are assembled:

Penelope was both physically and morally above the gathered rabble—formidable, celestial, and tragic, all at once. She asked the bard to please not sing about the Trojan War, but then something surprising happened. Telemachus, in an icy tone, told his mother to shut up, go back upstairs, and tend to her weaving. Speaking, said Telemachus, was men's business, and he was the kingpin of the house, so he, in particular, had the prerogative to speak.

It's a strange, sad moment in the epic. Telemachus, possibly feeling emasculated by the suitors, may have been trying to puff himself up by disparaging his mother. It is the first, but not the last, time in the epic that Telemachus treats his mother dismissively and shoos her away from a conversation. And so up Penelope went to her quarters, crying, Homer tells us, until the goddess Athena put her to sleep.

Whether or not we interpret Penelope as a secret genius, there is something heartbreaking about the heroine of the *Odyssey*. She's a piece of property in a man's world, and even her own son disdains her. Confined to a few palace rooms, unheeded and powerless, Penelope, like centuries of highborn ancient Greek women who heard her story, was stuck in a gilded cage. With an absent husband; an angsty, chauvinistic teenage son;

and more than a hundred lecherous men after her money and her body, Penelope has a plight that is uniquely unenviable in the *Odyssey*.

THE SHROUD

Other than that she is Mrs. Odysseus, and that there are suitors after her, the thing that many of us remember about Penelope is that she's weaving a shroud. The ringleader of the suitors (his name is Antinous) lays out the situation with the shroud in a long speech to Telemachus (2.92–139).

In the speech, Antinous grumbled that Penelope was the trickiest woman in the world! Why, she had been leading the suitors on for almost four years, and communicating privately with each of them. And Penelope, almost four years back, had announced that since Odysseus was obviously deceased, she would marry one of the suitors. It was just that first, she said, she needed to weave a funeral shroud for Odysseus's father, Laertes. She wove and wove, and wove and wove, and it wasn't until the fourth year of weaving that one of her maids discovered that Penelope was *unweaving* the robe every night, even though she was indeed working on it during the day. And so (the suitors' ringleader Antinous concluded), the suitors, having had enough, had forced her to finish the robe. Antinous then said she'd been torturing them, and that Penelope had a cleverness beyond that of any woman who had ever lived. Wouldn't Telemachus tell her to marry one of them already? Because she was developing a reputation as a coquette, and not doing Telemachus any favors in the process!

Antinous's revelation to Telemachus tells us more about the suitors' stupidity than it does Penelope's boundless brilliance. Laertes, Penelope's father-in-law, is still alive, and he lives through the whole story, and so his need for a funeral shroud is likely not insurmountable. That the suitors would believe a robe would take four years to make suggests that their lust and gluttony are not matched by a commensurate common sense. The chief of the suitors here, in short, along with his cronies, appears as an idiot as well as a thug, and perhaps that was Homer's predominant intention.

Dullards though they might be, the suitors are still in Penelope's palace, and she has to deal with them. And as the story proceeds, they prove increasingly ruthless. Toward the end of Book 4, with Telemachus off making friends, Antinous laid out an ugly plan. The suitors decided to wait for Telemachus in a narrow channel he had to pass through on the way to Ithaca. Then, they would ambush him and take him out.

In a single scene, Penelope learned that her son had gone out over the same dangerous sea that had claimed her husband—and about the suitors' plot to assassinate Telemachus. And, agonizingly, she couldn't *do* anything about it. Homer writes that her heart ached, pain sank into her bones, and Penelope collapsed on the worn hallway floor that led into her room. As is so often the case in the epic, Penelope was stuck, and she had no options. As the suitors gloated downstairs about the looming assassination, Penelope could only pray to Athena.

Athena heard her. The goddess assumed the shape of Penelope's sister and told Penelope that Telemachus would make it home safely. Still half asleep, Penelope said she was distraught to be missing both her husband and her son, but the disguised Athena assured her that Telemachus had a powerful ally with him—the goddess Athena! Awakening, and realizing that her visitor was something supernatural, Penelope asked the disguised Athena about her missing husband—was he alive or had he perished? The goddess refused to say anything one way or another, and then she vanished. Homer tells us that the conversation brought some comfort to Penelope. Book 4 ends with the suitors planning to kill Telemachus, and the unfortunate Penelope still cornered in her palace.

Then comes the central portion of the *Odyssey*. For *eleven* books of the epic (more than two hundred pages in the recent Emily Wilson translation), Penelope is off-screen. Presumably, she continues to quietly suffer as Odysseus bolts around the Aegean in his perilous, blockbuster escapades. Once, he mentions Penelope to his captor Calypso. But otherwise, she does not enter the narrative again until Book 16, when she learns from a pair of messengers that Telemachus *did* make it home safely, just as her divine visitor promised.

The news marks a modest turning point for the heroine. Once again coming downstairs to make herself heard, Penelope stood next to a door and focused her wrath on Antinous (16.419–36). She knew he was behind the plot to kill her son. She called him a ruffian and a madman. She told Antinous that Odysseus once saved his father's life, and growled that Antinous was a despicable person, telling him to get out and stop hurting her family. The venom of her speech was sudden and unexpected, and another suitor, the oily, well-spoken Eurymachus, assured her that they weren't trying to hurt Telemachus. (Eurymachus was lying, and he was in on the whole thing.) And then in a repeat performance from Book 1, Penelope went upstairs to her room, wept, and fell asleep only through the help of Athena.

This mic drop speech to the chief suitor Antinous seems to suggest the emergence of a firmer, more assertive Penelope. But when the heroine reunites with her son once more, we're keenly reminded of the uphill battle she is fighting. When Telemachus returned to the palace, the servants and slaves all flocked to him, embracing him. Penelope, also, rushed to greet her son, grateful beyond measure that the youth had made it home, after all. Hugging her boy and kissing him, she asked Telemachus where he'd gone and what he'd learned. And in one of the most needlessly chilly speeches in Homer, Telemachus told Penelope (as he had sixteen books before) to go upstairs with her women. Go take a bath, change clothes, and prepare sacrifices to the gods, said Telemachus. He had guests he was bringing to the palace. And so, once again, up to her room Penelope went to bathe, change clothes, and pray.

There is some evidence, *later* in the epic, which we'll discuss later in this book, that there's more than meets the eye with Penelope. But for most of the story, her tale is almost that of a martyr. Stuck in an unending cycle of baths and changes of clothing, derogated by her own son, trapped by an inexorable, four-year-long home invasion, Penelope can only sit by and hope that her truant husband, off on an endless string of murderous, adulterous adventures, will show up and save her. This is her story in most of the *Odyssey*—a case study of an unfortunate person, as strong and intelligent as anyone else, who's nonetheless crammed into the periphery of society. Ancient Greek art that depicts her shows a figure hunched and shawled, seated and often working at a loom, her eyes downcast, an icon for so many of us, ancient as well as modern, who show considerable heroism merely by enduring and surviving.

NOW YOU KNOW

Homer's language is incredibly rich. Ancient Greek syntax is flexible, and the language allows for a great compression of meaning in just a few words. In a key scene with Penelope, Homer writes, ἀλλ᾽ ἄρ᾽ ἷζε ἐπ᾽ οὐδοῦ πολυκμήτου θαλάμοιο ὀλοφυρομένη, or, as Stanley Lombardo translates it, "but [Penelope] sat curled / On the worn threshold of her bedroom / And wept" (4.718–9). In the tiny details of the original language (ἐπ᾽ οὐδοῦ πολυκμήτου θαλάμοιο, literally "on the threshold of the worn-in apartment"), the setting (a doorway trodden by years of foot traffic) matches the character (an oppressed woman, stuck there). Homer's language always abounds in meaning, just like this!

ODYSSEUS: THE HERO

THE APPEALING SIDE OF ANCIENT GREECE'S MOST FAMOUS SEAFARER.

PRONUNCIATION: oh-DISS-ee-us

LIKES: Ithaca, Penelope, His Friends

DISLIKES: Being Waylaid, Underestimated, and Disrespected

SPECIAL POWERS: Relentlessness, Resilience

NARRATIVE ROLE: A careworn protagonist trying to get home.

In the *Odyssey*'s first line, Homer describes Odysseus as ἄνδρα πολύτροπον (*andra polytropon*), which literally means "man of many turnings" or "man of many ways." Later, he is πολυμήχανος (*polymechanos*), or "of many devices," and πολύτλας (*polytlas*), or "much enduring." Perhaps best of all, Odysseus is ποικιλομήτης (*poikilometis*), which can be translated as "dapple skilled," meaning that Odysseus's skills are as varied and adaptable as the sunlight coming down through branches and leaves.

Together, these famous Homeric epithets tell us what kind of person Odysseus is. He is slippery. He's complex. He never holds still for long. He never even remains the same person for very long. He evolves from scene to scene and moment to moment, and is a mesmerizing figure who can become whatever he needs to, as skilled in lying as he is in its close cousin elegant social deportment. Conan the Barbarian and the Incredible Hulk might be the cinematic great-grandsons of the ancient Greek hero Heracles. As for Odysseus, he's a little bit closer to James Bond.

Odysseus moves through his epic in a long sequence of disguises, telling hours of fake origin stories about himself. The most famous part of the *Odyssey*, that four-book-long comic strip in which we meet the Cyclops, the Sirens, and Circe and follow Odysseus to Hades, is narrated by *Odysseus*, and not by Homer. Odysseus recounts his signature waterborne adventures to a people called the Phaeacians over a long evening of wine and games, and for all we know, he's made up every single word of the long narrative.

Still, beneath the many disguises, and behind the constant torrent of duplicitous narratives he offers anyone who will listen in the epic, there is something like a stable person, with characteristics that persist throughout the *Odyssey*. The epic is a νόστος (*nostos*), or "homecoming" story, and in it, Odysseus endures two returns. The first is the ten-year-long physical journey he takes back to Ithaca following the Trojan War. The second is the equally challenging journey that he must undertake as a deeply traumatized combat veteran back to the everyday world of civilian life. While Odysseus says many things and becomes many things over the course of the *Odyssey*, from the beginning to the end of the epic, he is on the move, and he is scarred by his past.

There is a vulnerable, human Odysseus in the *Odyssey*, then, just as there is an enigmatic, chameleon Odysseus. And it is the former whom we first meet in Homer's story, midway through Book 5, which proceeds as follows.

ODYSSEUS THE EVERYMAN

Odysseus sat on the shore of Calypso's island, his eyes damp with tears. Imprisoned there, he felt the years passing by, and his days were spent sitting on the sand or rocks, looking morosely out at the sea. From time to time in the *Odyssey*, the protagonist is just such a figure. He may be a multifaceted person with many layers, capable of weaving unending tapestries of lies. But he's also exhausted. He's lost too many friends. The glories he earned for himself on the battlefield, including devising the Trojan Horse that won the war, have left him a stranger in a long sequence of strange lands.

Newcomers to the *Odyssey* might giggle at Odysseus's plight on Calypso's island. After all, there are far worse fates than being stuck with a gorgeous sea nymph. But when the epic's first scene with Odysseus begins, the wanderer has been imprisoned there for seven years. The narrative makes it clear, in an ominous aside, that Odysseus did not enjoy the sex that Calypso demanded of him. When she told him that he was allowed to leave, Odysseus shuddered with incredulity, and in spite of being given nothing more than a few simple tools with which to build his own raft, Odysseus leapt at the chance to depart.

During his first days at sea, the hero's heart soared with hope. Keeping his eyes on the constellations of Pleiades and Ursa Major and Orion, Odysseus made his way west over the deep water with no land in sight for seventeen days. He is an everyman at this moment in the *Odyssey*, enveloped by the sky and open sea. At night, the stars shined on the water so that it seemed the ocean and constellations were all one and the same. Then, on the morning of his eighteenth day of sailing, the starlight on the water gave way to dawn, and Odysseus saw cliffs rising out of the mist and waves. A terrible storm struck, and Odysseus's humble vessel was capsized and broken. He swam, first for a day, and then a second day, and then a third, helped along, only *just* enough, by a small breeze from Athena. Then, finally, the hero glimpsed the shore again, as Homer describes in one of his epic similes:

As when a father

lies sick and weak for many days, tormented

by some cruel spirit, till at last the gods

restore him back to life; his children feel

great joy; Odysseus felt the same joy

when he saw land.

—Odysseus glimpses land, *Odyssey* (Wilson translation, 5.394–99)

Even after seeing dry land, Odysseus still struggled to get ashore. Scraped on sea rocks and reefs and confronted by tall cliffs, eventually, due once more to a tiny spark of help from Athena, Odysseus swam to the mouth of a river. Then, swollen, aching, and broken, he staggered out of the brine and onto the shore of Phaeacia, and passed out.

These are the events of Book 5 of the *Odyssey*. We first encounter Odysseus as a sad, solitary man pitted against the awesome forces of gods and nature. His pluck and grit are admirable. And yet as he misses his home and family, and struggles pitifully to stay afloat early on during his adventures, Odysseus seems as though he could be anyone. At this point, the protagonist is an uncomplicated, sympathetic, relatable person. We want him to survive his voyage across the sea because oceans are big and scary, and no one deserves to drown. We want him to get home because homesickness hurts.

Odysseus the Charmer

Our first impressions of Odysseus as an everyman hero—a guy trying to get home—soon give way to a better understanding of who he is, in one of the epic's most beloved scenes, in Book 6. Poor, battered, naked, soggy Odysseus had collapsed in a leaf pile. The sounds of nearby voices woke him up. He had no idea where he was. He managed to get up and cautiously peered through some foliage. Down by a river, he saw a number of young women. Only partially clad, they were washing their clothes and playing a game. One of them, Homer tells us, was the princess of the Phaeacians, Nausicaa.

Modern sensibilities (and perhaps ancient ones too) might read this scene with squeamishness. Here, after all, was a grimy, middle-aged man spying on a bunch of undressed young ladies who didn't know they were being watched. Yet Odysseus, to his credit, didn't linger there. As politely as he could, he grabbed a leafy branch to cover his crotch and then announced his presence. Understandably, the Phaeacian girls all fled, excepting Princess Nausicaa herself. Then, Odysseus addressed the young woman. His overture to the startled princess was generous, humble, and kind—a characteristic cocktail of flattery and self-effacement, of truth and falsehoods, so eloquent that when it was over, Nausicaa concluded that the filthy stranger was a decent fellow in spite of the fact that he had just stepped out of the woods in the nude with twigs in his beard. Soon thereafter, Odysseus won over the Phaeacian noblewoman so completely that Princess Nausicaa gave him clothes to wear and resolved to take him to meet her parents. The social ingenuity he exhibits in this wonderful scene is almost as impressive as the seafaring skills that brought him to Phaeacia in the first place.

As the story continues, Nausicaa's parents, King Alcinous and Queen Arete, took the wanderer in and cared for him, even though he showed up wearing clothes he received from their daughter! The *Odyssey* is rife with scenes of sadness and struggle up until Book 6, but when Odysseus reached the land of the Phaeacians, everything was suddenly as it should have been. A gracious propriety governed the Phaeacian palace. At the center of its court was Odysseus, who pretended to be nothing more than a shipwrecked nobody trying to get home. No one in Phaeacia knew who he was. In fact, as Odysseus's visit to Phaeacia continues, we get the sense that Odysseus *himself* may no longer have known exactly who he was.

ODYSSEUS THE VETERAN

During the second day of Odysseus's visit to Phaeacia, two things happened that spoiled his flawless etiquette. First, he cried while a bard sang a ballad about the Trojan War. The song stirred up awful memories for Odysseus, and though he tried to conceal his tears, King Alcinous saw them. Later that same day, the Phaeacians decided they'd pass the time with some recreational athletic competitions. The games started out smoothly enough. There was a race, and then some wrestling and discus throwing—all the usual sports associated with the ancient Greeks. Then, a young man started prodding Odysseus. Odysseus, the youth said, looked pretty burly. He looked like he could handle himself. Wouldn't Odysseus like to participate in the games? Odysseus declined. The young man needled the hero. Maybe, the youth taunted, Odysseus really was just a nobody, and not the gentleman everyone seemed to think he was!

Something snapped in Odysseus. He seized a discus larger than the competition size and hurled it so hard that it hummed in the air as it flew, landing vastly farther out than the other discuses that had been thrown. He looked around, the blood suddenly pumping in his veins, and asked if anyone wanted to try and beat his throw—or whether anyone present would like to box him, or wrestle him, or race him. For a moment in this scene, the genteel Odysseus, silver-tongued and debonair, melts away, and we see the Odysseus of Homer's *Iliad*, a killer who spent ten years with thousands of other killers in a long war that was hell on earth.

King Alcinous, fortunately for everyone, defused the situation. The Phaeacians switched to dancing. The young man apologized for goading Odysseus and gave him a sword to make amends. Odysseus accepted the apology and blessed him, and all was well in Phaeacia. Yet we remember this moment as the narrative moves forward. Odysseus, reintegrated into civilian life, doesn't quite fit anymore. He bears deep psychological scars from what happened at Troy, and he is a very dangerous person. Odysseus's sudden ferocity in the Phaeacian court shows us that the traumatized hero will never be the same again, even if he does make it home.

Odysseus isn't always an appealing character. In the *Odyssey*, it's very often hard to tell what Odysseus is thinking, as he dons disguises and makes up falsehoods about himself, even, later on, to his son, wife, and father. At times, Odysseus is outright sadistic. Yet when we first meet him in the story, Odysseus is just a small person, adrift in a big world, doing his best to stay afloat. He has a long journey ahead of him, and one that will involve psychological recovery as well as physical travel, because coming home, as the ancient Greeks well knew, is often far more complicated than it seems.

NOW YOU KNOW

Odysseus has a younger sister named Ctimene (15.363), whom his servant Eumaeus mentions in the epic. Although Odysseus's brother-in-law Eurylochus is a minor character in the *Odyssey*, Ctimene's name only appears once in the story. It's a shame. If Ctimene were anything like her brother, she would have been an interesting character to read about!

Later mythological traditions attested that Odysseus didn't want to fight in the Trojan War. He feigned madness, but men sent by the Greek leaders were able to prove that he was still sane, and off he went.

CALYPSO

THE PROS AND CONS OF AN OUTDOOR SEX DUNGEON.

PRONUNCIATION: kuh-LIPS-oh

LIKES: Long Walks on the Beach, Sunsets, Being Dominant

DISLIKES: Following Orders, Dressing Modestly

SPECIAL POWERS: Insatiable Lust, Singing

NARRATIVE ROLE: Calypso keeps Odysseus as a prisoner for seven years and finally lets him go in Book 5 of the *Odyssey*.

The long-suffering Odysseus, who took ten years to get home, spent *seven* of those years in the island paradise and erotic buffet of a gorgeous sea nymph. Calypso contributed to the hero's misery chiefly by feeding him and making love to him every night. Eventually, the gods decided it was time for Odysseus to go home, and so Calypso packed him lunch, slapped his heroic tush one last time, and sent him on his way. And that, more or less, is Calypso's role in the story.

Let's get to know Calypso a little better, though. Because although Book 5 of the *Odyssey* is always worth a good giggle, there are some pretty interesting and very dark aspects of Odysseus's steamy stayover with Homer's horniest nymph, not the least of which is the fact that he genuinely didn't want to be there. To begin with the basics, this is what happens with Calypso in the *Odyssey*.

Odysseus originally met Calypso when he was at rock bottom. As Odysseus made his many hairsbreadth escapes from the Cyclops, the Laestrygonians, the Sirens, and finally the monster Scylla and the whirlpool Charybdis, he lost more and more men. During this spin cycle around the eastern Mediterranean, a combination of bad luck and tactical mistakes led to Odysseus eventually losing every single one of his crewmen. Having drifted alone for nine days after a long string of disasters, he was lucky enough to wash up on an island called Ogygia, where he met a very, *very* friendly nymph named Calypso, who toweled him off and saw to his needs, and then to her own.

Amusingly, it is with the narrative of how he met Calypso that Odysseus breaks off his four-book-long "story within a story" to the Phaeacians. The Phaeacian court listened, rapt, as Odysseus laid out the epic's seminal island-hopping sequence. Then, the hero reached the part about how the frisky nymph pulled him out of the sea, and perhaps not wanting to draw attention to the length or nature of his sabbatical, he cut himself off.

The story about how Odysseus met Calypso may or may not be true. (After all, Odysseus tells it, and only a small percentage of what comes out of his mouth is reliable throughout the *Odyssey*.) More dependable, of course, is Homer, who gives us about a dozen pages describing what Odysseus's life was really like on Ogygia.

Book 5 of the *Odyssey*, the Calypso book, opens with a beautiful, sinister allusion. Eos, the goddess of dawn, Homer writes, languidly rose from the bed that she shared with her lover Tithonus (pronounced tih-THOAN-uhs), and the morning blossomed in fiery splinters. It's a characteristically stunning opening. Ancient Greeks had wonderful ways of describing daybreak! But who was Tithonus, and why would Eos, the goddess of dawn, leave him in bed?

Ancient Greek audiences would have known that Tithonus was the mortal lover of Eos. When Eos, smitten with the mortal Tithonus, asked Zeus to make Tithonus live forever, Zeus consented. Eos forgot, however, to secure a guarantee for Tithonus's immortal *youth*, and so in spite of living forever, Tithonus grew so old and feeble he could only lie in place and babble. That's the myth of Eos and Tithonus, and in it, the mortal ends up living in eternal and deepening decrepitude, all due to his divine lover's small mistake.

Homer thus begins Book 5 of the *Odyssey* with a menacing reference to what Odysseus might become. Odysseus, like Tithonus, will live out his days as the powerless pawn of a greedy goddess, unless help arrives. He's also like Penelope because he's backed into a corner due to the sexual

agendas of the powerful, and at this point, both hero and heroine are desperately hoping for rescue.

While Penelope is confined to a handful of upstairs palace rooms and chastened for leaving them, Odysseus's penitentiary is larger and, in all likelihood, far more pleasant. In one of the most celebrated set descriptions in the *Odyssey*, Homer writes:

> *A great fire*
>
> *blazed on the hearth and the smell of cedar*
>
> *cleanly split and sweetwood burning bright*
>
> *wafted a cloud of fragrance down the island.*
>
> *Deep inside she sang, the goddess Calypso, lifting*
>
> *her breathtaking voice as she glided back and forth*
>
> *before her loom, her golden shuttle weaving.*
>
> *Thick, luxuriant woods grew round the cave,*
>
> *alders and black poplars, pungent cypress too,*
>
> *and there birds roosted, folding their long wings . . .*
>
> *And round the mouth of the cave trailed a vine*
>
> *laden with clusters, bursting with ripe grapes.*
>
> *Four springs in a row, bubbling clear and cold,*
>
> *running side-by-side, took channels left and right.*
>
> **—Homer describes Calypso's island, *Odyssey***
> **(Fagles translation, 5.64–81)**

Granted, Odysseus doesn't *want* to be there, but Ogygia still sounds like a pretty nice place to spend time. Over these babbling brooks and lovely woodlands, in Homer's narrative, flew Hermes. The messenger god of Greek mythology first enjoyed the enchanting scenery on the island. Then he headed into Calypso's cave and got down to business.

Hermes told Calypso that she couldn't keep Odysseus any longer. Zeus had issued an order, and Calypso had to release her catch. Hearing this, the nymph was irate. The gods, Calypso sneered, were a jealous bunch! They couldn't stand it when goddesses enjoyed liaisons with mortals, even in cases when the goddesses in question were earnestly in love! Plus, Zeus was the one who had caused Odysseus's ship to sink! (She was telling the truth.) The sea nymph's anger crescendoed into a tantrum. She had taken care of Odysseus after Zeus had condemned him to die! Finally, Calypso's tone changed, since she knew she could do nothing against the will of Zeus. Very well, then, she concluded, to hell with Odysseus, he could go back out to sea! She'd at least give Odysseus really good directions to get him home. Hermes, watching the sea nymph's zigzagging blowup, was diplomatically silent, and eventually told her to go ahead and give Odysseus a nudge seaward so that the hero could get home. The droll interplay between the gods in Book 5 then darkens to a sadder scene. Odysseus, we learn, really wasn't doing well. He cried a lot. At night, he served his mistress's kinky needs, but, as Robert Fagles translates, "he had no choice— / unwilling lover alongside lover all too willing" (5.172). He saw Calypso approaching, and learned that she was bringing information, rather than demanding another unwanted liaison. She had good news and bad news. The good news was that Odysseus was allowed to leave. The bad news (though Calypso didn't seem to think anything of it) was that Odysseus would be departing on a raft. He would be required to build the raft. She would give him some clothing and food. Then he could make his way home across the Aegean.

Odysseus, hearing the nymph's dubious plans for his future, tried to be polite. But any ancient Greek, hearing this scene, would have either winced, laughed, or both. Calypso's offer was akin to telling someone who needs to cross a thousand-mile desert that you'll give them some trail mix and a windbreaker, and even let them build their own skateboard.

Still, Odysseus was in no position to bargain, and after he expressed his reservations and confirmed the goddess's earnest goodwill, the two sealed the agreement. A farewell dinner proceeded, during which Odysseus remained cautious not to incur his captor's resentment, and after some goodbye sex, the next morning, Calypso gave him some tools.

A four-day raft-building montage ensues. Odysseus, who was nothing if not resourceful when motivated, got to work, using various carpentry tools provided by Calypso. Though she was presumably watching the hardy hero's construction site with both ambivalence and sadness, Calypso, clad in her sexiest silver and gold, still helped him out with whatever he needed, and even supplied cloth for the sail toward the end of the project. When Odysseus was ready to go, she gave him a bath, dressed him up in the promised clothing, furnished him with some food, and handed him a skin of water, and one of wine. (Because ancient Greeks knew that navigating perilous waters on a slapdash raft is best undertaken with a decent buzz.)

Calypso then saw Odysseus off, and he sailed out without looking back. And that's Calypso's appearance in the *Odyssey*. It's a memorable cameo, simultaneously erotic, morally uncomfortable, funny, and tragic. We can imagine that way back during the 600s or 500s BCE, a few drinks into the evening, ancient Greeks might have requested a performance of this more adult-themed slab of the *Odyssey*. In one of the often-forgotten ironic factoids of ancient Greek literature, it is neither Zeus, nor Poseidon, nor human warriors, nor monsters that give Odysseus the most trouble in his long journey home, but instead, a middleweight immortal cougar who just can't get enough of him.

NOW YOU KNOW

Calypso's name actually comes from the same root word as "apocalypse." The name Καλυψώ (*Kalipso*) comes from the same root as καλύπτω (*kalupto*), which means "cover" or "conceal," as she is responsible for concealing Odysseus for quite a while. Relatedly, the word ἀποκάλυψις (*apokalupsis*) means "uncovering" or "revelation," as in the final book of the New Testament, the *Apokalupsis* of John, meaning the "Apocalypse" of John or "Revelation" of John.

POSEIDON

BLUE HAIR. HUGE TRIDENT.
IN A VERY BAD MOOD.

PRONUNCIATION: po-SIGH-don

LIKES: Seismology, Marine Biology, Horses

DISLIKES: Hubris, People Who Call Tridents Pitchforks

SPECIAL POWERS: Cannonballs, Hurricanes

NARRATIVE ROLE: Poseidon is angry at Odysseus for wounding the Cyclops and does his best to keep Odysseus from getting home.

Poseidon, the brother of Zeus and the god of the sea, spends the middle part of Homer's *Odyssey* sloshing around in the waves, stalking Odysseus, and occasionally hurling storms, death threats, and tsunamis at him. Terrifying, inexorable, scatterbrained, and slightly preposterous, Poseidon fits in rank and file with all the other Homeric gods.

In the *Odyssey*, Homer makes Poseidon's role clear immediately, in Book 1. Poseidon's anger at Odysseus was *immense*. Poseidon would pursue Odysseus all the way to Ithaca, despite the fact that Poseidon was, at that moment, down in Ethiopia, attending a big barbecue being held in his honor. With the god of the sea set against him, how would Odysseus ever make it home?

The answer to this question is, of course, with help from Athena. Athena, in the *Odyssey*'s opening scene, called a back-channel meeting with Zeus. She taunted Zeus, telling Zeus that although Odysseus always revered him, the poor mortal was still marooned out there somewhere far away from Ithaca, thanks to Poseidon. Zeus, in reply, thundered that Poseidon had good reason for being angry at Odysseus. Odysseus had really hurt Poseidon's son Polyphemus (pronounced paw-lee-FEEM-us),

the lord of the Cyclopes—Odysseus *blinded* the poor creature. Then Zeus, suddenly reconsidering in mid-monologue, reasoned that Poseidon would back down if the rest of the gang were set against him. Zeus said he could get behind Athena's plan. He could absolutely get behind this. Wait, what were they talking about? (Keep in mind that in the Homeric epics, Zeus is like a nuclear warhead piloted by a housefly.) Nonetheless, off Athena went, with the dubious assurance of her licentious, erratic father that it was absolutely fine to derail Uncle Poseidon's schemes and ignore his feelings.

What happens between Odysseus and Poseidon in the *Odyssey* thereafter is a little bit confusing, because it happens out of order. The sea god seems to lurch out of the Mediterranean once in a while, fling some kelp and some whitecaps at the hero, and then return to snorkeling. But if you read the Poseidon episodes of the *Iliad* and *Odyssey* closely, and watch the relationship between Odysseus and Poseidon evolve, you find that the entire sequence of events is carefully thought out and, really, one of the sadder parts of the whole story. So let's retrace the complex relationship between Poseidon and Odysseus and try to understand the spat between the two of them in the *Odyssey*.

During Homer's earlier epic, the *Iliad*, Odysseus and Poseidon were on the same side. Ancient Greece's most renowned mariner and the god of the briny depths both fought against Troy. There was a problem, though. Zeus had promised a nymph that he would support Troy. And at a crucial moment, tired of being steamrolled by his lightning-wielding brother, Poseidon essentially called Zeus an unelected despot.

Poseidon roared at a climactic moment of the *Iliad* (15.187–95) that when he, Zeus, and Hades were born from the titans ages ago, it had been decided that he'd rule the sea, Zeus would rule the heavens, and Hades the underworld, and they'd *share the rule of the land* between them. Zeus, however, persistently ignored the old covenant, and so (Poseidon said in this tirade) Zeus had better back down and stop threatening the god of the sea. Poseidon was speaking to a messenger goddess in this conversation, and when she cautioned him against a declaration of war, he slowly, and with great effort, collected himself. Poseidon said he was disgusted and bitter but that he would withdraw his challenge. The sea god's de-escalation was good news, because a conflict between Poseidon and Zeus would have been cataclysmic.

Eventually, the Greeks won the Trojan War. As the victors shook hands and headed home, we can imagine that Poseidon's feelings toward Odysseus were rather positive, since Odysseus was instrumental to the Greeks' success. Here's what happened next, although some of this happens off camera in Homer.

Odysseus lingered in Troy for a while with King Agamemnon, even though many other Greeks sailed off into the sunset (we find this out in Book 4). Then Odysseus and his men finally headed west (the next part of this narrative is in Book 9). They sacked and raided a town in the northern Aegean, then fled when warriors from neighboring areas chased them off. Next, Odysseus and his fleet, back at sea again, were pummeled by a massive storm *sent by Zeus*. The mariners' sails were heavily damaged. They beached the ships for a while close to the island of Cythera, but the wind battered them for nine days, driving them to the island of the Lotus-Eaters, and then to the island of the Cyclopes. It's interesting to pause here and note that Odysseus's first divine opponent in the *Odyssey* (for undisclosed reasons) is not Poseidon, but *Zeus*, a deity who, throughout the Homeric epics, works in mysterious, and possibly schizophrenic, ways.

In the remainder of Book 9, we read of Odysseus's fateful encounter with the Cyclops Polyphemus, son of Poseidon. Odysseus and his men got stuck in the cave of the Cyclops, who was gobbling them up in pairs and planned to eat all of them, saving Odysseus for the last. Odysseus got the creature drunk, he stabbed it in the eye, and he and the bulk of his men fled to their ships and got away. At the end of this famous confrontation, Odysseus told the maimed monster his name, and Polyphemus then shrieked a curse at the hero. The Cyclops prayed to Poseidon that Odysseus would never reach Ithaca, and that if Odysseus ever did, that he would arrive there battered, degraded, and having lost all his men.

The earsplitting curse that ends Book 9 explains events that have already taken place in the *Odyssey*, because by the time we read about old one-eye, Odysseus's main run-in with Poseidon has already taken place back in Book 5. The hero, having set forth in his little dinghy from Calypso's island, had been at sea for seventeen days. Odysseus saw friendly territory. But at just that moment, Poseidon, heading back to Greece from his honorary cookout in Ethiopia, spied Odysseus rowing home and hit the hero with everything he had. Poseidon glowered and fumed. He called to the clouds and began stirring the sea with his trident. The sky grew black, and mountainous waves rolled down from the north. Odysseus had time for a brief lamentation, and then his raft was dashed to pieces, and he was at the mercy of the heaving ocean, with chaotic storm currents pulling him all over the place. He struggled to breathe and coughed up salt water. It's one of the *Odyssey*'s most unforgettable moments, this struggle between a single person and the amassed forces of gods and nature. Ancient Greeks wrote marvelously about the sea.

As this principal confrontation scene draws to a close, Poseidon dusted off his hands, assuming Odysseus was taken care of. A nymph, however, came to the hero's rescue and ultimately helped spirit him shoreward. And although the sea remained a consistent threat to Odysseus throughout the remainder of his adventures, this confrontation in Book 5 is his most climactic run-in with Poseidon. It happens confusingly early, before we entirely understand *why* Poseidon is shooting coral reefs at him.

To return to the subject of Poseidon in the Homeric epics as a whole, what happens to Poseidon in the *Iliad* ultimately happens to Poseidon in the *Odyssey* too. In both epics, Poseidon has an itinerary. In both epics, Zeus bullies his younger brother into submission. And in both epics, Poseidon has to swallow his pride. Poseidon's fearsome quest for revenge in the *Odyssey* has a finale that is both anticlimactic and odd. Here's what eventually happens to Poseidon in the *Odyssey*.

After the Phaeacians dropped Odysseus off in Ithaca in Book 13, Poseidon and Zeus had a talk. The sea god was angry. Poseidon grumbled that Odysseus had not only made it to Ithaca; he had made it to Ithaca *in a Phaeacian flotilla, disembarking with all kinds of gifts*! Poseidon said he realized Zeus had ultimately intended for Odysseus to make it home. But did his bossy brother really have to let Odysseus return to Ithaca with crates of linens and fine carpets? All the mortals were going to think that Poseidon's threats counted for nothing!

In return, Zeus offered a monologue that was simultaneously warm, comforting, and deranged, like a tall uncle with body odor and wine on his breath leaning in way too closely. Zeus told his younger brother that things would be *fine*. Poseidon could take his wrath out on the *Phaeacians*, Zeus said. Poseidon (for unspecified reasons) liked the idea and proposed destroying the last ship in the Phaeacian convoy as the helpful sailors returned home to their island. Zeus told him to instead *petrify* (meaning, turn to stone) the trailing Phaeacian ship, just as it was about to dock in the Phaeacian harbor. The proposed petrification took place, with the innocent Phaeacian mariners who'd helped Odysseus apparently turned to stone too. The Phaeacian monarch, King Alcinous, threw up his hands in resignation and concluded that they'd better stop helping victims of shipwrecks, and vowed to make a substantial sacrifice to Poseidon. And thus, Poseidon ends his time in the *Odyssey*, once again steamrolled by his older brother, and on the way to another complimentary barbecue.

Poseidon's last scene in the *Odyssey*, in which he petrifies a ship full of sailors for no discernible reason, is, to put it charitably, puzzling. The Homeric gods frequently don't make a lot of sense. And yet in their erratic behavior and ugly power dynamics, there are important lessons for modern readers new to ancient Greek history. The Olympians in the Homeric epics are gods, lumbering around and doing things. But they're also metaphors for abstract forces out there in the world, indifferent to humanity. Thunder over the mountains, bountiful harvests, dawn breaking over a meadow, and loved ones lost at sea—these were all things that the Homeric gods helped explain. Homer's earliest audiences would not have expected an omnipotent, omniscient god doling out justice evenly to all. The world was demonstrably inequitable, turbulent, and chaotic, and a pantheon like the Olympians suited it perfectly.

NOW YOU KNOW

Poseidon fought on behalf of the Greeks during the Trojan War because the Trojans owed him money. Long ago, the sea god had, along with Apollo, helped build some of the walls of Troy. The Trojans refused to pay their divine contractors for services rendered, and so when the Trojan War began, the two deities jumped at the opportunity to pulverize the city.

A frequent epithet for Poseidon in the Homeric poems is Ἐνοσίχθων (*Enosichthon*), or "earth shaker." The title is a little bit confusing, at first, as he is the god of the *sea*. But like all the Olympians, Poseidon was the god of a number of different things, including earthquakes, horses, and storms, in addition to the sea.

NAUSICAA

SHE OFFERS ODYSSEUS KIND WORDS, HOSPITALITY, AND PANTS.

PRONUNCIATION: now-SIK-uh or now-SIK-uh-a

LIKES: Hanging with the Girls, Doing Her Own Work, Sports

DISLIKES: Dirty Clothes

SPECIAL POWERS: Eloquence, Generosity, Crushes

NARRATIVE ROLE: She welcomes Odysseus to Phaeacia when he washes up there and takes him to meet her parents.

Once upon a time, there lived a beautiful young princess named Nausicaa. One morning, Nausicaa was sleeping in her richly adorned chamber, with her lovely attendants drowsing near the door. The goddess Athena, disguising herself as Nausicaa's young friend, appeared before the girl in a dream, telling her that it was time to get up. There was work to do, the disguised Athena chided. All of Nausicaa's fine clothes were lying around her chamber, neglected, and they needed to be washed. It was time to have a wagon loaded with all the laundry that needed to be done, and to go to the calm river bend where clothes were washed. Nausicaa needed to look her best, Athena added, because the princess might soon be married!

Thus begins Book 6 of the *Odyssey*, the tale of Nausicaa. Nausicaa is the second of three women in the middle books of the *Odyssey* who help Odysseus. Sandwiched between narratives involving lusty vixens, deadly monsters, ruthless gods, and the churning ocean, Nausicaa's story slows things down and offers us a captivating look at something we don't very often see in ancient Greek literature: everyday life.

Nausicaa woke up after her strange, portentous dream. It was by all appearances an ordinary morning in the palace, but Nausicaa felt suddenly shy. Athena's talk of marriage made the girl feel awkward around her father. Princess Nausicaa, however, still managed to voice her request. Could she borrow the wagon—the one with the good wheels and high sides? After all, the Phaeacians, including her brothers, needed clean clothes, didn't they? Her dad, a likable fellow throughout the *Odyssey*, said of course Nausicaa could use the wagon. The princess's mother was also supportive. The queen packed her daughter and the servants some food and other niceties for the morning outing, and Nausicaa set out to get to work.

The mules then clopped and jingled down to the river, pulling the cart. As Homer narrates:

> *They reached the lovely river with its never-failing pools, in which there was enough clear water always bubbling up and swirling by to clean the dirtiest clothes. Here they unharnessed the mules and drove them along the eddying stream to graze on the sweet grass. Then they lifted the clothes by the armful from the wagon, carried them to the dark water and trod them down briskly in the washing-pools, vying with each other in the work.*
>
> **—Nausicaa washes clothes, *Odyssey* (Rieu translation, 6.85–94)**

This isn't one of the epic's blockbuster sequences. Laundry montages, in general, have not proved big moneymakers in literary or cinematic history. However, it's still a beautifully written pastoral scene. Young women are washing clothes, the livestock is grazing happily, and a tinge of romance is in the air. Homer could sing stupendous passages about peace as well as war.

Once the girls finished washing, they left the clothes drying nearby and proceeded to have lunch on the riverbank. They played some sort of a game to pass the time. Nausicaa sang. The girls all removed their veils as they tossed a ball around. Homer tells us that the young princess looked like Artemis. It's a deft comparison. Artemis, the virginal goddess of the hunt, enjoyed bathing in forest pools with her handmaidens too. Then, the commotion of the ballgame awakened Odysseus. The old warhorse had fallen asleep in a nearby thicket. For a moment, as the heroic veteran at

the center of the *Odyssey* peers through the foliage at the young ladies, the tenor of the whole scene changes.

Ancient Greek literature has a number of famous stories involving beautiful women in woodsy or pastoral settings. Human women and nymphs, if they stray into the forest or wilderness in Greek myths, often fall victim to the lusts of satyrs and gods. On the flip side, human men who happen upon virginal huntresses sometimes find themselves hunted. Ancient Greek audiences, then, hearing a bard sing of Odysseus spying on Nausicaa and her companions as they bathed, would have understood that danger and eroticism were in the air.

However, Odysseus was no lusty satyr, and Nausicaa was no woodland murderess in a chastity belt. The hero covered himself. And then he flattered the princess. Odysseus said he was on his knees before her. Was she even mortal? She was as beautiful as Artemis. If she were human, Odysseus said, how lucky her family was to be able to see her dance. And the man who won her hand in marriage would be more blessed than anyone! Wouldn't Nausicaa please have pity on him and direct him to town, and give him a rag to cover himself? Wrapping up his overture, Odysseus said he wished her his very best, and that he hoped that the gods would provide her with a fitting husband and a fine home someday.

Now, if we put ourselves in Nausicaa's shoes, "Sure, mister, have a towel. Good luck out there" would have been a perfectly appropriate response to Odysseus's unsolicited torrent of compliments. Nausicaa, however, moved by the stranger's polite comportment, told Odysseus she'd be happy to help him with clothes and get him safely to town. On the *Odyssey*'s ongoing spectrum of characters who are hospitable to strangers and those who are not, Nausicaa is definitely one of the former.

Odysseus then emerged from the thicket, heroically covering his privates with a piece of foliage. The Phaeacian maids, at Nausicaa's bidding, gathered around the stranger, who had proved harmless, and supplied him with clothes and some oil. Odysseus asked if the girls would please turn their backs while he bathed and dressed. And while Nausicaa was looking away, Athena did something she does at several other junctures of the *Odyssey*. She enhanced Odysseus's appearance, so that he looked taller and more muscular, with thicker hair. Thus bedazzled, Odysseus told the

Phaeacian ladies they could turn around, and Nausicaa swooned, seeing the hero having gone from grungy vagrant to sea hunk.

Odysseus, she said to her handmaidens, had looked a bit sketchy at first, but now he looked like a deity. Why, if only *she* could have a man like Odysseus for a husband! But a man like Odysseus would never stay in Phaeacia. Well, Nausicaa concluded to the other girls, whoever he was, they'd better give him some food.

After Athena gave him the makeover, Nausicaa told Odysseus that she *couldn't* just walk back into town with Odysseus. He was *far* too tall and handsome, and *everyone* would think that he was her future husband (hint, hint). *Everyone* knew she didn't want to marry a mere Phaeacian, but instead, perhaps, a *foreigner* who washed up in Phaeacia (hint, hint, hint, *ahem*). Odysseus, Nausicaa insisted, had to arrive in town *after* her and act like he was just showing up there out of the blue. The hero listened to the young woman's speech and then, following her instructions carefully, parted ways with her before they got to town. (We have no idea what he was thinking, other than perhaps that he'd just gotten out of a *really* bad relationship with the nymph Calypso.)

Odysseus takes center stage from this point onward, with Nausicaa becoming supporting cast. But as the long sequence of books set in Phaeacia proceeds (Books 6–12), she is around, watching the hero, listening to him, and in her only other appearance in the epic, definitely flirting with him. A bit later in the story, after the Phaeacians had enjoyed some athletic games, Odysseus had a bath and a change of clothes. Nausicaa, tall and naturally beautiful, stood near a column and watched the hero pass by, admiring him. She asked Odysseus to please not forget about her. He did owe her his life, so Odysseus told the princess he would never forget her as long as he lived, and that he would pray to her as a goddess. And that's it. The young woman's crush is brief and unrequited, and off goes Odysseus into the wild blue yonder after staying in Phaeacia for a few days.

Nausicaa's tale in the epic is a standalone story—a brief pastoral romance in the midst of a more operatic tale of glory and homecoming and fate. In it, the monsters and dangers of the *Odyssey* are far away, and only foreigners have great adventures in distant lands. A girl likes a boy, and the boy doesn't give her the time of day. An innocent young person is, for a moment, swept up in a great tornado of heroes and gods, only to be set safely back down again.

Readers love the *Odyssey* because it shows us strange things and a dangerous, fascinating man whom we can inhabit vicariously as he goes places we'll never visit and does things we'll never do. But the *Odyssey* is also full of things that aren't strange at all. In it, there are families, workdays, mornings and evenings, chores and duties, houses and huts, rude slights and things said just right, and all the cadences of the lives we actually live. Set over an enormous swath of the ancient world, from Mount Olympus to Hades, Homer's epics are fairy tales, but they also chronicle what's close by and commonplace. Their touching tableaus of everyday life tell us that although there may be Odysseuses out there, most of us are Nausicaas, taking care of our families and daily obligations, and that all of that is as it should be.

NOW YOU KNOW

The Greek poet Sappho, who flourished circa 600 BCE, also wrote about unrequited love (Fragment 1, Fragment 31). Though it was not a common theme in ancient Greek epics or classical Athenian theater, Greek lyric poetry like Sappho's contains both homo- and heterosexual speakers wishing for unions they cannot have. Later Roman love poets influenced by Sappho, like Catullus and Ovid, had a formative effect on the Italian Renaissance through Petrarch, who in turn influenced the sonnet sequences of Shakespeare and his contemporaries. Every generation, it seems, spends some time crying heartbrokenly into pillows, and writing poems about being rejected and dumped.

The possibility of Odysseus marrying Nausicaa would have had a certain logic to the *Odyssey*'s early audience. As Greek colonists established communities in the eastern and central Mediterranean during the 700s and 600s BCE, diplomatic marriages between prominent Greeks and Indigenous aristocrats helped secure political relationships between the natives and newcomers.

ARETE & ALCINOUS

MODEL MONARCHS WHO LISTEN TO ODYSSEUS'S LONG, LONG STORY.

PRONUNCIATION: ah-REE-tee and al-KIN-oh-us or al-SIN-oh-us

LIKE: Each Other, Hosting, Defusing Situations

DISLIKE: Who Knows? They're Too Polite to Tell You

SPECIAL POWER: Being Normal and Civil in a Crazy World

NARRATIVE ROLE: The king and queen of Phaeacia take Odysseus in and preside over one of the main parts of the *Odyssey*.

From Books 6–12 of the *Odyssey*, Odysseus rests and refuels in Phaeacia. During these books, through social tact and some sorcery by Athena, the hero goes from being a crusty drifter to a lionized guest. He does so by making a tremendously good impression on the Phaeacian royal family: first, the daughter, Nausicaa; then, her parents, Queen Arete and King Alcinous.

ODYSSEUS MEETS THE KING AND QUEEN

Just prior to Odysseus's arrival in the Phaeacian capital, Athena offered Odysseus an overview of the queen and king whom he was about to meet. Both of the Phaeacian monarchs, Athena explained, were descendants of Poseidon. Queen Arete's father had been killed by Apollo, and afterward, she'd married her uncle, Alcinous. The union is, of course, bizarre and incestuous by modern standards, but Athena's main point of emphasis

was that King Alcinous was utterly devoted to Queen Arete, and that the Phaeacian queen was wise, judicious, and revered by all. If Odysseus won over Arete, Athena said, he'd win over the Phaeacians.

What happens next is a curious moment in the *Odyssey*. A sort of over-the-shoulder camera follows Odysseus as he walks, concealed by magical mist from Athena, into the Phaeacian palace. The hero had won a war and survived terrifying ordeals, but even so, as he looked at the radiant gates of the royal estate, he felt apprehensive. The walls were bronze and blazing with blue enamel toward their tops, and further inside, golden doors were hinged to silver posts. Odysseus saw tall chairs with fine covers, and golden statues holding torches that burned with real fire. Past the outer entrance to the palace, there extended a courtyard full of fruit trees, where something was always perfectly ripe and where grapes and vegetables were watered by two fresh springs. Heading in for an audience with the Phaeacian monarchs, Odysseus observed a wonderland of perfect comfort and prosperity. We get the idea that the hero, notwithstanding his considerable accomplishments, suddenly felt out of his depth. The estranged king of a small island nation, Odysseus had spent almost two decades of his adult life far from the posh peacetime civilization that the Phaeacian estate represented, and his hobnobbing skills weren't at full strength.

Still, he gave it a shot. Odysseus made it to the throne room, sank down in front of Queen Arete, and embraced her knees. The mist that had been hiding him vanished. In his second effusively complimentary appeal of the day (the first was to Princess Nausicaa), he introduced himself as a humble supplicant and asked if the great queen might help him get home. Then, Odysseus shuffled over to the fire and awaited a reply.

The room was dead quiet. We might expect profanity-laden incredulity from the startled queen, but caught off guard by the sheer strangeness of what had just happened, everyone simply stared. It's one of the *Odyssey*'s immortal moments, a moment that, like so many others, could really have gone south for the protagonist. Finally, a nobleman spoke up. Give the guy a chair, he said, and get him some wine and food. The gods were good to those in need. (If the *Odyssey* were a Western, this would be where the off-pitch piano music would resume and the background noises of glasses clinking and conversation would start up again.)

The king got Odysseus a chair, and Alcinous commenced an ostentatious display of courtesy to the newcomer, almost as though the king was showboating in front of his court. Get the newcomer some wine, yes, of course, Alcinous told a squire. But the stranger's presence in Phaeacia, and what to do with him, would require *more* Phaeacians. They needed to call all the elders, Alcinous said. They wouldn't just help him. They would stay by his side until he reached his home soil. The stranger might be a god in disguise! They would reconvene the next morning.

Odysseus, who at this juncture might have been thinking, "Holy [expletive], I just wanted you to call me a cab," remained polite. He said he wasn't a deity but that he *was* pretty hungry and thirsty, and would accept the Phaeacians' help. The Phaeacian nobles headed home, leaving the hero with Queen Arete and King Alcinous.

ODYSSEUS SETTLES INTO PHAEACIA

The queen, at this point, hadn't said anything, but she had definitely noticed something. She'd noticed that Odysseus was wearing clothes that she had made. (Princess Nausicaa had loaned them to Odysseus that morning.) More direct and warier than her husband, Arete asked Odysseus who he was and where he was from, and—um—why, exactly, was he wearing that clothing? The hero offered her a mostly true narrative, telling the monarchs about Calypso and his lengthy incarceration on her island, about how he had washed up the previous night in Phaeacia, and how their daughter Nausicaa had more or less saved his life. Alcinous wondered why Nausicaa hadn't escorted Odysseus into the palace herself, and Odysseus, telling a white lie, said it was his choice to arrive separately.

Alcinous, hearing Odysseus's remarks, was fantastically impressed, because he told Odysseus, "Father Zeus . . . if only– / seeing the man you are, seeing that we think as one– / *you* could wed my daughter and be my son-in-law / and stay right here with us" (Fagles translation, 7.356–9). Nothing wrong with offering your daughter's hand in marriage to a man whose name you don't know, whom you just met a few minutes ago, and who has just told you he spent the past seven years as the prisoner of a dominatrix who enjoyed tropical-themed foreplay. Whatever exactly Odysseus thought of his host's exceptional generosity, the hero thanked

Alcinous. Queen Arete, more reserved and prudent than her backslapping husband, had what sounds like a wonderfully snuggly bed made up for Odysseus, and then everyone retired for the night.

As the next day dawned and Odysseus's time with the Phaeacians proceeded, so, too, did the delicate social dynamics of his presence in the court there. Queen Arete was pretty quiet. King Alcinous, however, started showing off Odysseus as though he were a giant and miraculous fish the king had just caught. With Athena's help, Alcinous called all the Phaeacian nobility to court. At an outdoor assembly area just adjacent to the Phaeacian harbor, Alcinous had a ship brought out, promising that precisely fifty-two excellent young rowers would be aboard to pilot the hero back home. Then, the king said he wanted Odysseus to see what fine athletes the Phaeacians were, so some athletic games were staged for the visitor's enjoyment. A bard offered two different performances, singing a song about the Trojan War and then telling a story about Aphrodite and Ares enjoying an illicit love affair. Odysseus mostly enjoyed himself. Although the tune about Troy made Odysseus sad, and a young braggart taunted him and made him grouchy, Alcinous kept things light and friendly.

The Phaeacians also offered Odysseus lavish gifts. At some point, poor Odysseus must have realized that they were keeping him for another night, in spite of the ship waiting out in the harbor, because Alcinous had everyone return to the palace. The Phaeacian king continued walking a thin line between being hospitable and obsequious. Odysseus had received so many gifts, Alcinous said, that they'd better give him the finest chest they had to carry all the presents too! He asked his wife to fetch the chest in question, and to include luxurious garments of their own as gifts, and also to heat up a bath for the stranger, so that Odysseus could enjoy a night of music. Also, Alcinous said, he'd give Odysseus a fine golden chalice. A bath was heated. The chest was brought out. Odysseus was given even more ancient Aegean bling. Phaeacian maids bathed and oiled Odysseus.

Another night of heroic mingling commenced. When Odysseus began weeping during a second song about the Trojan War, Alcinous stopped the bard from playing. They'd been hosting Odysseus for two days, said the king. Could Odysseus, maybe, tell them his name? Perhaps where he was from? And it is at this juncture, freshly bathed, well fed, dressed in Phaeacian clothing, and possibly perched atop a pile of Phaeacian presents while the ship idles outside and the rowers warm up, that Odysseus throws down the longest speech in the Homeric epics, and the Phaeacians fade into the background for the remainder of the *Odyssey*.

As Odysseus speaks for the next 70–150 pages, depending on the edition you're reading, and the big-budget special-effects part of the *Odyssey* proceeds, you almost forget about the kindly seaside people who have taken Odysseus in and almost literally given him the clothes off their backs. Other than a short sequence when the seafolk finally wave goodbye to Odysseus from their docks, they have just one more appearance in the *Odyssey*.

Poseidon, furious that the Phaeacians had offered Odysseus safe conduct home, turned one of their ships to stone in the harbor. Poor King Alcinous took it as a warning. He decided that the Phaeacians had better cool it with the luxury gifts and eight-course meals given to every vagabond who washed up there. The Canadians of the Homeric world, the poor Phaeacians' only offense is that a grouchy god deems them a bit *too* nice.

NOW YOU KNOW

Various Greek islands have been theorized as the home of the Phaeacians, including Crete and Corfu. Near Corfu is a very small island called Pontikonisi that has historically been claimed as the remains of the ship that brought Odysseus to Ithaca, petrified just as it returned from its mission. If you fly into Corfu today, you pass right over this little island, which, while probably not a ship turned to stone by a wrathful sea god, is still a nice part of the landscape.

There's a strange narrative quirk in the *Odyssey* involving Queen Arete of the Phaeacians. When Odysseus arrives in Phaeacia, Athena tells the hero that he absolutely, positively has to get on Arete's good side, and that if Odysseus wins over the queen, he'll win over the Phaeacians. Although Odysseus voices his initial appeal to Arete for hospitality and help getting home, afterward, the queen hardly says anything or does anything, and it seems as though King Alcinous is the head honcho of the Phaeacians, after all.

OLYMPIC ATHLETES

SWEATY HUNKS DOING EPIC THINGS.

LIKE: Discus Throwing, Footraces,
Nude Wrestling, Glamour Shots

DISLIKE: Losing, Wimps

SPECIAL POWER: Interrupting Epics to Win Prizes

NARRATIVE ROLE: An athletic competition is a customary
part of ancient Greek and Roman epics, and
one happens in Book 8 of the *Odyssey*.

The epic poets of ancient Greece and Rome loved writing about athletic games. The heroes of Homer and his successors invariably spend a dozen pages boxing, wrestling, dashing around racetracks, and throwing things. Athletic-games sequences are quite an odd convention for those of us who are new to ancient literature. We expect heroes to continue their dire quests, not to pause for an entire book to race chariots and outjump one another. And yet, following the example set by Homer, numerous ancient epics contain long, detailed processions of athletic games, in which epic poets pause the action, stretch out, and show off their poetic ability, even as many modern readers wonder what on earth happened to the main story.

The *Odyssey* contains one of the tamer athletic-games sequences in antiquity. Here's how it goes down. At the outset of Book 8, the Phaeacian court had gathered to honor the arrival of Odysseus. King Alcinous paused all the operations of government and gave his entire civilization a day off because a polite drifter (Odysseus) showed up. First, of course, there was a feast. We are told that the king had two oxen, eight boars, and a dozen sheep sacrificed for breakfast—enough livestock for a respectable farmstead. It should be noted here that in classical epics like the *Odyssey*, characters never just *eat*. They always *feast*. You never read "Odysseus and his companions had some soup and then got on with their day." It's "Odysseus and his noble companions slaughtered [large numbers] of [types of quadrupeds] and roasted them, adding to their feast skins of noble wine." Even though real ancient Greeks ate a lot of fish, grain, fruits, and vegetables, Homeric characters seem to eat only wheelbarrows full of red meat, and to do so every few hours.

Anyway, following the fleshy, caloric extravaganza at the Phaeacian court, the Phaeacian bard played some songs, and then King Alcinous announced that it was time for some athletic games. Some fit young guys lined up. Homer helpfully informs us that "There was no lack of fine young men to compete—Acroneos, Ocyalus, Elatreus, Nauteus, Prymeneus, Anchialus, Eremeus, Ponteus, Proreus, Thoon, and Anabesineos" (Rieu translation, 8.111–13), and that wasn't even the full list. Neither we nor Odysseus have any idea who all these people are, and in ancient Greek, their names are all puns, which we would translate as, for instance, "Seaman," "Paddle," and "Oarsman." (The Phaeacians were all sailors.) Perhaps if Odysseus had visited a colony of forest-dwelling lumberjacks who competed in athletic games, Homer would have named them "Axeman," "Leafmaster," "Stumpguy," "Woody," and so on. Anyway, the goofily named Phaeacian beefcakes started the competition.

There was a footrace, which kicked dust up into the seaside air. There was some wrestling. There was a jumping competition. There was a discus-throwing contest. In a long scene that's important for Odysseus's characterization (discussed earlier in this book), an impetuous young Phaeacian man started taunting Odysseus and asking the mysterious guest to compete. Odysseus, after attempting politeness, eventually lost his cool, seized a discus, and outthrew all the Phaeacians who had already competed. To bring the temperature down, King Alcinous proposed that the Phaeacian assembly watch some dancing, and that's what they did.

The *Odyssey*'s games sequence is short, and within the context of other ancient epics, it's tightly written and appropriate to the plot. Other epics have far longer ones. The entirety of Book 23 of the *Iliad* (the epic's second-to-last book) is an athletic-games sequence. Achilles' companion Patroclus has just been killed, prompting Achilles to kill the Trojan champion Hector.

Rather than pressing their advantage, astoundingly, the Greeks pause for a while to eat a herd of hoofed mammals and then spend an absurd amount of time and energy chariot racing, boxing, wrestling, sprinting, dueling with real weapons, throwing heavy things, shooting arrows, and throwing javelins. We might think that the long-suffering Greeks would want to conserve their energy, as at that moment, they are in between the harrowing final battles of the ten-year war, but no—athletic games are a convention of ancient epics, and so off go the Greeks, punching one another in the face and cartwheeling around the battlefield while the Trojans up on the walls perhaps wonder what on earth their opponents are doing.

For ancient Greeks, narratives involving athletics were intrinsically riveting and required little narrative justification. The first Olympic Games in ancient Greece are traditionally said to have begun in the city of Olympia, in the west central Peloponnese, in 776 BCE. Athletes came from all over the Greek-speaking world to compete there. By the time the Homeric epics came together, the Olympic Games were a fixture of ancient Greek society. And as the centuries passed, more recurrent games were established in Greece. Most famously, in the 580s BCE, Greeks founded both the Pythian Games (in Delphi) and the Isthmian Games (near Corinth). By the 570s BCE, a fourth interregional Greek (or "Panhellenic") competition was established in Nemea, in the northeastern Peloponnese. In short, the mainland and Peloponnese had four major competitions by the middle of the 500s BCE, and Greeks traveled from all over the eastern Mediterranean to attend them.

And yet, there were far more athletic games in ancient Greece than these four major festivals! Ruins from almost every ancient Greek settlement have tracks for footraces, amphitheaters for various athletic contests, and most famously, gymnasiums, where men gathered to hone their athletic skills, particularly in wrestling. A rich part of everyday life, athletic competitions were parts of religious and civic festivals, private parties, and improvised get-togethers alike. Today, we tend to think of ancient Greeks as intellectuals and innovators, scratching their beards and puzzling out the secrets of the universe. But they were also jocks who loved a good body slam, photo finish, and close, dramatic race, just like we still do today.

The word "gymnasium" comes from the ancient Greek word γυμνάσιον (*gymnasion*), which itself derives from γυμνός (*gumnos*), meaning "naked." In ancient Greece, then, the word "gymnasium" meant something like "nakedarium."

The ancient Greek poet Pindar (518–438 BCE) wrote a type of poem called the "ode." "Ode" simply meant "song" in Pindar's time, but Pindar's odes were so distinct and complex that they created a genre of poetry called the "ode"—a genre notorious for its dense, literary style. As challenging as Pindar's odes are to read, the ones that survive are all about *sports*! Pindaric odes are from an ancient Greek genre called ἐπινίκιον (*epinikion*), from the Greek words *epi* ("on") and *niké* ("victory"), and each one celebrates the triumph of a specific athlete in a competition.

DEMODOCUS

THE *ODYSSEY'S* FRIENDLY BARD.
HE TAKES REQUESTS.

PRONUNCIATION: deh-MOD-oh-kus

LIKES: The Spotlight, Playing in Tune, Memorization

DISLIKES: Breaking Strings, Stingy Crowds

SPECIAL POWER: Taking the Lyre Higher and Higher

NARRATIVE ROLE: The Phaeacian bard figures into a couple of key episodes in the middle of the *Odyssey*.

If you went to a party in ancient Greece, you'd be likely to hear an ἀοιδός (*aoidos*), or "bard." Just as skalds in long-ago Scandinavia and rawis in ancient Arabia performed songs and poems, ancient Greece's bards offered musical and narrative entertainment to audiences. In Homer's *Odyssey*, after Odysseus cleans the sand and plankton out of his ears and returns to civilization, one of the first things he hears is a bardic performance by a revered minstrel named Demodocus. The character Demodocus, a blind virtuoso storyteller, may have actually inspired the many tales told about Homer himself in antiquity. Here's the story of Demodocus in the *Odyssey*.

Dawn broke over Phaeacia, and as the sun rose, the Phaeacians all convened to honor the arrival of their king's mysterious guest. No one knew who Odysseus was, and yet everyone seemed glad to take the day off. The Phaeacians enjoyed a large, greasy Homeric breakfast. Then, a duo of new characters made their way into the Phaeacian palace. An assistant led a blind man along, guiding him to an ornate chair in the center of the room. This blind man was Demodocus the bard. The assistant hung Demodocus's lyre on a pillar behind him and made sure the bard could find it. Then, adjacent to Demodocus, the assistant set out a bowl of bread and a glass of wine. The musician had everything he needed, and once the clamor of the assembly had died down, Demodocus reached behind him to retrieve his lyre, and he began a song.

The song was about an event in recent history. Ten years prior, toward the end of the Trojan War, Odysseus and Achilles had quarreled. The quarrel was soon mended, but nonetheless it touched off a dire period of the war, during which the assailing Greeks suddenly began losing ground to their Trojan foes.

Hearing Demodocus's song, Odysseus was overwhelmed with emotion. He pulled his cloak up to hide his head and conceal his tears. At intervals, the bard paused his performance. During the breaks, Odysseus applauded politely and poured out libations, as was the custom. Yet each time the bard Demodocus continued his narrative about the Trojan War, Odysseus lost control of his emotions, until the king of Phaeacia felt sorry for his guest of honor. Not wanting Odysseus to be down in the dumps, King Alcinous proposed that they watch some athletic competitions to pass the time. The bard Demodocus, presumably, took a break, rested his hands, and had a bite to eat himself.

After athletic games and dancing, Odysseus and his Phaeacian hosts were ready for some more bardic entertainment. The king summoned the bard Demodocus again, and some youthful dancers stationed themselves near the singer. This time, the production wasn't about recent history. Instead, Demodocus sang a crowd-pleaser about a pair of horny, adulterous gods who were caught in the act together. Here's what Demodocus sang.

It was a tale as old as time, concerning a homely husband, a wanton wife, and a lustful lover. Hephaestus, the god of smithing, was married to Aphrodite, the goddess of love. Aphrodite, however, had a wandering eye, and she was having an affair with Ares, the god of war. When Hephaestus learned that his wife was cuckolding him in his own bed, the smith god stomped into his workshop and began a new project. Hephaestus most often made things like armor and shields. This time, his creation would be subtler. The smith god crafted a web of chains so thin that they were unable to be seen. Hephaestus, his clever snare completed, left it all around the bedroom he shared with Aphrodite. Then, Hephaestus pretended to leave town.

Ares, aroused and impatient, had been waiting for the smith god to depart. The god of war hurried to Aphrodite and Hephaestus's house. She opened the door. Her husband, Aphrodite said, wasn't home. Wouldn't Ares come to bed with her right away? (It's amusing to remember that R-rated stories like this were accompanied with music and choreographed dancing in ancient Greece!) As Demodocus's story seemed about to reach its erotic crescendo, however, Hephaestus's booby trap did its work. Aphrodite was stuck. Ares was stuck. Hephaestus came in and bellowed in anger, calling for all the gods to come and see the lecherous pair.

Livid, Hephaestus ranted that he'd worked hard to win Aphrodite, and that he wanted Aphrodite's father to return her bride price to him. The male gods soon arrived (the female gods didn't wish to see the ugly scene). And as Poseidon, Hermes, and Apollo ogled the compromised lovers, they burst into laughter, appreciating how Hephaestus, though modest in appearance, had made a fool of handsome Ares. After some more guffawing and dirty jokes, Poseidon told Hephaestus to undo the gossamer threads that held the lovers in place, guaranteeing that he would pay Ares's adulterer's fine if necessary. Hephaestus consented, and the randy lovers, once freed, went off to different parts of the Aegean to recover from the embarrassing experience.

This was Demodocus's second song, and it went off well with the crowd. In ancient Greece, everyone could rally around a story about the gods behaving like horndogs, voyeurs, and dirtbags. With the mood of the Phaeacian party thus heightened, the day lengthened, and the generous Phaeacians bestowed more and more gifts onto Odysseus.

In the evening, the revelers convened again, including the bard Demodocus, who sat in his customary place in a fine chair with its back to a pillar, on which his lyre was suspended within easy reach. Odysseus gave the bard a large piece of pork as a tip (perhaps throwing it, such that Demodocus caught it out of the air in his mouth?) and complimented him. Demodocus, he said, was supernaturally talented, and sang about the Trojan War as though he'd been there. Could Demodocus sing one more song? Odysseus asked. Could he sing about the Trojan Horse?

Once again, Demodocus knocked it out of the park. Singing about events that never actually take place elsewhere in the Homeric epics, Demodocus recalled how the Greeks set fire to their camp as they pretended to depart from Troy for good. Demodocus described how a knot of assassins, including Odysseus himself, hunkered down inside the infamous wooden sculpture and listened to the Trojans debating whether to punch spears through the Trojan Horse or to haul it over to a nearby cliff and toss it down to the rocks below. In the end, though, the bard Demodocus sang, the Trojans kept the gift, and later, Odysseus was one of the first ones out, cutting his way through the enemy city with all the ferocity of the god of war.

Hearing this second tune about Troy, Odysseus, once again, lost control of his emotions, barely concealing the flow of his tears from the greater assembly, although King Alcinous, once again, observed that his guest was crying. The king gently asked Demodocus to stop his performance, and the bard, a thorough professional, did so. At this point, the main bardic figure in the story—that's Odysseus himself—takes over after Demodocus has loosened up the audience.

By the time Odysseus takes his turn at the microphone, so to speak, the Phaeacians have already enjoyed three substantial bardic performances. Odysseus's four-book-long soliloquy dwarfs Demodocus's performance by a considerable margin, and most of the *Odyssey*'s readers accept the hero's long tale as a factual recounting of things that Odysseus has actually done and said. Nonetheless, Odysseus is absolutely conscious of his story as a performance. Just as Demodocus performs for tips, Odysseus's recitation is transactional as well. He's telling tales with the ultimate aim of getting home. At one juncture, it's pretty clear that Odysseus is grandstanding, and that he knows he has his listeners on the edges of their seats.

Odysseus is in the midst of telling the Phaeacians about his trip to Hades when he suddenly breaks off for a moment. He saw the murk of the deepest underworld! he tells them. And thousands of souls swimming through the darkness! He saw Jocasta, and Phaedra, and Ariadne, and met and spoke with a great many imposing and terrifying doomed souls, *but you know, it was getting late, and they probably didn't want to hear about everything he saw in Hades.*

This trick—building up to a tantalizing climax and then stopping— is one of the oldest bardic maneuvers in the book. The bard sings and sings about a fateful secret behind a door, and then just before the door opens, he pauses, pretending to think the audience isn't interested, only to milk them for applause and tips before continuing. Thus, when Odysseus halts his story while describing the depths of Hades, he knows he has the Phaeacians in the palm of his hand, and after securing Alcinous's renewed resolution to get him home safely and securely, Odysseus, the real bard of the *Odyssey*, presses forward with his story.

Demodocus functions as a sort of warm-up bard for the epic's main tale within a tale. The blind Phaeacian minstrel reminds audiences, past and present, that bards were the stewards of ancient myths and legends, and that without them, there would be no epics at all.

NOW YOU KNOW

Penelope calls songs sung in the *Odyssey thelkteria*, or "enchantments," and the root of this word is the Greek verb *thelgein.* This verb was associated with divine transformations of humans into other creatures, as when Circe changes Odysseus's men into animals. There is, then, throughout the *Odyssey*, a sense that songs enchant and transform those who listen to them, which is a wonderful way to describe how music and narrative can sometimes move us.

Books 9–12 of the *Odyssey* make up a section of the epic that scholars, ancient and modern, often call the *apologoi*, or "stories." Whether or not Odysseus's long yarn about his adventures is entirely true, it's definitely a whopper of a story!

THE CICONES

JUST SOME TOWNSPEOPLE ODYSSEUS BUTCHERED AND ENSLAVED.

PRONUNCIATION: sick-OH-nees

LIKE: Living in the Region of Thrace

DISLIKE: Being Slaughtered by Homeric Protagonists

SPECIAL POWER: Being Forgotten by Most Readers of the *Odyssey*

NARRATIVE ROLE: Odysseus's encounter with the Cicones is the first adventure he relates to the Phaeacians during the *Odyssey*'s central sequence.

In the ninth book of the *Odyssey*, the main character begins telling a very long story. Sitting in the Phaeacian court, after athletic games, bardic performances, and dinner, Odysseus finally reveals his name to the Phaeacians and explains what happened to him after he left the city of Troy when the war ended. The story that he tells eventually includes the epic's most famous scenes—the Sirens, Scylla and Charybdis, and so on. Before he gets to the monsters and magic, though, Odysseus tells of murder.

Just after they left Troy, Odysseus said, he and his men went to a place called Ismarus (likely near the border shared by modern-day Greece and Turkey). Ismarus was, in antiquity, situated in a region called Thrace—essentially the northern Aegean rim, up to and including parts of present-day Bulgaria. The first lines of Odysseus's lengthy flashback tale to the Phaeacians were as follows:

Thus, the very first thing Odysseus told his Phaeacian hosts was that he was quite literally a pirate, having killed all the men in a town, looted it, and enslaved the women, giving them to his men as property. That wasn't the end of the tale either. The hero told his hosts that after the butchery, his men, ignoring his order to hop back on the ships, drank excessively and began feasting. As the Greeks feasted, some survivors of the slaughter managed to make it to neighboring Thracian towns. The Thracians mustered up fighting forces in large numbers, and they attacked Odysseus's troops furiously. A battle ensued that lasted much of the day, and at its end, when the bloody morning fell into afternoon, the Greeks lost the battle. Six men from each ship died in the fighting, and as the fleet made it back out to sea, they mourned their lost comrades.

This short Cicones narrative is, again, the *first* story Odysseus tells the Phaeacians: a grim narrative of mass execution, sex slavery, mutiny, and dead crewmates. It reminds us that the heroes of ancient epic narratives, including the biblical David and Solomon, were warlords more than they were chivalric knights. Odysseus's initial story is unadorned and brisk, as though the decimation of civilians in a town isn't worth much more than a minute's narration. But the story of the Cicones in the *Odyssey* is still an important one to remember.

Why should we remember it? First of all, the opening of Odysseus's four-book-long narrative reminds us where he's coming from. Ten years of war have made him into a killing machine. The *Odyssey* is full of monsters. He's one of them. Though Odysseus has many dimensions in the epic, one of them is that he's an executioner with little regard for human life. This version of Odysseus takes center stage during the epic's finale.

The short narrative about the Cicones also introduces a recurring pattern in the central books of the *Odyssey*. Odysseus tells his men to do something. They don't listen, and disaster strikes. It happens again and again—so many times that the *entire fleet* with which he leaves Troy is gone by the end of the story that he tells. The folkloric tale of mortals ignoring a warning or breaking a covenant is all over ancient narratives, from Adam and Eve to Prometheus and Pandora, and the *Odyssey* uses this archetypal plotline in many of its most prominent episodes.

Careful readers of *both* of the Homeric epics have a better understanding of why Odysseus and company may have attacked the Cicones. The Cicones are briefly mentioned in the *Iliad* (2.965–6) as spearmen who fought on the side of Troy. When Odysseus disembarked in Thrace to raid their town, he was attacking a settlement in enemy territory, and a people against whom he'd been fighting already for a long time.

All told, then, the Cicones episode doesn't paint Odysseus in very flattering colors—neither to modern readers nor, we can imagine, to his Phaeacian hosts. Nonetheless, it perfectly demonstrates where he's been and who he is, and placed where it is at the outset of Book 9 in the *Odyssey*, it starts to open up the vastness of the Homeric world that we're about to see a whole lot more of as we turn the pages of the epic.

NOW YOU KNOW

The Cicones live up in Thrace (the northern Aegean rim) in the Homeric epics. These epics actually mention *hundreds* of different peoples dwelling in the eastern Mediterranean in cities, villages, tribes, and islands, all with unique names and attributes. Book 2 of the *Iliad*, often called the "Catalog of Ships," lists all the many tribes and cities that fought in the Trojan War, and reading it carefully, scholars and archaeologists have acquired a sense of just how pervasive and diverse ancient Greek civilization was, even as early as 700 BCE.

THE LOTUS-EATERS

ANTIQUITY'S MOST BELOVED STONERS.

LIKE: Chilling, Hospitality, Psychoactive Fruit

DISLIKE: Short-Term Memory Tests, Sobriety

SPECIAL POWER: Narcotics

NARRATIVE ROLE: Odysseus's second stop in the epic's central portion is a land where his men are nearly seduced by friendly addicts.

One of the *Odyssey*'s most well-known episodes is only about twenty lines long. Here's what happens. Following their departure from Troy, Odysseus and company had a bloody run-in with the Cicones in Thrace, or the northern Aegean, and barely escaped. Once they were out at sea again, a gale bore down on them from the north. Taking every measure they could to stay afloat, including beaching their ships during the worst of it, the Greeks were driven clockwise through the Aegean, around the mainland, and down past Cythera, a large island south of the Peloponnese.

The storms continued battering them for nine more days, until they reached a place Homer calls the land of the λωτοφάγοι (*lotophagoi*), which means "lotus eaters." The Greeks disembarked there in order to get water. As often happens in the *Odyssey*, Odysseus sent some of the crew farther inland to look around and see if anyone lived there. And also, as often happens in the *Odyssey*, the sailors sent to scout the new territory ran into trouble. Three men went in. Zero returned.

Odysseus, narrating his own story in this part of the epic, explains what happened to them. The scouts he sent inland met some people called the Lotus-Eaters. The Lotus-Eaters were peaceful, and they offered the Greek explorers some sweet fruit. As Odysseus puts it in the Fagles translation, "Any crewman who ate the lotus, the honey-sweet fruit, / lost all desire to send a message back, much less return, / their only wish to linger there with the Lotus-eaters, / grazing on lotus, all memory of the journey home / dissolved forever" (9.106–10). Dopey and numb, Odysseus's trio of scouts made themselves comfortable and had no plans of leaving.

Fortunately, there were ultimately no casualties on the island of the Lotus-Eaters. Odysseus, evidently saying no to drugs, followed his men's trail inland, seized them, and dragged them back to the ships, although the men wept all the way there. Their hysterics were so intense that Odysseus had to tie them up and wedge them under the rowers' benches, and then the Greeks headed out again, another perilous adventure behind them.

The Lotus-Eaters episode, short as it is in the actual *Odyssey*, has rich, universal overtones. A narrative about forbidden fruit, like several others roughly contemporary with the Bible's book of Genesis, Homer's tale of the Lotus-Eaters also contrasts leisure with duty. Ancient Greeks knew that there are ups and downs to intoxicants, just as we do today, and that what brings ease and comfort can also bring apathy, amnesia, and addiction. Later interpreters of the *Odyssey*, including Neoplatonists, read the epic's temptation scenes as allegories for pleasures that the noble philosopher must resist, and Christian readers found Odysseus's staunch resistance noble in many of the poem's central episodes.

Yet Homer's land of the Lotus-Eaters is more than a cautionary tale against narcotics. The world of the *Odyssey* is a perilous one, and one in which violence and loss are never far away. The land of the Lotus-Eaters, by contrast, is stable and timeless. Numbed by the lotus, and indifferent to any prior memories and aspirations, the Lotus-Eaters are peaceful and satisfied. The episode ultimately leads us to ask whether, if there were an off-ramp available from the wear and tear of the human condition, we would want to take it, like the Lotus-Eaters do.

NOW YOU KNOW

The ancient historians Herodotus (400s BCE) and Polybius (100s BCE) theorized that the island of the Lotus-Eaters was in North Africa, either in Libya or Tunisia. The geography makes sense based on references in Homer's *Odyssey*. The epic tells us that southbound winds pressed Odysseus all the way to the bottom of the Peloponnese. But of course, although the ancients loved it, Homer's *Odyssey* is a fable, and there was probably no land of Lotus-Eaters.

The later ancient Greek writer Lucian of Samosata (circa 125–180 CE) wrote a mock epic partly based on Homer's *Odyssey*. In it, a crew of adventurers embark on escapades that tend toward the wild and zany more than the violent and harrowing. In an episode with parallels to Homer's story of Lotus-Eaters, Lucian's crew stops in a land where fish made of wine swim in streams made of wine, and where women partly made of grapevines seduce the crew. It's a funny, bizarre scene, reminding us that in the original Homeric epics, some of Odysseus's rest stops are in pretty weird places.

THE CYCLOPS

BIG. HUNGRY. HEARTBROKEN.

PRONUNCIATION: SIGH-klops

LIKES: Farming, Peace and Quiet, Alcohol, Human Flesh

DISLIKES: Gods, Liars, Freeloaders

SPECIAL POWERS: Animal Husbandry, Murder

NARRATIVE ROLE: The eyeconic monster almost eats Odysseus and gang in Book 9.

He's a giant cannibal with one eye who gets stabbed in the face. That's what most of us remember about the Cyclops of Homer's *Odyssey*. In Book 9 of the epic, Homer's most famous monster stomps onstage, and his exceedingly violent confrontation with Odysseus and his men is one of the most well-known episodes in literature. The Cyclops, a wine-swigging, cheese-munching, skull-crushing terror, nearly ends Odysseus's journey. But, crafty as always, Odysseus gets away.

The story of the Cyclops—in the *Odyssey*, at least—is straightforward. Here it is.

About a third of the way through the epic, the travelers landed on the coast of Sicily at night. It was a fertile place where a natural abundance of barley and grapevines covered the hills and valleys. The next morning, the Greeks happened upon a massive cave entrance lined with laurel trees, and Odysseus surmised that someone lived there—someone very large. The Greeks headed into the cave. Inside, they helped themselves to a stock of goat milk and cheese. Although the other men wanted to leave, Odysseus, for whatever reason, hoped to meet the giant denizen of the cavern. The hero soon got his wish.

In clomped the Cyclops, and the creature sealed the entrance to his home with a massive boulder. Seeing the pint-sized intruders in his cozy quarters, the Cyclops accused them of being pirates and troublemakers. Odysseus lied and said he and the other Greeks were merely shipwrecked travelers seeking hospitality. The gods of Olympus, Odysseus warned the monster, prized hospitality above all other virtues. At this, the Cyclops chortled. The race of Cyclopes, the monster said, were stronger than the gods. Then the creature seized two of Odysseus's men, crushed their heads on the ground, tore them to pieces, and ate them.

The Cyclops then went to sleep. Odysseus considered stabbing the monster in the liver, but he realized that wouldn't be smart because a dead Cyclops would mean that the Greeks would be trapped in the cave. The next morning, the monster awakened, ate two more of the travelers, and left, sealing the giant door behind him. Then, Odysseus did what he did best. He made a plan.

A dreadful, tense day passed for the Greeks. Late that afternoon, the Cyclops lumbered back in and gobbled up two more of Odysseus's men. The hero kept his composure. Odysseus persuaded the monster to drink wine. The evening lengthened, and as the Cyclops grew increasingly inebriated, he asked Odysseus for his name. "Noman," said Odysseus. And the Cyclops, drunk and belching burps that reeked of human flesh, passed out.

Odysseus and his men wasted no time. They smashed a sharpened mast of wood into the snoring creature's eye. Shrieking with agony, up rose the Cyclops, and he wrenched away the boulder that sealed his cave's exit, crying out to his brethren for help. No one replied. Menacingly, the Cyclops guarded the way out, allowing sheep to pass beneath his wary hands and feeling for any human escapees. The Greeks tied themselves to the undersides of some sheep, and in this fashion, they escaped the clutches of the furious Cyclops.

A short, cinematic coda follows this story in the *Odyssey*. The Greeks paddled out to their ships. Once safely aboard, Odysseus shouted to the now-distant monster that the Cyclops had made a terrible mistake. The monster had abused guests, committing an impiety in the eyes of the gods. The Cyclops, realizing he'd been duped, tore loose a section of shoreline and hurled it toward the Greek ships, nearly capsizing them. The adventurers, however, stayed afloat and won the day. And as they drifted farther out into the sea, Odysseus mocked the defeated monster, telling the Cyclops that if anyone ever asked how the creature had lost his eye, "Tell him that Odysseus . . . did it . . . Son of Laertes, whose home is on Ithaca" (Lombardo translation, 9.140–1). These words later came back to haunt Odysseus. The Cyclops was the son of Poseidon, and in many of the hero's subsequent adventures, the god of the sea prevented Odysseus from getting home.

And that's the story of the Cyclops in the *Odyssey*. It's a self-contained episode–a trickster narrative, today sometimes read by classicists as an ethnocentric fable for Greeks encountering more primitive civilizations during the colonizations of the Archaic period and triumphing over them with what ancient Greeks perceived to be their superior intellect. The Cyclops episode is the kind of thing you'd hear if you were at a Greek party in, say, 500 BCE. A few jugs of wine into the evening, someone might tell the bard, "Let's hear some Homer!" And the bard would tune up his or her lyre and sing something like Book 9–a part of the epic, rather than the entire thing. You'd enjoy a harrowing but morally coherent story of humans triumphing over a monster.

It's important to know that the Cyclops himself was a major character in ancient literature–far beyond the pages of Homer's *Odyssey*. His name was Polyphemus. And rather than being a mere monster, in antiquity, Polyphemus was also understood as a lover!

The later Greek poet Theocritus, and his Latin successors Virgil and Ovid, all tell the sad story of how the Cyclops Polyphemus passionately loved a sea nymph called Galatea. The giant carefully combed his hair, practiced his romantic speeches, and then confessed his feelings to her. The nymph Galatea, not bothering to be nice about it, rejected the giant. Off Polyphemus went, his single eye swollen with tears. Though crestfallen, the Cyclops–again in later Greek and Latin poetry–resolved that he still liked himself and that he'd be okay on his own. It's a sad but endearing story about the creature, and it all happened before Polyphemus met Odysseus. Thus, while the *Odyssey*'s popularity has led many of us to remember Polyphemus as an angry monster, in ancient Greek vases and mosaics, it's not uncommon to also see him depicted as a lovelorn, lonesome shepherd, clutching his pipes and staring wistfully off into the distance. Just as so many of the *Odyssey*'s heroes have significant faults, the epic's monsters and villains have redeeming qualities as well!

NOW YOU KNOW

"Cyclopean" is an adjective that archaeologists use to describe buildings made of giant hewn stones—rocks so large that the structures seem to have been made by giants. The Greek word κύκλωψ (*kuklōps*), from which we get the word "cyclops," means "round eyed," from *kuklos* ("circle") and *ōps* ("eye").

AEOLUS

DON'T OPEN THE BAG. DON'T OPEN THE BAG. THEY OPENED THE BAG.

PRONUNCIATION: ee-OH-luhs

LIKES: Family Time, Cholesterol, Windbags

DISLIKES: People Who Can't Follow Simple Instructions

SPECIAL POWER: Controls the Winds

NARRATIVE ROLE: The god of the winds offers Odysseus a breeze home, along with a bag of winds.

In the central portion of the *Odyssey*, after Odysseus and his men barely survived their encounter with the Cyclops, they pressed onward. Lost and in an unfamiliar stretch of the Mediterranean, they spotted an island with sheer cliffs jutting up from the salt water. Atop the bluffs, a bronze wall encircled a palace. The palace, Homer writes, was that of Aeolus, the god of the winds. The Aeolus episode of the *Odyssey* is short, tightly written, and, if you read it carefully, quite weird.

Aeolus had six sons and six daughters. The six sons were married to the six daughters. All day long, every day, Aeolus, his wife, and his pairs of married children feasted on meat. Their house was always filled with the savory odors of roasting flesh. At night, they slept on comfortable beds, covered with copious rugs.

A little worse for wear from their most recent adventure, Odysseus and his troops disembarked on this island and joined the happy, meaty, incestuous household of Aeolus for an entire month. Aeolus asked Odysseus all sorts of questions about the recent war in Troy, and Odysseus answered them. When the month was up, Odysseus had made a sufficiently good impression on Aeolus that the god of winds offered to help Odysseus get

home. Aeolus blessed the hero with a slight breeze to nudge Odysseus toward Ithaca. But much more famously, Aeolus gave Odysseus a bag of winds.

The bag was large—in fact, Odysseus stated that it took an entire ox hide to make it. Aeolus sealed the bag airtight with a silver wire and then stowed it in the hold of Odysseus's ship. Evidently, off camera at some point, Aeolus *also* told Odysseus not to open the bag of winds, no matter what, although Odysseus doesn't explain this in Book 10 of the *Odyssey* as he tells the story of Aeolus.

Well rested from their month within the wind god's bronze walls, Odysseus and his companions set out with the aid of an eastbound breeze to guide them home. Nine days brought them within sight of Ithaca, and Odysseus could actually see the fires of homesteads along the shoreline. But he was exhausted, having stayed up manning the rudder for over a week, and he collapsed, just as they prepared to land in Ithaca. Then, things went awry.

His crewmen, predictably, opened the bag of winds. (Just as they had lingered too long in Ismarus in the previous book, and just as they would eat the cattle of Helios later in the journey, Odysseus's men weren't great at following orders.) Why did they open the bag of winds, though?

Odysseus says his men were jealous of him. His crewmates had left Ithaca with him ages ago, fought with him through the whole Trojan War, and endured the long road home by his side. They speculated among themselves that the great bag of winds within the hold of Odysseus's flagship actually contained hoards of gold and silver, and that the king planned to keep the plunder for himself. Although Odysseus doesn't say this, the men may also have been angry at him for insisting on going into the Cyclops's cave during their previous stop, which resulted in a number of them being eaten. And thus, wanting to see how much Odysseus was cheating them, and perhaps resenting their leader for other reasons besides, they opened the bag.

As soon as the bag of winds was opened, a typhoon engulfed the hero's fleet, spinning and sloshing the ships westward, away from Ithaca once more. Odysseus was distraught and considered suicide, but in the end, he covered himself with his cloak, and the storm-battered fleet eventually careened all the way back to the island of Aeolus. The men scrambled ashore and collected fresh water, and then Odysseus and two of his shipmates went to try and negotiate with Aeolus.

The wind god, his wife, his six sons (also sons-in-law), and his six daughters (also daughters-in-law) were chowing down in the feasting hall. The hero and his men, penitent, sat on the floor near Aeolus's door. The wind god's family asked them why on earth they had returned. Odysseus told them the truth. He'd fallen asleep, he said, and his crew had proved unscrupulous! Could they perhaps give him another nudge eastward?

Aeolus, furious, told Odysseus to get out. He said no one was more accursed than Odysseus, and that Odysseus was obviously detested by the gods. And so the hero and his men climbed back aboard their ships and, deflated, began laboriously rowing homeward, no longer helped along by the tailwind Aeolus had provided. As their adventures continued, and more and more of Odysseus's men perished, the mistake they had made with Aeolus's bag began to seem more and more severe.

Odysseus ends the story of the god Aeolus with a small coda. He tells his listeners that he and his men brought their subsequent misfortunes on themselves. It was neither the caprices of the gods, nor the impersonal power of nature that did them in, but instead, their own shortcomings.

It's easy to blow past the Aeolus episode in Book 10 and go on to the next adventure. But what happens with Aeolus still sets the stage, thematically, for a lot of what's to come in the *Odyssey*. The bag of Aeolus, an unexplained, dangerous talisman stuffed into the hull of a ship by a god, seems almost like a trap. It is a forbidden-fruits story, certainly, but it's also a tale about the unpredictability and incomprehensibility of divine will. Ancient Greeks, who met with priests and oracles to help them understand what gods wanted, would have found Odysseus's fraught negotiations with the divine amply relatable.

In addition to being a boilerplate forbidden-fruits tale like others in the epic, the Aeolus story in the *Odyssey* also gives us a glimpse of something darker: Odysseus's relationship with his men. Loyal though those men might be, the hero's followers have also served beneath him for more than a decade. Though they haven't deserted him, Odysseus's shipmates are clearly beginning to look out for their own interests. As the story continues, and he loses more and more of them, tensions only increase.

NOW YOU KNOW

Later Greek and Roman poets imitated nearly every aspect of the Homeric poems. One of those aspects was using Aeolus, the god of winds, as a character. The ancient Greek poet Apollonius of Rhodes, in his *Argonautica* (200s BCE), has the wind god Aeolus make a little cameo to help Jason and the Argonauts along on their waterborne journey. In the *Aeneid* (19 BCE), the Roman epic poet Virgil wrote a scene about Aeolus hurling the winds at the hero Aeneas.

THE LAESTRYGONIANS

HUNGRY GIANTS WITH ANGER-MANAGEMENT ISSUES.

PRONUNCIATION: lie-stru-GOAN-ee-uns

LIKE: Violence, Cannibalism

DISLIKE: Trespassers, Refugees

SPECIAL POWERS: Xenophobia, Rage

NARRATIVE ROLE: The Laestrygonians destroy Odysseus's entire fleet, excepting one ship.

At this point in the story, Odysseus and the other Greeks have weathered a run of pretty bad luck. Tripping out with the Lotus-Eaters back in Book 9 wasn't so bad, but then they got attacked by the Cyclops and, after that, were blown way out into the sea after nearly reaching Ithaca. Six days and nights after departing from the wind god's island for the *second* time, they caught sight of Telepylus, the land of the Laestrygonians, likely hoping for a good reception and directions back home.

Telepylus, however, was an eerie place rather than a welcoming one. Night there seemed to only last a moment. Herdsmen bringing in their flocks at dusk greeted those escorting other flocks out at dawn. Odysseus's fleet rowed through a narrow passage and into a large natural harbor that was wreathed by sheer cliffs. The bay was so still that the Greeks could moor ships right next to each other. Ship after ship entered and tied down its sails—every ship except for that of Odysseus himself. The hero left his own vessel *outside* of this natural harbor, tying it to a rock and then

making a steep climb up the cliffside. At the top, all around him, Odysseus only saw empty wilderness, although in the distance, he caught sight of a small whorl of smoke.

Some of the *Odyssey*'s most magical moments are just like this one. The protagonists arrive somewhere new. We're right there alongside them. Things could go very badly. Things could go very well. Imagine an ancient Greek bard, 2,700 years ago, pausing at a moment like this in the story, perhaps just playing a few extra measures on the lyre to build tension, with the audience leaning in and waiting to find out what Odysseus would discover! The earliest audiences of the Homeric epics lived during a period of colonial expansion, and some of them knew just what it was like to step off a ship and onto the shore of a strange land, not knowing whether they'd find friends or foes.

Odysseus sent a trio of men inland to investigate the source of the distant smoke. The Greeks discovered a wagon track that led to a town. Before they reached the town, they saw a girl drawing water from a spring. The Greeks asked her questions: What was the name of the country to which they'd come? Who was the ruler? The girl, eerily, said nothing. She only pointed to a very large dwelling down the path. The Greeks, following her directions, investigated, and, entering, they met the first full-grown Laestrygonian.

The woman was gigantic, and her appearance terrified the Greeks. She roared to summon her husband, and he appeared. The tribe's chief (for that was who the enormous man was) immediately pounced on one of Odysseus's three men and began eating him alive. The other two, mortified, ran for their lives. As the Greeks dashed along the wagon track back toward their leader and flagship, all hell broke loose in the Laestrygonian town. The chief howled out an alert for all the Laestrygonians, and they suddenly appeared from everywhere. The giants thundered toward Telepylus's main harbor. They heaved huge stones down at Odysseus's fleet.

It became a massacre. The natural harbor, seemingly secure with its high walls and narrow entrance, was impossible for the Greeks to escape all at once. The sounds of screams joined those of snapping masts and breaking boards, and the Laestrygonians not pelting the fleet hurried down close to the water to skewer the sailors who had gone overboard. Eleven of Odysseus's twelve ships were destroyed.

Remember, Odysseus's ship was the single vessel *not* moored within the Laestrygonian harbor. He dashed back down from the headland, sliced his mooring rope with a sword, and ordered his men to row for their lives. The crew didn't have to be told twice. Soon, the sole surviving ship of the hero's fleet was out to sea, and the glowering cliffs of Telepylus, and all their dead comrades, were left behind.

The episode with the Laestrygonians is a pivotal one, but like a lot of important scenes in the book, it's pretty short. Odysseus loses his entire fleet, excepting one boat, in about two pages, and he doesn't explain why he chose to tie up outside the Laestrygonian harbor while all the other ships went in.

All told, the Laestrygonians episode, and the Cyclops sequence that precedes it, have the tenor and cadence of a horror movie. A small armada of veterans lands in unknown territory. Mystery and spookiness turn to horror and carnage, and the body count climbs. Within the *Odyssey* are dozens of narratives of different genres, and some of them, like that of the Laestrygonians, are very grim and dark!

NOW YOU KNOW

The nearly unending daylight of the island of the Laestrygonians may be based on stories of Bronze or Iron Age explorations to Orkney, Shetland, the Faroe Islands, northern Scotland, or even Iceland. A Greek explorer named Pytheas, in the fourth century BCE, sailed around what is today Ireland and the United Kingdom. Perhaps even earlier, in Homer's day, news of the midnight sun was already circulating in the central Mediterranean.

James Joyce's novel *Ulysses* (1922) famously follows the overall structure of Homer's *Odyssey*. The eighth section of the novel, called "Lestrygonians," takes place in Davy Byrne's pub in Dublin. Byrne's pub is full of people noshing and drinking, and the book's protagonist, Leopold Bloom, gobbles down a cheese sandwich and drinks a glass of burgundy.

HERMES

BEARING NEWS AND WEARING WINGED SHOES.

PRONUNCIATION: HER-mees

LIKES: Traveling, Communication, Sneakers

DISLIKES: Explicitly Taking Sides

SPECIAL POWERS: Being Slippery, Moving Between Worlds

NARRATIVE ROLE: Hermes has a couple of cameos in the *Odyssey*, the most important of which is preparing Odysseus for his meeting with Circe.

At first glance, Hermes is sort of a benchwarmer god in Greek mythology. Effectively a mailman in a lot of stories, Hermes helps move the action along without personally doing anything spectacular. Yet he is a fixture in so much ancient Greek literature that when we read everything about him that's been left behind, we get the sense that even by Homer's time in roughly the 700s BCE, Hermes was a very ancient god with many different attributes.

In the *Odyssey*, Hermes has three appearances, and all of them are awesome. First, he is the deity whom Athena and Zeus dispatch to help Odysseus escape from Calypso. In one of the *Odyssey*'s most fabulous descriptions, Hermes zooms down to earth from Mount Olympus to go and find Odysseus:

Quickly under [Hermes's] feet he fastened the supple sandals,

ever-glowing gold, that wing him over the waves

and boundless earth with the rush of gusting winds. . . .

Swooping down from [Olympus], down the high clear air,

[Hermes] plunged to the sea and skimmed the waves like a tern

continued

Ancient Greek literary scholars praised something called ἐνάργεια (*enargeia*), which meant using language to create a vivid, lifelike impression, and this description of Hermes certainly does just that.

The messenger god's mission at this point was a jailbreak, and landing on Calypso's island, he told the goddess it was time to let Odysseus go home. Calypso, knowing that Hermes was conveying orders from the boss, agreed to do so, albeit with some grumbling.

That's all at the beginning of Book 5. In Book 10, Hermes showed up again, in order to help Odysseus deal with another dangerous goddess: the witch Circe. Hermes found Odysseus wandering around on Circe's island and offered him advice. The goddess, Hermes said, was going to drug Odysseus and cast a spell on him in order to transform him into a pig. What Odysseus needed to do was gobble down a special herb (Hermes provided it). The herb would immunize Odysseus from Circe's drugs, and when Circe saw Odysseus unaffected by her narcotics, she would seduce him. Odysseus then had to sleep with Circe, but to do so carefully, because the witch could harm Odysseus while he was naked.

Odysseus's meeting with Hermes takes place right before the hero actually meets the witch Circe. The scene is funny, creepy, and morally sketchy all at once, and it begins to give us a sense of who Hermes was in Greek mythology beyond merely being a messenger. Hermes's most frequent Homeric epithet is Ἀργεϊφόντης (*Agreiphontes*), which is usually translated as "giant killer" but which literally means "slayer of Argus." Argus was a hundred-eyed giant stationed to guard a nymph with whom Zeus wanted to have sex. Hermes blinded and killed the giant, allowing Zeus access to the nymph. And in other Greek myths, along these same lines, Hermes is the messenger of seedy, lecherous, spiteful peers, and he

helps the Olympians through various deceptions, thefts, and cover-ups. Another one of his epithets in Homer is πολύτροπον (*polytropos*), or "of many turnings," and Odysseus, also a trickster, gets described with the same word. Hermes, then, is the perfect emissary to convey schemes and strategies to Odysseus. The messenger god and the wily hero are birds of a feather.

Yet Hermes was also more than a dodgy intermediary in Greek mythology, and in his third and final appearance in the *Odyssey*, we encounter the messenger god in one of his often-forgotten roles. This final role is that of a shepherd of the dead, or "psychopomp," to use the technical word. Following the battle toward the end of the *Odyssey*, in Book 24, Hermes guided the spirits of the deceased out over the ocean, past the orbit of the sun, through the realm of dreams, and into the meadows on the fringes of the underworld. This, too, was one of Hermes's roles—to guide the souls of the departed into the afterlife. Homer calls Hermes the "healer" in the god's final appearance in the book, suggesting the range of attributes associated with ancient Greece's messenger god.

Hermes is very often depicted wearing a *petasos* (round hat) in ancient Greek art. But really, Hermes, and many Greek gods, wore a number of proverbial hats. Understanding ancient Greece means understanding how much gods like Hermes had many different sacred legends associated with them, and how much each god evolved over the centuries.

NOW YOU KNOW

At some point in the ancient world, there arose a deity called Hermes Trismegistus. Hermes Trismegistus was a combination of the Greek god Hermes and the ancient Egyptian deity Thoth. Hermes Trismegistus allegedly wrote a body of works called the *Hermetica*, which were mystical, pseudo-scientific texts dealing with alchemy, magic, astrology, and medicine. The texts, likely written by devout mystics in and after the 200s BCE, are still an important part of esotericism and the occult today.

CIRCE

ODYSSEUS'S LONG ROAD HOME
REQUIRED MORE SEX AND DRUGS.

PRONUNCIATION: SIR-see

LIKES: Animals, Singing, Sketchy Hookups

DISLIKES: Neighbors

SPECIAL POWERS: Pharmacology, Seduction

NARRATIVE ROLE: Odysseus and his men stay on the island of the witch
Circe for an entire year during their trip home in the *Odyssey*.

Of all the secondary characters in Homer's *Odyssey*, Circe easily had the
largest impact on later art, showing up in dozens of poems, plays, novels,
operas, and ballets, long after Homer told her story in the *Odyssey*. People
of all ages, it seems, love the story of a witch, and Circe is the most famous
witch in ancient literature.

The truth is that Circe is more of a druggist (φαρμακίς, or *pharmakis*),
dealing in potions and poisons, than she is a cackling sorceress wearing a
pointy hat. Her occult powers are all related to the brewing of concoctions
(φάρμακα, or *pharmaka*) and the performance of rituals rather than divine
miracles such as those of Athena and Zeus. She's not the only druggist in
the *Odyssey*. Homer's Helen mixes a certain νηπενθές φάρμακον (*nepenthes
pharmakon*), or "anti-sorrow drug," into wine at dinner in Sparta. Later in
ancient Greek history, the word φαρμακεία (*pharmakeia*) was used in the
New Testament to describe sorcery and witchcraft. Back during Homer's
time, however, drugs, chemistry, and sacred rites were all in the same general wheelhouse. Circe, schooled in all of them, is more associated with
herbs and potions than evil and malice in the *Odyssey*.

The lengthy Circe episode forms the heart of Odysseus's waterborne adventures in the central part of the *Odyssey*. The hero disembarks on Circe's island for a rest stop, and his subsequent bender there ends up being the second-longest stayover in the *Odyssey*. Here's the story as Homer tells it.

Following their catastrophic encounter with the Laestrygonians, the single remaining ship of Odysseus's fleet arrived at an island called Aeaea. Exhausted, the Greeks tied their vessel in a natural harbor, staggered out onto the beach, and collapsed. Morale was terrible. The Greeks mourned their lost comrades. After two days, Odysseus left his men in order to explore the forested island. Climbing atop a crag, the hero saw a column of smoke in the distance, but caution kept him from investigating it right away. Instead, Odysseus went to speak with his men. On the way, he was able to kill a large stag, which he brought back to the boat to share with his shipmates.

The food bolstered the men's spirits. And to hearten them further, Odysseus announced that although they were certainly lost, he'd seen signs of civilization on the island. The men were, understandably, not overjoyed. Recent experience had taught them that Homeric islands were perilous places. Still, they had to investigate if they wanted to find out how to get back home. Odysseus divided the men into two parties. He led one, and his brother-in-law Eurylochus led the other. A drawing of lots resulted in Eurylochus's party leading the scouting expedition inland. Odysseus planned to stay with the ships.

Eurylochus led his men into the island's interior, and soon they found a house made of polished blocks of stone. All around it there were wolves and lions, but the predators did not attack. Instead, the animals watched the Greeks approaching the house and greeted the men as friendly puppies would, many standing on their hind paws. Inside the homestead, the men heard the haunting sound of a woman singing.

Though the Greeks were apprehensive, they called out a greeting to determine the source of the music they heard. A woman answered the door and ushered them in. The adventurers did not know who she was, but, as Odysseus informs his listeners, she was Circe, daughter of Helios, the god of the sun. Circe offered the men some food and wine. But the food and wine, the Greeks soon discovered, were drugged, because the men began changing. They grew bristles, floppy ears, and snouts. And, losing all their memories of home and duty, they changed into pigs. Circe goaded the pigs into a paddock, and there they stayed.

One member of the scouting party, as it turned out, had not gone into Circe's house. Something about the tame wolves and eerie singing had led Odysseus's brother-in-law Eurylochus to not follow the others into the extremely dubious drug den. Eurylochus dashed back to the ships and offered Odysseus a report of the disaster. The hero heard the news stoically, shouldered his weapons, and headed inland to help his men, although his brother-in-law proposed leaving the island right away. Hurrying through an oak forest to confront the witch, Odysseus was surprised to instead see Hermes, the ancient Greek messenger god.

Hermes warned Odysseus that Circe was dangerous. Odysseus needed to be prepared to meet her, or he'd end up in the pigsty with his crewmen. Hermes also had *bad* news, *good* news, and *weird* news for the hero. The bad news was that Circe was going to drug Odysseus. The good news was that Hermes would give Odysseus a drug to immunize him from the witch's concoction. The weird news was that Odysseus, after warding off the witch's black magic, would need to have sex with her in order to free his men. The sex, Hermes said, would be dangerous, and Odysseus needed to make Circe swear not to harm him during intercourse. With that, Hermes handed Odysseus an antidote and wished the hero good luck with the drugs and sex.

The hero, with considerable apprehension, knocked on Circe's door. She admitted him and offered Odysseus a silver chair and a golden bowl filled with a mysterious drink. After first quaffing the antidote, and perhaps crossing his fingers, Odysseus gulped down Circe's poison. The witch prepared to exile him to join the hogs. But Odysseus, unaffected, drew his sword and made as if he were going to attack her. Circe, suddenly terrified, sank down onto her knees and began talking to Odysseus in a rather different tone. (Here, perhaps, an ancient bard performing this portion of the *Odyssey* would have struck up a sultry melody on the lyre.)

Circe exclaimed that she'd *never* met a man who could take her drugs and not be affected by them. He was *quite* a man. He must be Odysseus! She'd heard about him. Put down the sword, Circe purred, and come to bed, so that they could get better acquainted through sex. Odysseus, after making her promise not to harm him during the proposed encounter, complied.

After Odysseus had some sort of Homersexual experience off camera, four maids came and offered the hero linens, a fine table setting, a bath, a massage, new clothing, bread, and scrumptious foods. Before too long, the hero admitted he didn't want to eat anything because his men were out there rooting around in the pigpen. Circe said she understood, and she went outside and rubbed the pigs with an enchanted ointment, and they transformed back into men. As the men cried and Odysseus hugged them, Circe had a change of heart, and she told the Greeks to go ahead and fetch all their men—even the ones back on the boat. She'd see to everyone's comfort.

Odysseus went to collect them. Reuniting with his men was an emotional experience, and soon, all the Greeks were gathered beneath Circe's roof. Having attacked them initially, the witch now treated them to all the hospitality at her resources, and the men grew very comfortable there. In fact, they grew so comfortable that they stayed on the island of Aeaea, bewitched, as one might say, for an entire year.

Eventually, Odysseus's men told him he really ought to think about pulling up the anchor and getting back to Ithaca. The hero agreed, and told Circe that his men wanted to leave. She said she certainly wouldn't keep him there unwillingly. He could go.

It was just that he had to go to hell.

In Hades, Circe recommended, a sage would be able to offer Odysseus an overview of how the hero could reach home. The witch offered him extensive instructions on how to open a portal to Hades. Odysseus, though he couldn't have been very excited about the prospect, agreed to go and ask some dead guy in the underworld for directions. His men were devastated that the next stop would be so dark and dreary, but having no say in the matter, they got on the ship, and the Greeks left Circe's island.

Interestingly, after the *Nekyia*, or visit-to-the-underworld sequence, Odysseus and the gang went back to Aeaea to collect a shipmate's body. Before the group left the island the first time, Odysseus's youngest crewman, Elpenor, had an accident. The youth, Odysseus explains, got so drunk that he decided to sleep on Circe's roof. (Perhaps the Greeks were having a going-away party and Circe was spiking the drinks.) Unfortunately, on the morning of their departure, Elpenor staggered off the roof and fell to his death. The Greeks came back to Circe's island after visiting Hades to offer the young man a proper burial, at which time the witch gave Odysseus strategic instructions on what was to come next on his journey. Then, finally, the hero and the witch parted for good.

And that's the story of Circe in the *Odyssey*. She's *almost* a major character in the epic. And in the *Odyssey*'s original sequel, an epic called the *Telegony*, Circe *was* a main character and the mother of Odysseus's son Telegonus. (The *Telegony* is discussed at the end of this book.) Though she's been interpreted and staged in many different ways in subsequent centuries, in the *Odyssey*, she is an ambiguous figure: on the one hand, dangerous, mysterious, and solitary; on the other, happy to enjoy an adulterous relationship with Odysseus and host the Greeks for an entire year.

The *length* of Odysseus's stay on Aeaea, in the home and bedchamber of Circe, is one of the *Odyssey*'s narrative quirks. He's not being held prisoner there, as he is on Calypso's island. To be fair to the Greeks, they've suffered some awful experiences just prior to landing on Aeaea, and so they could use a break when they disembark on the island. At the same time, though, the fact that it's Odysseus's *men* who urge him to leave the witch's sumptuous forest mansion suggests that his homesickness is not unconquerable under the right circumstances!

NOW YOU KNOW

Circe was the aunt of ancient Greece's *other* most famous witch. This younger witch was Medea. Circe's brother Aeëtes was the king of Colchis in present-day Georgia. In Greek mythology, the hero Jason went all the way to Colchis in the eastern Black Sea to get the Golden Fleece, and Medea came back home with him. Medea, like Circe, was associated with black magic, herbs, and concoctions, and both women are mighty, formidable figures in ancient Greek mythology.

TIRESIAS

FRIENDLY, GENDER-FLUID, AND ALL OVER ANCIENT GREEK LITERATURE.

PRONUNCIATION: tie-REE-see-us

LIKES: Blood, Prophecies

DISLIKES: Offering Clear, Actionable Advice

SPECIAL POWER: The Original "Blind Guy Who Sees All" Archetype

NARRATIVE ROLE: Tiresias offers Odysseus visions of things to come, describing events both in the *Odyssey* as well as afterward.

In Book 11 of the *Odyssey*, Odysseus opens a portal to Hades in order to speak with the dead. Though he ends up chatting with a lot of departed mortals, he opens the portal to Hades specifically in order to consult with a dead prophet named Tiresias. Here is the story of how Odysseus meets Tiresias.

Sailing away from Circe's island, the Greeks passed into a territory called Cimmeria, at the edge of the earth, a land of perpetual darkness. Odysseus and his men beached their ship and then went inland into the night, and found the spot that the witch Circe had described—a spot where a gateway to the underworld could be opened, if the right protocol were followed.

Odysseus had learned the correct portal-opening procedure from Circe. The hero dug a small trench. In it, he poured honey, then milk, then wine, then water. He sprinkled barley atop the sludgy mixture and prayed to the dead, telling the unseen spirits that he would sacrifice fine animals to them if and when he returned to Ithaca. Then, the Greeks brought sheep forward, and Odysseus slashed their throats over the open trench, so that dark blood pooled atop the prior concoction.

Scenting the blood, spirits surged up from the trench, and Odysseus grew pale at the cacophony of wailing coming out of the ground. First, the hero saw young Elpenor, that crewman who had died the morning of their last day with Circe. Listening to Elpenor's story, Odysseus promised to return to the witch's island and bury him. Then Odysseus caught sight of the blind prophet Tiresias—the very man he had come to see.

Tiresias asked Odysseus why he had come to the forlorn realm of the dead, and without waiting for a response, the sage stepped forward and sipped blood from Odysseus's trench. (Nothing wrong with slurping up a nice mouthful of blood from a trench before having a conversation about the future.) Thusly fortified, old Tiresias offered his counsel.

The sage reported that Odysseus had angered Poseidon and that the sea god would be a big problem for the hero in days to come. However, Tiresias added, Odysseus and his shipmates still had a chance to get back to Ithaca, though they'd have no shortage of suffering. They would come to the island of the sun god Helios, where the god's herds of beautiful cattle grazed. Odysseus needed to keep his men under control and make sure that they didn't kill and eat the cattle. Also, said Tiresias, Odysseus would face dire problems when he arrived at home, because his palace was full of greedy, horny suitors courting his wife.

Now, so far, this information is all pretty straightforward. Tiresias, maybe with a bit of hemoglobin and soil in his beard, was telling Odysseus what to expect. But while the *Odyssey* ends with Odysseus getting home and defeating the suitors, *Tiresias's prophecy does not*. Though many readers forget this moment in the book, the old sage *also* offered Odysseus revelations about what would happen to him *after* the *Odyssey*.

Tiresias told Odysseus that once the hero defeated the suitors, Odysseus had to leave Ithaca again. Odysseus needed to travel somewhere far inland, where people knew nothing of the sea, and bring an oar with him. When he met someone who did not recognize the oar for what it was, but mistook it as something to winnow grain, Odysseus needed to root the oar in the earth and offer a sacrifice to Poseidon. *Then* Odysseus could go home, and would die peacefully and at an advanced age.

These were the words that Odysseus had traveled to the edge of the world to hear. Odysseus milked the sage for one more answer. Odysseus told Tiresias that he'd noticed that not all of the dead would speak to him.

Tiresias offered the hero a quick rundown on communing with the dead. The prophet told Odysseus that the dead had to drink the sacrificial blood, and only then would they speak. With this, Tiresias departed. Odysseus then took the opportunity to speak with numerous other Homeric characters who had passed away, making sure each one got a decent swig of blood ahead of time.

Tiresias only gets a short part in the *Odyssey*, but like so many other Homeric characters, he would have been a familiar figure to the epic's original audiences. In the Greek myths, Tiresias was associated with the city of Thebes. More than any other mythological event, the Trojan War was the root of many stories that survive today in ancient Greek literature. But a close second was a war at the Greek city of Thebes, just thirty miles northwest of Athens (not to be confused with the Egyptian city of Thebes). From Sophocles's Oedipus Cycle and Euripides's *Bacchae* during the 400s BCE all the way down to the Roman poet Statius's *Thebaid* (90s CE), many ancient Mediterranean stories are set in Thebes and based around a few mythological generations that lived there.

While Tiresias's cameo in the *Odyssey* is one of his major appearances in literature, a second one occurs in the Oedipus story cycle. The blind sage has the unenviable responsibility of telling Oedipus that the king has killed his father and married his mother, and over the course of subsequent events in the city, poor Tiresias is tasked with telling other people things they really don't want to hear.

The sage is also, in Ovid's *Metamorphoses* (3.408–51) and other ancient Greek and Latin stories, one of several characters from antiquity who changes from a man to a woman, or a woman to a man (Tiresias does both!). Having been changed from a man to a woman, and then back, Tiresias was able to answer an important question posed to him by Zeus and Hera. The gods asked the prophet whether men or women enjoyed sex more. Tiresias's response was definitive: Women did.

The sage Tiresias, then, had an unusually long and strange resume in ancient Greek mythology. When he appears in Homer's *Odyssey*, he crosses between what we might call cinematic universes, moving from the Theban story cycle over to the Trojan War story cycle to offer Odysseus news about what's coming his way. A colorful figure in the Greek myths, Tiresias should also remind us that ancient Greeks really did consult with oracles and augurs—at famous sites like Delphi and Eleusis, but also in towns and trading hubs all over the Aegean where prophets could make a profit.

THE GHOST OF ACHILLES

"SO, WHAT'S IT LIKE BEING DEAD, ACHILLES?"

PRONUNCIATION: uh-KEEL-ees

LIKES: Glory, His Mother, Dismemberment

DISLIKES: Being Dead, Having a Body Part Named after Him

SPECIAL POWERS: Combat, Whining

NARRATIVE ROLE: Odysseus speaks with Achilles and other departed spirits in Hades, and learns much from them.

When you have a portal to Hades open, you want to get as much mileage out of it as possible. At least, this is the attitude that Odysseus seems to take to his doorway to the underworld in Book 11 of Homer's *Odyssey*. Because after Odysseus completes his official mission of speaking with the seer Tiresias, he leans in as far as he can go through his doorway to the dead and has conversations with a number of ghosts. The Hades sequence of the *Odyssey*, after the hero's initial consultation with Tiresias, is as follows.

Odysseus first met his mother, Anticleia. He had numerous questions for her, and she answered many of them. She had died, she said, of heartbreak from missing him, and his father, though still alive, dwelt mournfully in the shacks and pastures of Ithaca, also in unending lamentation of Odysseus's absence. The hero's wife and son were alive and well, however, so that was decent news. Odysseus leaned in to hug his mother. He had only just learned of her death, so it was a tragic moment for the protagonist. But when he tried to embrace her, he found that she had no physical form. Odysseus's mother faded and disappeared, and then the hero saw a long procession of famous figures from Greek mythology.

Odysseus first looked upon the founders of Thebes, and Jocasta, the mother of Oedipus. He saw Pasiphae, the mother of the Minotaur, and Ariadne, the Minotaur's sister (who helped the hero Theseus through its famous labyrinth). And though Odysseus saw many imposing figures from bygone days, most pivotally, he saw men whom he had known during the war at Troy.

The first of these was Agamemnon, the king of the Greeks. For a dead guy, Agamemnon has a fair amount of on-screen time in the *Odyssey*. Agamemnon had essentially been Odysseus's boss for ten years, and Odysseus, his right-hand man and fixer. Seeing his former commander, Odysseus was overwhelmed with grief, and he asked how the leader of the Greeks had come to be in Hades. Agamemnon explained, telling Odysseus a tale that Homer's original audience would have known–the tale of Agamemnon's own homecoming.

Agamemnon revealed to Odysseus that he'd come home to catastrophe. His wife was cheating on him with his cousin. This cousin welcomed the victorious Agamemnon home, feasted and toasted the king in his own palace, and then butchered him, along with his companions. Agamemnon's wife, Clytemnestra, had been there, and even shared in the slaughter. The king's ghost told Odysseus that the two men had seen grisly sights during the war in Troy but that what had happened to him at home had been worse than any horror they'd encountered abroad.

The most piercing part of the betrayal, Agamemnon growled, was that of his wife. The dead king told Odysseus to be very careful about Penelope when Odysseus came home to Ithaca. Odysseus needed to exercise caution when he reached Ithaca, and to approach his former household in secret. Otherwise, Odysseus, too, might meet a gruesome end. Agamemnon had a son, and asked Odysseus if he knew of the young man's whereabouts, but Odysseus didn't. Overcome with loss–one of them dead, and the other off course and heartbroken–the two heroes wept and commiserated with one another.

Hades held another of Odysseus's dear friends, and this was the Greek champion Achilles. Achilles, the hero of Homer's first epic, the *Iliad*, only shows up for a moment in Homer's *Odyssey*, but his appearance still prompts one of the most well-known scenes in ancient literature. The great hero Achilles, seeing Odysseus, asked what the latter was doing in Hades. Odysseus told him the truth, explaining that he was lost and that he'd come to talk to Tiresias in order to find his way home. Then Odysseus changed the subject, wanting to discuss Achilles. The heroes of the two Homeric epics shared this immortal exchange:

[Odysseus said:] "But you, Achilles, are the most fortunate man that ever was or will be! For in the old days when you were on Earth, we [Greeks] honoured you as though you were a god; and now, down here, you have great power among the dead. Do not grieve at your death, Achilles."

"And do not you make light of death, illustrious Odysseus," [Achilles] replied. "I would rather work the soil as a serf on hire to some landless impoverished peasant than be King of all these lifeless dead."

—Odysseus speaks to Achilles in Hades, *Odyssey*
(Rieu translation, 11.483–91)

In other words, Odysseus learned that even though Achilles had been the most glorious hero of his time, none of it counted for anything after death, because he'd plummeted down to the same dingy penitentiary as everyone else. Like King Agamemnon had a moment before, Achilles asked about his son. Odysseus told Achilles that the young man had distinguished himself at the end of the Trojan War and made it out alive. This assurance, at least, gave the grieving Achilles some comfort. The mighty hero of the *Iliad* turned and went off through the gloomy meadows of the underworld, becoming indistinguishable among the rest of the departed.

This was the last conversation of any length that Odysseus had with the dead, though he lingered there in the periphery of Hades a short while longer. He saw his old comrade-in-arms Ajax, but the giant warrior refused to speak with him. Odysseus caught glimpses of Tityus, Tantalus, and Sisyphus, describing the distinct punishments each had to endure due to their betrayals of the gods. He saw Heracles, and the muscle-bound giant told Odysseus briefly about how in years past he'd caught the three-headed dog Cerberus and dragged the creature up out of Hades as one of his labors.

Even after this, Odysseus lingered for a perilously long time, hoping to see and learn more about the forbidden realm of Hades. In the end, though, so many withered spirits swarmed up to where he stood that fear overtook him, and he fled to his ship, sailing with his men far, far away from Cimmeria and the gateway to the underworld.

That's the story of Odysseus and his visit to Hades. Later epic poets imitated the convention of having a hero visit the underworld. The American scholar Joseph Campbell theorized about something called the "monomyth," a story of a heroic journey shared by many different cultures, in which heroes like Odysseus went through a sequence of archetypal experiences, one of which was a descent to an abyssal realm where they learned secrets pertinent to their quests. And while it's fun to speculate about theoretical models that explain all literature, it's equally fun to observe how a scene or sequence in one story influenced many later stories.

In the case of Homer's *Odyssey*, Book 11 ended up having an absolutely massive impact on all subsequent cultural history, influencing how we still imagine the afterlife today. What happened was as follows. In addition to many other ancient writers, the Roman poet Virgil (70–19 BCE) carefully read Homer's *Odyssey*. Virgil wrote an epic called the *Aeneid*, which, during the Middle Ages, was a lot more popular than Homer's works in Europe. (The *Aeneid* was in Latin, and European scholars could still read Latin, while Greek had fallen out of use.) The *Aeneid* also had an underworld book (Book 6), in which *its* hero went down to Hades, and this underworld was very much influenced by Homer's.

While many of us today forget that ancient Greek and Latin epics had long scenes depicting what we would call "hell," for Dante Alighieri (circa 1265–1321 CE), the underworld sequences of ancient epics were the most influential scenes of all. His *Inferno*, a long narrative poem about a descent to hell, had as one of its primary sources Virgil's *Aeneid*. Dante's hell is made with pieces from Virgil's *Aeneid*, which is built with blocks from Homer's *Odyssey*. The Christian afterlife has deep, often-forgotten roots in ancient Greek literature. In fact, the Greek word for "hell" that's used numerous times throughout the Gospels and the rest of the New Testament is Ἅιδης (*Ádis*), or Hades!

NOW YOU KNOW

Reading the underworld sequence in the *Odyssey*, we can't help but notice that there's no corresponding heaven. In Homer's universe (as in Sumerian mythology and in Old Testament books like Job and Ecclesiastes), everyone goes down to the same somber subterranean holding tank, and that's it. Later scholars have often assumed that the Homeric underworld encapsulates precisely what all ancient Greeks believed about the afterlife. But really, ancient Greeks, who inhabited multiple time zones and multiple continents over a thousand-year period of history, believed all sorts of stuff about the afterlife, depending on when and where they lived.

THE SIRENS

DON'T LISTEN TO THEM. DON'T LISTEN TO THEM. HE LISTENED TO THEM.

LIKE: Singing, Seducing, Human Flesh

DISLIKE: Hearing Protection

SPECIAL POWER: Luring People over to Their Dubious Island

NARRATIVE ROLE: Carnivorous creatures who try to stop Odysseus and his crew in Book 12 of the *Odyssey*.

Along with facing the Cyclops back in Book 9, Odysseus's short encounter with the Sirens in Book 12 might be the *Odyssey*'s most iconic episode. And while paintings and on-screen depictions of the scene might lead us to imagine it in certain ways, in the actual *Odyssey*, the episode with the Sirens is surprisingly short and enigmatic. So let's go through the actual Sirens scene in the *Odyssey* and also, importantly, the events that led up to it.

Having completed his journey to the underworld and his consultation with the sage Tiresias, Odysseus piloted his sole remaining ship back to Circe's island. The heroes returned because their young crewmate Elpenor had died just before the Greeks left Circe's island. Elpenor had accosted Odysseus in Hades and asked for a proper burial. Accordingly, as soon as they arrived on the island of Aeaea, the Greeks burned Elpenor's body and built the poor young man a burial mound, at the top of which was his oar.

Circe realized that the Greeks had come back, and she greeted them with the usual platters of meat and jugs of wine requisite to any hospitality scene in the Homeric epics. As the heroes chowed down, got tipsy, and mellowed out a bit after quite literally going to hell, Circe secreted Odysseus away to give him a summary of what was next on his journey. This

short, secondary meeting between the hero and the witch is a very strange and sometimes forgotten moment in the epic. Circe *just* sent him all the way to the distant land of Cimmeria so that Odysseus could convene with the dead sage about what was going to happen next on his long boat trip. Then, just as he arrives back in Aeaea, Circe herself seems to have the power of foretelling, because she gives him a *much longer* play-by-play of what's to come than the sage Tiresias did. Anyway, Odysseus, maybe scratching his head and wondering why the witch had sent him to Hades if she knew more than Tiresias, nonetheless listened politely.

First, Circe told him about the Sirens. They lurked in a meadow stacked with the rotting bones of those who had listened to them. Anyone who heard their music never went home. Odysseus *could* listen to the Sirens and enjoy their song if he wanted to, said Circe, but only if the hero was tied tightly to the mast of his ship. That was the advice that Circe gave Odysseus about the Sirens. (She also counseled him about other upcoming dangers, but let's stick with the Sirens.)

When it was time to leave the next morning, Circe saw the Greeks off, filling their sails with a magical tailwind. Odysseus had the men stow everything for the voyage. Then he explained what was going to happen with the Sirens. Interestingly, Odysseus told his crewmen that Circe *ordered* him to listen to the Sirens. (In reality, the witch told Odysseus that he *could* listen to them if he wanted to.) He told the rowers that when the time came, they should tie him up and not listen to him, regardless of what he said during that part of the day's voyage. The men, perhaps shaking their heads a little bit at their captain's weird instructions, agreed to do what Odysseus said.

As they drew closer to the Sirens' island, the wind stopped. The sea grew still, as though the waves themselves had been soothed into silence. Odysseus sliced off a piece of wax from a block of it, let the sun warm it, and then personally squished wax into each of his men's ears. Thus, given hearing protection, the men, as per Odysseus's instructions, tied him hand and foot to the mast, and the hero was ready. The crew then paddled forward. And soon, the Sirens became aware of their presence.

The creatures hailed Odysseus immediately, greeting him by name. They sang for him to come to them. They said he was a legend, and that he was indeed glorious. The Sirens told Odysseus:

This would have been a showstopping moment in ancient bardic performances of the *Odyssey*, as performers played and sang the song of the Sirens, dancers mimed out the events of the story, and listeners got the titillating sense that *they*, like Odysseus, were enjoying something arcane and forbidden!

To return to Book 12 of the *Odyssey*, the Sirens' song was indeed enchanting, and Odysseus writhed in his bounds, wanting to halt and hear more of what the creatures knew. Odysseus wriggled and glowered and made it clear that he was ordering his men to stop rowing. But they ignored him, and the oars splashed onward through the waves, and soon the Siren song faded into the distance. When they were safely out of earshot, the Greeks removed the wax from their ears and untied their commander, and thus ended Odysseus's short, oblique encounter with the Sirens.

The passage describing this episode in the *Odyssey* is only about a page long. Though the Sirens are often depicted as bird women in ancient Greek art and, in later European paintings, as topless beauties languishing among breaking waves, *Homer does not visually describe the Sirens at all.* They are an unseen presence in the *Odyssey*, disembodied voices more than creatures that actually physically threaten the crew, and the only thing we really know about them in the actual epic is that they waylay travelers by offering joy and knowledge.

As such, then, the Sirens fit into the central part of the *Odyssey* perfectly. They are perhaps the clearest "forbidden-fruits" narrative in the entire epic, and ancient Greeks loved stories about mortals who reached too far for the knowledge or the nectar of the divine and suffered as a result. In the *Odyssey*, Odysseus is tempted to stay on the islands of Calypso and Circe, though as a mortal, in the arms of either goddess, he'll grow old and never reach home. His men are tempted by the lotus fruit, though that episode does not end in disaster. More consequentially, his men are tempted by the god Aeolus's bag of winds, and by forbidden cattle in an episode to come. Hades, as Odysseus sees it, is crammed full of mortals who succumbed to temptation and ambition. Tantalus, in the *Odyssey*, is tantalized by food and drink he can never reach, as a punishment for taking the food of the gods and giving it to humans. Sisyphus, also in the *Odyssey*, cheated death, and so in Hades he must push a boulder again and again up the same hill.

The Sirens scene in the *Odyssey* is as famous as it is because it's familiar. Forbidden apples, Pandora's boxes or jars, intoxicating substances or songs that make us forget our burdens and homes and our very mortality—these myths seem to strike a chord in readers of any age. Odysseus, the wily trickster that he is, gets to walk the line between mortal and immortal at many different junctures of the *Odyssey*, bedding goddesses, peering down into the murk of Hades, and hearing a song that other mortals may not hear. In reading his story, and so many other works of ancient Greek literature, we learn of other heroes who push against the bounds of their own mortality. Most of them are chastened for it, while some of them, like Odysseus, get away scot-free.

NOW YOU KNOW

Ancient Greece and Rome were home to many skeptics who rejected various myths, as well as religion itself. The Roman naturalist Pliny the Elder (circa 23–79 CE) wrote that the Sirens were a silly fable, even though people still believed in them.

Christian interpreters later saw crucifixion imagery in the scene of Odysseus tied to his ship's mast, resisting the temptations of the Sirens. It's a bit of a stretch, but it's still an endearing example of how, during the early centuries CE, Christian readers who loved pagan classics tried to retroactively inject Christian themes into them.

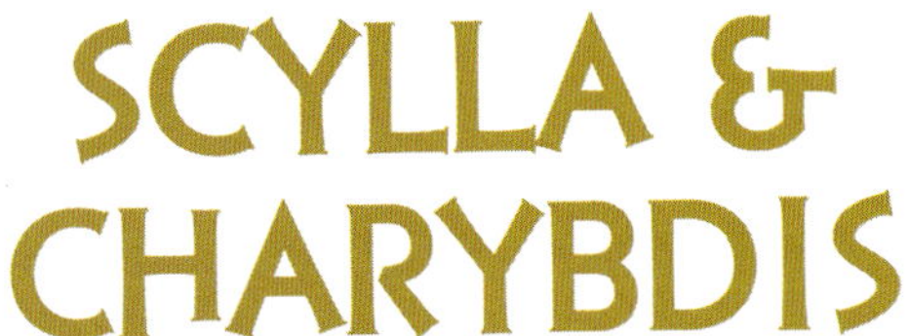

SCYLLA & CHARYBDIS

THE CLASSIC STORY OF TWO EQUALLY CRAPPY CHOICES.

PRONUNCIATION: SILL-uh or SKILL-uh and kar-IB-diss

LIKE: Smashing, Devouring

DISLIKE: Getting Confused with One Another

SPECIAL POWER: Making Heroes Morally Uncomfortable

NARRATIVE ROLE: Odysseus has to sail between a large whirlpool and a hungry six-headed monster in one of the *Odyssey*'s most well-known scenes.

A rock and a hard place. A frying pan and a fire. Between the devil and the deep blue sea. There are numerous idioms out there describing what Odysseus faces in Book 12 of the *Odyssey*, but to ancient Greeks, "Scylla and Charybdis" said it best: facing a dilemma in which neither alternative is appealing. The *Odyssey*'s tale of a monster, a whirlpool, and a ship full of poor suckers who have to sail between them is as follows.

Odysseus first learned about Scylla and Charybdis from the witch Circe. After returning to Circe's island, the witch ushered Odysseus aside to offer him a preview of his upcoming journey. First, Circe told the hero about the Sirens. As dangerous as they were, if Odysseus's crew made use of some crude earplugs, the songstresses were not going to be a problem. The next part of Odysseus's road home, however, would be far more dangerous.

Out of the turbulent sea, Circe said, rose a pair of sheer cliffs called the Πλαγκταὶ (*Planktai*), or "Wandering Rocks." Between them, the sea was so violent that even birds had trouble flying through, and fierce waves and currents smashed all ships that entered into splinters. Only one ship, Circe said, had threaded the needle through the Wandering Rocks, but this had been a very unique occurrence. The hero Jason, along with his Argonauts, had made it through the Wandering Rocks, but only barely, and with aid from the goddess Hera. The first of Odysseus's choices, then, was to sail between the Wandering Rocks.

The second choice, Circe explained, was to sail between Scylla and Charybdis. In the sea, out past the Sirens and in the other direction from the Wandering Rocks, a gargantuan crag rose up into the sky. The stone was sharp and smooth as glass, and so tall that black clouds wound around its peak. Halfway up this crag, and on the east side, there was a deep cavern. The cavern was home to Scylla. Scylla was a deadly creature with twelve feet and six heads, and each hideous head had a hungry mouth with three rows of sharp teeth. Scylla hid in the darkness of the cave, high over the turbulent water, her heads darting down into the sea to snatch up dolphins, seals, and unsuspecting travelers. Most eerily of all, Scylla did not roar or bellow. Instead, her heads emitted small barks, like those of puppies. No ship, said Circe, made it past Scylla without losing six men—one for each of Scylla's famished heads.

A bowshot away from Scylla there was another, smaller rock. Atop this rock there was a fig tree, suspiciously serene and healthy among all the turbulent seawater. Circe said that Odysseus might be tempted to paddle close to the fig tree in order to steer clear of the monster Scylla. But, the witch warned, the monster Scylla was a far better alternative, because beneath and all around the smaller rock was a maelstrom called Charybdis—a whirlpool that, three times a day, yawned open and pulled anything nearby to the bottom of the sea.

Odysseus didn't like what he heard. Couldn't he and his men fight the monster Scylla off, so as to not lose any crewmates? Circe scoffed. There was no defense against Scylla, she said. When it came to the six-headed horror that lurked high up on the crag, the only hope Odysseus and his men had was to flee, and pray to Scylla's mother that the creature wouldn't descend a second time in order to devour more men.

Given what Circe told Odysseus about the monster Scylla and the whirlpool Charybdis, the hero was understandably distressed as he set out the next morning with his crew. They made it past the Sirens unscathed. But ahead of them, Odysseus heard the booming crash of breakers. The air was thick with ocean spray. The rowers were so terrified at the great calamity ahead that they stopped, and Odysseus addressed them as the last remaining ship of his fleet bobbed in the choppy water. In the distance, the men could see Scylla's ominous rock looming out of the mist. Odysseus reminded them they had made it past the Cyclops and told them they now had to do exactly as he ordered to make it past this next obstacle. They were to row at full speed past the tall rock, avoiding the other rock with the fig tree on it. They were not to stop under any circumstances.

This was all Odysseus told his men. He did *not* mention that six of them would inevitably be seized and eaten by Scylla.

Although he had surrendered himself to paying a heavy price for passage past Scylla's rock, Odysseus still put on armor and gripped a spear, looking up to try and catch a glimpse of Scylla as the monster rushed down to get them. As they rowed, the nearby whirlpool Charybdis roared and churned, descending so low that Odysseus could see the seabed beneath it. Then it suddenly closed and sent geysers of salt water into the air. At just such a moment when Charybdis smashed back together, Scylla struck. The creature darted downward and grabbed six sailors. In a passage that's piercingly tragic in the original Homeric Greek, Odysseus keenly heard his sailors screaming his name in terror and watched them borne upward toward Scylla's den. The men shrieked and reached out to the hero as they were eaten alive, and Odysseus said that although he had seen a lot in his long life, their awful deaths was the worst thing he'd ever witnessed.

Circe's prediction had come true. Paying a grim and exacting toll, Odysseus and his crew had made it between Scylla and Charybdis. Odysseus loses many men in the central books of the *Odyssey*, but these six deaths seem to pierce him the most, perhaps because he knew that they were coming and still pushed his men forward. One of the greatest scenes in the *Odyssey*, and perhaps the greatest jump scare of ancient literature, the Scylla and Charybdis episode is also about the awful choices that leaders sometimes have to make, and how regardless of what they choose, they have to live with themselves afterward.

NOW YOU KNOW

According to the Roman poet Ovid (circa 43 BCE–18 CE), the witch Circe was *responsible* for the monster Scylla's existence. In Ovid's *Metamorphoses* (14.1–105), Circe became jealous that the sea god Glaucus loved a beautiful woman named Scylla. Always handy with drugs, Circe brewed up a potion and splashed it into a pool where beautiful Scylla liked to bathe. Sometime later, Scylla washed herself there, and was terrified to find that below the waist, she had turned into a ravenous pack of dogs. While this story came along much later in antiquity than the *Odyssey*, Greek mythology is full of tales of jealous goddesses doing awful things to their rivals.

HELIOS

DON'T EAT THE CATTLE. DON'T EAT THE CATTLE. THEY ATE THE CATTLE.

PRONUNCIATION: HEE-lee-ows

LIKES: Livestock, Fair Weather, Photosynthesis

DISLIKES: Hubris, Cloudy Days

SPECIAL POWER: Controls the Sun

NARRATIVE ROLE: Odysseus's encounter with Helios is the final episode in the *Odyssey*'s central flashback sequence.

Helios was the ancient Greek god of the sun. Helios had a long, complex history in antiquity, and later, he was equated with Apollo and associated with other important gods as well. In the Homeric epics, Helios's home is an idyllic island called Thrinacia. There, Helios presides over sacred herds of cattle when not resting from his day job of hauling the sun across the sky in a chariot. Helios has a short but important appearance in the *Odyssey*, and his island is the last place Odysseus visits before the hero ends up on Calypso's island. Here's the story of Odysseus's encounter with Helios.

After their horrifying run-in with Scylla and Charybdis, Odysseus and his diminished crew paddled onward. For the captain and sailors, morale was at an all-time low. They'd spent a year on Circe's island and then gone to Hades. Then, even though they'd made preparations and fortified themselves with directions, on their first day of outbound travel back home, they'd seen six of their men eaten alive. Odysseus had kept secrets from them, and he knew more secrets about what was to come. There were tensions between the commander and his men, and something soon happened that brought those tensions to the surface.

Up ahead, Odysseus and his crewmen saw an island. It was not, like the Sirens' island, littered with skeletons. It was not, like Scylla's rock, a deadly promontory, always battered with waves and surf. The island that the men saw was beautiful, and all they could make out there were cattle and sheep grazing in broad pastures. Odysseus, however, told his men they would not be stopping on Thrinacia. The men grumbled, and then the grumbling stewed into a near mutiny. Odysseus's brother-in-law Eurylochus spoke up.

Odysseus, said Eurylochus, was a dreadful person if he would deny his crew a brief anchorage on such a peaceful island. Did Odysseus really expect them to keep rowing into the night? After the traumatizing day they'd just faced together? They couldn't see weather coming in the dark. Odysseus had to understand, they needed rest. They needed to anchor for the night on Thrinacia.

The other men applauded Eurylochus's speech, and Odysseus, admitting that he was outvoted, said that they could stop on one condition. The men could not, under any circumstances, catch and slaughter any of the sheep or cattle on the island. Every man needed to promise not to do so. They had plenty of provisions with which Circe had just stocked them. Odysseus's men, hearing these requirements, shook hands on the matter, and the ship pulled over for the night.

Both Tiresias, in Book 11, as well as Circe, in Book 12, had emphatically told Odysseus that he and his men must not harm the cattle of Helios on the island of Thrinacia. And having stopped there for a single night, and elicited a promise from his men, the hero thought it reasonable to suppose that no livestock would be harmed. But then, as sometimes happens in the *Odyssey*, Odysseus and the gang ran into some good old-fashioned bad luck.

The first night on the island of Thrinacia allowed the men some time to mourn the loss of their comrades and rest. But as the night lengthened, a storm blew in, whipping up waves and making the sea dangerous to navigate. In the morning, the Greeks beached their ship to protect it, securing the vessel in a natural cave. There, once again, Odysseus repeated his warning. Don't eat the sheep, he said. Don't eat the cattle. His men understood.

Unfortunately, the storm continued, first for days, and then for weeks, and then a month, until the provisions Circe had given them wore down to nothing. The men foraged as best they could, but hunger was shortening tempers. As the storm continued to batter the island of Thrinacia, Odysseus went to pray to the gods, and after doing so, the deities cast him into a deep sleep. As he slept, his men, led by his brother-in-law Eurylochus, discussed what to do.

They were ravenous. Eurylochus said he'd rather take his chances than starve. They would kill and eat some of Helios's cattle, and when they returned to Ithaca, they would build the sun god a fine altar by way of remuneration. The men agreed. Soon enough, Odysseus's crew broke their promise to the hero, slaughtering and eating many of the cattle of the sun god Helios. (Being red-blooded Homeric warriors, of course, they couldn't eat just one animal, or forage and catch some fish, like real ancient Greeks would have.)

When Odysseus woke up, he smelled barbecue, immediately exclaiming in terror and praying to Zeus. High above, the gods had witnessed what had happened. Odysseus rushed to his men and rebuked them, but it was too late. Ominously, the hides of the slaughtered cattle began to writhe and squirm, and the meat emitted the lowing sound of living cattle, though it was cooking over fire. And incredibly, as Odysseus's men ate and ate, the monthlong gale continued to blow. Eventually, a week after the slaughter of Helios's livestock, the storm finally stopped. And Odysseus's men, hoping against hope to finally make it home, pushed their ship out to sea on a clear day and charted their course to Ithaca. Unfortunately, it was not to be.

Zeus, filled with wrath about the killing of Helios's cattle, sent a cataclysmic storm down on Odysseus and his last ship. The mast and its supports snapped, and tumbling lumber killed the helmsman. Lightning sheared down from the roiling sky and into the boat, leaving the air filled with the scent of sulfur. The ship and its crew were doomed. In Odysseus's last glimpse of his longtime comrades, they looked like seagulls floating on the moving sea. The hero himself managed to lash a rope around the keel and mast of the ship, but the rest of his boat and his crew were dragged into the maw of the sea. Nine days later, Odysseus told his Phaeacian listeners, he ended up on the island of Calypso.

The episode on Thrinacia and its aftermath is Odysseus's final story to the Phaeacians at the heart of the *Odyssey*. The tale of the cattle of the sun is a tragic one, but it's also rather predictable. Mortals, when warned not to do something in the *Odyssey*, don't follow instructions. We hope they won't eat the cattle. We also know they're going to eat the cattle, because over the course of their long, calamitous journey, Odysseus's men have disobeyed his orders again and again.

The story of Odysseus and his men, which lasts from Books 9–12 of the *Odyssey*, is an epic within an epic—a story of attrition and increasing tension between a commander and his fleet. When Odysseus's men finally begin ignoring him, first demanding that they stop the ship and then eating the cattle in spite of his instructions not to, the heart of the *Odyssey* is over. The captain has lost control. The Odysseus of the *Iliad*, a military commander indispensable largely due to his sway over men, goes down with his ship, and what is left is a solitary person still, just as before, trying to make it home.

NOW YOU KNOW

The Colossus of Rhodes, one of the seven wonders of the ancient world, was a statue of the sun god Helios. It was allegedly a bronze statue taller than any other in the ancient world, but after standing for barely half a century, it was brought down by an earthquake in 226 BCE.

The sun god Helios's most famous appearance in literature is in Ovid's *Metamorphoses* (1.748–2.400). Helios promises his son, Phaëthon, to grant anything Phaëthon wishes. Phaëthon asks to take over Helios's job for one day, towing the sun across the sky in the sun god's chariot. Phaëthon does so, and loses control, perishing in the great conflagration that results. In grief, the sun god causes a daylong eclipse.

ODYSSEUS: THE TACTICIAN

WHETHER YOU LIKE HIM OR NOT, ODYSSEUS GETS THINGS DONE.

PRONUNCIATION: oh-DISS-ee-us

LIKES: Lying, Manipulating, Winning

DISLIKES: Anything That Gets in His Way

SPECIAL POWERS: Espionage, Moral Flexibility

NARRATIVE ROLE: Comfortable with all sorts of skullduggery and morally murky situations, Odysseus will do anything or become anything in pursuit of a goal.

Odysseus is the hero of the *Odyssey*. He makes a long trip back home, and after a great struggle, he rejoins his wife, son, and father. But he was also *one* of the heroes in Homer's *Iliad*. The *Odyssey*'s ancient Greek audiences, familiar with the full story of the ancient Epic Cycle, would have remembered the role that Odysseus played during the Trojan War. Let's go back in time for a moment and learn about what sort of a character Odysseus is in Homer's *Iliad*.

ODYSSEUS IN THE *ILIAD*

Odysseus wasn't a leader during the Trojan War, like his boss, the Greek king Agamemnon. Nor was he a champion, like the Greek warrior Achilles and the Trojan defender Hector. He was what we might call a "fixer," a behind-the-scenes operative who handled ugly, messy situations, both with the enemy

and on his own side. By the *Iliad*'s end, we have met dozens of burly warriors—axmen and archers and swordsmen whose violent clashes form the epic's central action. In contrast to these musclemen, Odysseus's greatest weapon in the first Homeric epic is his mind. While the war is still raging onward at the *Iliad*'s end, it's clear that many warriors on both sides can win battles. Odysseus, however, can win wars. During the Greeks' darkest hour in the Trojan War, in Books 9–10 of the *Iliad*, Odysseus takes center stage. Here's a summary of Odysseus's longest appearance in the *Iliad*.

In the tenth year of the Trojan War, a rift between the Greek king Agamemnon and the Greek champion Achilles quickly proved catastrophic. Troy, after all, had a champion, and when the mighty Trojan hero Hector strapped on his jumbo sandals and drew his humongous sword, the Greeks who didn't run for cover soon regretted it. Hector was schooling all of the Greeks, and the whole problem was Agamemnon's fault. The Greek king had stolen Achilles' female slave. As a result, the indomitable Achilles had stopped clocking in for battle every day, and lacking Achilles, the Greeks had been losing ground. In Book 9 of the *Iliad*, Odysseus, who throughout the *Iliad* serves as King Agamemnon's henchman and troubleshooter, went to go and talk with Achilles to try and patch things up.

Odysseus didn't go alone. Along with him went Ajax, a giant man and one of the most formidable Greeks who'd come to fight at Troy. The stakes of their embassy to Achilles were quite high because the Greeks were going to lose without Achilles. It was the responsibility of Odysseus and Ajax to persuade Achilles to swallow his pride and serve King Agamemnon once more.

Achilles, Odysseus, and Ajax were friends and brothers-in-arms, and so Achilles bore the other two no ill will for their continued loyalty to the Greek king Agamemnon. Odysseus explained the dire situation of the war to the champion Achilles, using all the eloquence and logic at his disposal. Odysseus also offered Achilles great prizes from Agamemnon—limitless wealth, the return of his female slave and more women besides, and even marriage into Agamemnon's family. Finishing his flawless, respectful entreaty, Odysseus waited for a response. He was soon disappointed. Achilles said there was absolutely no way he'd ever serve Agamemnon again. Achilles and his men were leaving the war, and that was final. Crestfallen, the Greek peacemakers returned to Agamemnon and delivered the terrible news. The embassy to Achilles marks Odysseus's only significant failure in Homer's *Iliad*. As we turn the page from Book 9 to Book 10 of the *Iliad*, night has fallen, and it looks as though the Greeks are finished.

The Trojans, at this critical moment of the *Iliad*, were no longer behind their walls. They were camped down on the plain, sharpening their swords and planning a final assault on the Greek fortifications on the nearby beach. King Agamemnon, unable to sleep, and conscious that he'd made a terrible blunder with Achilles, called a nocturnal meeting, and one of his advisors had a suggestion. The advisor was Nestor, whom we meet in Book 3 of the *Odyssey*. The old fellow, always a fire hose of advice (roughly half of it good), proposed a surgical strike on the Trojans under the cover of darkness. The Greek powerhouse Diomedes volunteered, and Diomedes said he wanted Odysseus at his side during the attack.

It was almost dawn when Odysseus and Diomedes set out on what scholars call the *Iliad*'s *doloneia*, or "night raid." They were lucky enough to immediately come across a Trojan spy who was also doing reconnaissance work in enemy territory. Capturing the enemy agent, Odysseus and Diomedes questioned him, and after receiving intel, the Greeks murdered him. They'd learned something valuable. Close by, the Trojans had an enclosure full of fine horses that the Greeks could steal. Acting on this information, Odysseus and Diomedes skulked through the murk, killing as they proceeded. By the time they'd secured some of the horses, thirteen Trojans were dead, one of them a king. Though daybreak was visible on the horizon, Odysseus's comrade Diomedes wanted to continue. They'd only slaughtered fourteen people, after all. They could squeeze a few more in before sunup! Athena, however, a patron of Odysseus in the *Iliad* as well as the *Odyssey*, curtailed any further violence. The two Greek warriors, their night raid very successful, snuck back to the Greek camp and presented their spoils.

The nocturnal mission of Odysseus is a critical moment in the *Iliad*. Having failed in Book 9 to persuade Achilles to patch things up with Agamemnon, Odysseus throws himself into a bloody infiltration mission, and the success of this operation gives the Greeks a badly needed boost in morale. The Greeks dig deep the next day, and they're able to continue their war effort.

This sequence of events takes place in the middle of the *Iliad*, and in this central part of Homer's first poem, Odysseus briefly becomes the main character of the story. In the embassy to Achilles, Odysseus demonstrates that he can be eloquent, diplomatic, and politically savvy. In the night raid,

Odysseus proves that he can be sneaky, swift, and ruthlessly violent. Many Greeks and Trojans can do *some* of the things that Odysseus can do, but only Odysseus can do *all* of them, seeming, from time to time, to be better than everyone at everything.

THE ROMAN TAKE ON ODYSSEUS

As thoroughly impressive as Odysseus is in the *Iliad* and *Odyssey*, from ancient times to the present, he has always had his dissidents. Those dissidents have generally found the hero to be *too* cunning, underhanded, and self-serving. A Trojan Horse, after all, hurts as many people as it helps. Let's zoom out from the world of Homer for a moment and explore how later readers in antiquity responded to Odysseus.

Books 9–12 of the *Odyssey* are a flashback sequence. In them, Odysseus tells the Phaeacians about his travels from Troy, all over the Aegean, up until he came to be jailed on the island of Calypso. The flashback sequence contains the *Odyssey*'s most celebrated episodes—episodes involving monsters and magic and hairsbreadth escapes. A question that readers have asked over the ages, however, is as follows: *How much of the lengthy story that Odysseus tells in Phaeacia is actually true?*

The later Roman poet Juvenal, in the early 100s CE, called Odysseus out for lying. Juvenal (Satire 15.13–23) imagined the Phaeacians politely listening to Odysseus's interminable narrative until an observer in the court finally proclaimed what everyone else was thinking: Odysseus's entire story about Cyclopes and Laestrygonians and Circe was a ridiculous, insulting fairy tale. How could Odysseus stand up in front of everyone and yammer on about magical bags of wind and sexy nymphs and expect to be believed by anyone with any sense? Odysseus was the windbag! Also during the 100s CE, the Greek novelist Lucian of Samosata wrote that Odysseus's *apologia*, or "stories," to the Phaeacians were all baloney.

This is a fascinating interpretation of the epic's main course, but to be clear, in the actual *Odyssey*, the Phaeacians accept the flashback sequence at face value. Some of Odysseus's flashback *is* supported by the epic as a whole. Zeus says, in Book 1, that Poseidon is angry at Odysseus because the hero blinded the Cyclops, so at least *some* sort of encounter with the one-eyed, and then zero-eyed, giant must have taken place. But otherwise, there is a distinct possibility that only Odysseus knows what he was really doing in between Troy and Phaeacia.

Just as Spider-Man shoots webs out of his hands and Wolverine has an Adamantium skeleton and claws, Odysseus has a special power as well, and it might simply be called "deceit." In the *Odyssey*, he lies, omits information, sneaks, wears disguises, and never quite settles into being just one person. The entire second half of the *Odyssey* is a long series of fictitious performances by Odysseus, in which he first lies to Athena (she calls him out), then to Eumaeus the swineherd, the suitors, his wife, and finally, though it is completely unnecessary, his elderly father. It follows, then, that in considering the long yarn Odysseus tells the Phaeacians, many readers, past and present, have suspected that Odysseus never heard any Sirens, and never saw any cattle of Helios, and that he lost his fleet in some other way that he's keeping secret.

To be clear, *most* readers of the *Odyssey* have generally accepted the central adventure sequence to be true, or at least mostly true. Since the whole epic is just a fable, it doesn't really matter whether Odysseus went to bed with a witch. But the way that people interpret stories is important in human cultural history, and can tell us a lot about who we are.

BEWARE GREEKS BEARING GIFTS

Perhaps you've heard the phrase "Beware Greeks bearing gifts"? The phrase comes from the Latin line *Timeo Danaos et dona ferentes*. The words, which literally mean "I'm afraid of Greeks even when they bear gifts," were written by the Roman poet Virgil in Book 2 of the *Aeneid* (19 BCE). They are spoken at the most climactic moment of the Trojan War in Virgil's famous story. The Trojans, having received the Trojan Horse as a peace prize, are debating whether or not to bring the horse into their city. An old priest warns them not to, but they don't listen. And so the greatest of Odysseus's many deceptions is successful, and the Greeks win the war. Today, "Beware Greeks bearing gifts" is typically a general warning, like "beware enemies who give you a present." In ancient Rome, however, it was more of a statement about Greeks themselves.

Romans had a complex relationship with ancient Greek culture. Rome officially had sovereignty over ancient Greece after 146 BCE, when a long clash between the two civilizations led to Rome winning military and administrative control over the mainland and Peloponnese. However, long after the Roman conquest, Greek civilization was deeply rooted in the eastern Mediterranean, and ethnic Greeks and Greek speakers were still everywhere. Romans both adored and resented ancient Greek culture. On the one hand, they were enchanted with it. Wealthy Roman kids had Greek tutors who taught them the language and legacy of ancient Greek civilization. On the other hand, conservative Romans who spoke Latin and professed roots on the ancient Italian Peninsula didn't like the fact that so many Romans were spellbound with Greek culture. The Roman poet Horace succinctly wrote that "captive Greece took its captor captive" (*Epistles* 2.1.256), perfectly summarizing the long, strange relationship between Rome and Greece. Rome won all the wars. Then Greek culture won over the Romans.

To nationalistic Romans, who were fond of Latin and Rome's Italian roots, Odysseus was the ultimate emblem of the two sides of Greek civilization. The Greeks were clever and eloquent, but (at least some conservative Romans believed) they always had ulterior motives. The Greeks brought gifts, but the gifts, like the Trojan Horse, could be very dangerous. The Greeks, like Odysseus, had many great stories, but how many of them were actually true?

Beyond the *Iliad* and *Odyssey*, in the ancient world, to many, Odysseus was the archetype of an entire civilization. He was the most pervasive character in the Homeric epics, and more than Zeus, Athena, or Heracles, Odysseus emblematized what ancient Greece was: Smart. Adaptable. Amphibious. Dangerous. Interesting.

NOW YOU KNOW

There have been many wonderful film adaptations of Homer's *Odyssey*, but in many ways, the first is the most impressive. In 1911, a trio of Italian directors completed a silent film called *L'Odissea*. The film, forty-four minutes in length, was complete with hundreds of costumes, an ancient Greek ship that actually rowed, a forced-perspective gigantic Cyclops, Sirens, Scylla and Charybdis, and a tremendous climax quite faithful to the Homeric original. *L'Odissea* has also aged quite well, and you can watch it for free online!

EUMAEUS THE SWINEHERD

HOMER'S FAVORITE HOMERIC CHARACTER.

PRONUNCIATION: you-MAY-us

LIKES: Odysseus, Country Living, Cute Little Piglets

DISLIKES: Rich Douchebags, Having His Pigs Stolen

SPECIAL POWERS: Loyalty, Hospitality, Non-Kosher Cuisine

NARRATIVE ROLE: Odysseus's right-hand man in the epic's second half.

One of the most important characters in the *Odyssey* is a pig herder. Eumaeus the Swineherd, though often forgotten next to the Cyclops, Sirens, and Circe, nonetheless gets more airtime than all of them. Alongside Athena, crusty old Eumaeus is Odysseus's primary collaborator in the *Odyssey*'s second half, almost constantly by the hero's side, offering Odysseus intel on the dangerous situation afoot in Ithaca upon the wanderer's return to his homeland and, ultimately, helping the king win back his throne at the epic's end.

Here are the basics on Eumaeus the Swineherd, the most famous pig herder in all of literature. Eumaeus hadn't always been a peasant. He'd been born into a wealthy family, but at a young age, he'd been sold into slavery, and was eventually purchased by Odysseus's father, who put Eumaeus to work in Ithaca's pigpens. Though Eumaeus had suffered a fall in fortune, overall, he respected the leadership of Ithaca. When King Odysseus had left Ithaca decades before to go and fight in the Trojan War, Eumaeus, like many other Ithacans, had crossed his fingers and hoped for the monarch's safe return. But the war took ten years to fight, and ten years later, Odysseus still hadn't returned. Old Eumaeus waited and

watched as Penelope's greedy suitors disrespected the queen and her son Telemachus. Eumaeus grinded his teeth as the suitors ate all the food that workmen like him raised and grew for the rightful king of Ithaca. And the suitors even had the gall to abuse Eumaeus himself. They came down from the palace, time and time again, and stole the poor old man's best hogs.

That's what we know about Eumaeus upon first meeting him in the *Odyssey*. Unlike the epic's many braggarts and blowhards, Eumaeus is a hardworking country fellow just trying to do his job. From what you've heard so far, Eumaeus probably seems like a sympathetic, but perhaps not very riveting, character. But Eumaeus is actually a very unique and endearing figure in the *Odyssey* for a number of reasons.

First, Eumaeus epitomizes one of the great virtues of Greek epic poetry, and that is ξενία (*xenia*), or "hospitality," also translated as "guest-friendship." Odysseus hobbles up to Eumaeus's humble hut disguised as a shriveled old beggar. Eumaeus welcomes the disguised Odysseus in spite of the hero's shabby appearance, offering him a warm and considerate ear, not to mention food and lodgings. Odysseus decides the old yokel must be a really good person. Not long after, when Odysseus learns that Eumaeus has remained absolutely loyal to him in spite of the hero's twenty-year absence, Odysseus concludes that the epic's pig wrangler truly has a heart of gold.

And this is where things really get interesting, especially for geeks who love ancient Greek literature. The poet Homer actually addresses Eumaeus directly in the *Odyssey*, twice!

> *And you answered, Eumaeus, my swineherd:*
>
> **—the poet Homer to the pig herder Eumaeus,**
> ***Odyssey* (Lombardo translation, 16.66, 142)**

Eumaeus is the only character in the entire epic whom Homer addresses like this! In other words, normally, Homer would simply write, "And the swineherd Eumaeus answered." But instead, Homer writes, "And *you answered*, Eumaeus, *my swineherd*." Why on earth would Homer address only Eumaeus directly, and not, for instance, Odysseus, or Athena?

There are many answers to this question. Maybe Homer really liked bacon? Perhaps Homer, and other ancient Greek bards, serving rich patrons in performance settings, felt some kinship with Odysseus's working-class right-hand man, as they, too, served aristocrats for a paycheck? These are decent answers, but Eumaeus's sizable and unique role in the *Odyssey* also invites us to remember something very important about the epic.

The *Odyssey* is actually filled to the brim with scenes of country life and rural labor. Yet we tend to remember it only as a swashbuckling adventure story set on the deep blue sea. The remainder of the *Odyssey* is largely set in humble abodes, country crossroads, farm fields, and pastures. Even before Odysseus gets home, the *Odyssey* sparkles with wonderful little scenes of humdrum everyday living in the ancient Greek countryside, from the princess Nausicaa washing her clothes to the Cyclops tending to his own beloved herds.

The *Iliad* is a war story, in which predominantly highborn warriors taunt and slaughter each other. In the *Odyssey*, though, through characters like Eumaeus, we see a larger, richer world. Gods and heroes might slug it out, pursuing glory and ugly vendettas. But Homer's herdsmen and farmers remind us that the cadence of human life goes on peacefully in spite of human wars and divine strife. Maybe that's why Homer addresses Eumaeus directly in the book. A great poet, after all, would know that sagas of gods and wars pay a bard's bills. But at the same time, an ancient Greek poet would know that the real Aegean was home to a lot more Eumaeuses than Odysseuses, and that a pig herder was just as good a person as a warrior or king.

NOW YOU KNOW

The *Odyssey*'s rustic scenes helped inspire an entire genre of ancient Mediterranean literature, a genre we call "pastoral," after the Latin *pastor*, for "shepherd." In this genre, pipe-playing herdsmen (and sometimes herdswomen) sing songs to one another about grazing sheep and planting seeds, and later English writers like Shakespeare, Marvell, and Milton all wrote works in the pastoral genre.

Eumaeus is described as Odysseus's δμώς (*dmos*) or "slave" in the *Odyssey*. The Homeric epics, like most ancient Greek literature, present slavery as a natural social institution.

ANTINOUS, AMPHINOMUS, & EURYMACHUS

THE RINGLEADERS OF THE SUITORS.

PRONUNCIATION: an-TIN-oh-us, am-FIN-oh-muss, and yer-IH-muck-us

LIKE: Cholesterol, Imagining Themselves As the Stars of *The Bachelorette*

DISLIKE: Working, Accountability

SPECIAL POWERS: Disrespect, Hypocrisy, Imperceptiveness

NARRATIVE ROLE: Antinous, Amphinomus, and Eurymachus, though they have very different personalities, are the most prominent named characters among Penelope's many suitors.

There are a lot of suitors in Homer's *Odyssey*. Largely, they're a bunch of interchangeable deadbeats, loafing around the palace and eating all the time and, more maliciously, ignoring Queen Penelope's repeated entreaties for them to leave. While the suitors sometimes seem like little more than a termite infestation awaiting bug spray, Antinous, Amphinomus, and Eurymachus are more three-dimensional characters.

ANTINOUS (THE STRAIGHTFORWARD SCUMBAG)

A young Ithacan man named Antinous has the dubious honor of being the most infamous of Penelope's many aspiring husbands. His name, to ancient Greek audiences, would have said it all. Αντίνοος (*Antínoos*) means "against mind" or "hostile mind." Antinous, in other words, is rash and insolent and doesn't do a lot of thinking. He is the opposite of Odysseus, the Homeric character most known for mental acuity. Odysseus, in contrast to Antinous, is cunning, guarded, and tactical. From the moment that we meet the blustering chief of the suitors all the way up until Antinous's gory death in Book 22, we know that there's going to be a showdown between Odysseus and Antinous.

Antinous, more than any other suitor, was brazen and unapologetic about his presence in Queen Penelope's house. He bullied Telemachus relentlessly at the beginning of the epic and then engineered a plot to kill the young prince while Telemachus was off looking for leads in the Peloponnese. There's some evidence that the two once feasted and drank together (2.305), which makes Antinous's plotting against the prince all the more repugnant. In short, the first few books establish Antinous as an arrogant, hedonistic snake, and incredibly, Antinous somehow only gets worse as the story continues.

Halfway through the epic, we learn a bit more about Antinous. Queen Penelope, confronting the kingpin of the suitors about his botched plot to kill Telemachus, told Antinous he was ungrateful as well as malevolent. Penelope reminded Antinous that Odysseus had *protected* Antinous's *father*. Antinous's father had joined a squad of pirates harrying the allies of Ithaca, and when the Ithacans had come after Antinous Senior, Odysseus had stood up for the man in spite of his mistakes. Penelope's emphatic reminder, however, did not stop the shameless Antinous Junior, who soon proved that he could be as rude to strangers as he was to people he knew.

When Odysseus started casing his former palace, disguised as a beggar, Antinous, more than anyone, antagonized him. While the other suitors agreed to offer the disguised Odysseus food from their laden tables, Antinous insulted the drifter. Odysseus, incredulous, pointed out the plain fact that Antinous was stealing food from someone else and yet wouldn't share any of it. Out of comebacks, the chieftain of the suitors hurled a stool at Odysseus, shouting insults at him. The stool glanced harmlessly off of Odysseus's mighty shoulder, and the hero silently began envisioning ways of killing the repugnant intruder. Antinous's assault on the elderly beggar seemed a step beyond the pale for the other suitors. The other men exclaimed that Antinous had gone too far. Penelope prayed that Apollo would shoot him, emphasizing that Antinous was the very worst out of all the suitors.

If Antinous has an appealing quality, it's that he genuinely seems to admire Penelope. He describes his desired bride as someone with immense intelligence and artistic skill, and while his actions reveal a disgusting dismissal of what Penelope herself wants and requests, Antinous's pursuit of her is at least based on some inkling of her considerable merits.

AMPHINOMUS (THE DECENT-HEARTED SCUMBAG)

Antinous's confederates Amphinomus and Eurymachus, while not exactly appealing characters, are not quite as revolting. If there is a sympathetic character among the suitors, it's definitely Amphinomus. The prince of a small kingdom near Ithaca, Amphinomus is a voice of moderation among the suitors, attempting to rein in some of the worst of their impulses. After the suitors' plot to kill Telemachus abroad failed, Antinous proposed just murdering him on Ithaca. Amphinomus, however, spoke up. He said they shouldn't kill anyone without understanding the will of the gods. The men, finding Amphinomus's argument unassailable, decided not to try and kill Telemachus, and Homer also reveals that of all the suitors, Penelope preferred Amphinomus's speeches the best.

Among the extremely seedy ranks of the suitors, then, Amphinomus stands out as moderately okay. Toward the epic's end, Odysseus, who had found that Amphinomus ranked fairly low on the dirtbag meter, scooted over to the man at mealtime one day while still disguised as a beggar and advised Amphinomus to take a hike, because (Odysseus warned) Ithaca's leader was going to get home soon. The goddess Athena, however, did not let Amphinomus leave, and so sadly, the suitor with a good heart later got speared through the chest by Telemachus, even as Amphinomus pleaded for his life.

EURYMACHUS (THE LYING SCUMBAG)

Other than abominable Antinous and decent Amphinomus, one more suitor cuts a memorable figure in Homer's *Odyssey*: Eurymachus. His name, Εὐρύμαχος (*Eurúmakhos*), means "wide battle," denoting someone who has an array of martial skills, or perhaps someone who picks a fight everywhere he goes. And indeed, in comparison to the openly predatory Antinous, Eurymachus is more resourceful and more devious, covering his malevolent scheming with a friendly demeanor. A sort of stunt-double Odysseus, with some of the hero's wit and no small share of his ruthlessness, Eurymachus is perhaps the most dangerous suitor of all.

When poor Penelope discovered the suitors' plot to kill her son, she confronted them, letting Antinous in particular know that what was happening on Ithaca was horrifying. Antinous, for once, seemed flummoxed, but Eurymachus slid in and offered Penelope one of the slimiest speeches in ancient literature. He declared that he'd die before letting anyone lay a hand on Telemachus. Why, when he was young, Eurymachus said, he used to sit on Odysseus's lap, and the hero was very kind to him. Eurymachus said he loved Telemachus more than anyone. And as Homer adds, "He spoke to mollify her; all the while / he was devising plans to kill her son" (Wilson translation, 16.449–50).

Charming as well as heartless, Eurymachus did anything to get what he wanted. With a proverbial knife behind his back, Eurymachus was friendly and accommodating to Telemachus in the epic's opening books, telling the prince that Telemachus should keep everything that was his, all while probing the besieged prince for information. Shortly thereafter, we learn that one of Penelope's slaves, Melantho, gave up the secret of Penelope's habit of unweaving her signature shroud. This slave betrayed the secret because she was sleeping with the treacherous suitor Eurymachus. And unfortunately for the epic's protagonists, by the middle of the story, Eurymachus was perilously close to marrying Penelope. Athena told Telemachus that Penelope's dad and her brothers were pushing her to marry the dashing scoundrel.

The worst of the worst, Eurymachus antagonizes every member of Odysseus's family. Athena sees all of it. When Odysseus finally reveals his identity in Book 22 in the palace feasting hall and shoots an arrow through Antinous's throat, only Eurymachus can think of anything to say. Eurymachus, characteristically, lies. Why, Eurymachus says, it was all Antinous's plan. Antinous was going to try and kill Telemachus! The suitors would pay Odysseus back for everything. Eurymachus certainly understands why Odysseus is angry. (Hearing all of this, Odysseus, who has done his research and knows malarkey when he hears it, tells the suitors to draw their swords.)

All told, the suitors can seem like a uniform mass, one about the same as the next. The tale of 108 suitors invading the palace of an absent king feels like a piece of folklore from an earlier age, a bit too clunky for literature as advanced as the Homeric epics. Nonetheless, Homer deftly humanizes the story's antagonists, and Antinous, Amphinomus, and Eurymachus represent the range of personalities that Penelope's aspiring husbands had. Later in this book, when we explore the *Odyssey*'s climax, we'll learn a bit more about who the suitors were and how the strange tale of their rise and fall fits right into the Epic Cycle, of which the *Odyssey* was once a part.

NOW YOU KNOW

The suitor Eurymachus's pursuit of marriage with Penelope was a family affair. Eurymachus's father, Polybus, was also there in the palace, courting the queen of Ithaca. So, too, was Eurymachus's uncle Peisander. Perhaps if these ancient, fictitious Don Juans had careers and interests, they wouldn't have squandered multiple years on the 1 percent chance that the resentful queen of an extremely small island would marry them.

Some little grottos of the Homeric epics sound unintentionally funny to modern ears. Eurymachus, at one point, is lying to Penelope and telling her how fondly he remembers Odysseus. He recollects from his childhood, "Time and again Odysseus dandled me / on his knees, [and] the great raider of cities fed me / roasted meat and held the red wine to my lips" (Fagles translation, 16.490–2). The meaning, of course, is that Odysseus was kind to Eurymachus when Eurymachus was a kid, but the most insidious of suitors here sounds a bit like an alcoholic lapdog.

ARGOS

AT LEAST ODYSSEUS'S DOG REMEMBERS HIM.

PRONUNCIATION: AR-gohs

LIKES: Treats, Forests, Odysseus, Sniffing

DISLIKES: Being Ignored and Forgotten

SPECIAL POWERS: Slobber, Loyalty, Hunting

NARRATIVE ROLE: Argos recognizes Odysseus's scent in Book 17, but sadly, he passes away just after his reunion with the hero.

One of the most poignant and famous scenes in the entire *Odyssey* involves a dog. Other than the three-headed Cerberus, the most revered dog in Greek mythology is likely Odysseus's hunting hound, Argos. Though Argos only has a short cameo in the *Odyssey*, everyone tends to remember it. Here is the brief, touching tale of Argos.

Odysseus, back on the island of Ithaca, had partnered with the surprisingly clever and capable pig herder Eumaeus. Eumaeus had no idea who Odysseus was, but, civil and helpful, the swineherd escorted the disguised Odysseus to his palace. Playing the part of an old beggar, Odysseus shambled along, all the while noting how much home had changed while he'd been gone. Once they reached Odysseus's palace, the hero saw something.

A very, very old dog lay out in front of the estate. Seeing the two newcomers approaching, he raised his head and ears, watching them. He seemed to be a stray, unwanted and forgotten, for his resting place was a pile of manure. His coat was infested with bugs. When he saw Odysseus, the dog's ears fell back in a tired canine smile, and he wagged his tail in recognition, though Argos was too weak to rise. Odysseus restrained himself, though tears welled up in his eyes, for he recognized his dog. He asked Eumaeus about the animal.

Argos? said Eumaeus. The old hound had once belonged to an Ithacan who'd left a long time ago. Odysseus had trained him perfectly. The dog was, years ago, a magnificent hunting companion. His nose was impeccable, and he never let his prey escape. But, Eumaeus added, Argos had been forgotten, since Odysseus had been gone for so long. The palace's servants used to take care of him, but with the suitors there, no one ever did any work anymore, and so Argos had been left to fend for himself.

With that, Eumaeus went into the palace. Shifting the perspective to that of the dog Argos very briefly, Homer writes that, having waited twenty years to see his long-lost master, the shadow of death passed over Argos, and he was no more.

The scene with Argos is only about a page in length, but it's one that the *Odyssey*'s readers have tended to remember. On the simplest level, the *Odyssey*'s second half subdivides characters into those loyal to Odysseus and those disloyal to him. Argos is unambiguously one of the former. Argos's short, sad reunion with Odysseus is also one of the epic's moments of what ancient Greeks called ἀναγνώρισις, or *anagnorisis*; essentially, a "recognition," or revelation scene, in which characters suddenly understand the truth of a situation or the real identity of those around them. By the *Odyssey*'s end, there have been *eight* recognition scenes, in which Athena, then Telemachus, Argos, Eurycleia, Eumaeus, the suitors, Penelope, and finally Laertes each experience an *anagnorisis* of who Odysseus is.

Technical literary terms aside, more than anything, the scene with Argos is a devastating reminder of how quickly time has drifted by in Odysseus's absence. The hero met his son for the first time the previous night, and Odysseus is preparing a cunning, pitiless attack to claw back what's his from the suitors. At the same time, though, in some ways, Odysseus has already lost. He's lost twenty years at home with his parents, his wife, and his child. He's lost part of himself abroad, fighting a war that did far more harm than good to both sides. The wonderful dog that he raised, who seems to have clung to life just to see him one last time, is a tragic emblem of peacetime years and love and family that he'll never get back.

NOW YOU KNOW

One other dog from Greek mythology might approach the stature of Odysseus's heroic old Argos. The mythographer Apollodorus briefly set down a fascinating anecdote about a mythical dog named Laelaps (or "Hurricane"). The dog was so fast that it could catch anything. It was sent in pursuit of a magical fox that could not be caught by anything. In order that the universe not come to an end due to the confrontation between an ineludible predator and uncatchable prey, Zeus turned both the dog and the fox to stone. The dog became the constellation Canis Major, and the fox (he's called the Teumessian Fox) became Canis Minor.

MELANTHIUS & MELANTHO

AN ITHACAN BROTHER AND SISTER, AND THEIR GRIM, TRAGIC STORY.

PRONUNCIATION: mel-AN-thee-us and mel-AN-tho

LIKE: Social Climbing, Opportunism

DISLIKE: Slavery, the Social Order of Ithaca

SPECIAL POWERS: Rudeness, Hubris, Ambition

NARRATIVE ROLE: Melanthius antagonizes Odysseus and Melantho schemes against Penelope in the book's scenes set on Ithaca.

Once upon a time, when the young Princess Penelope married King Odysseus, her father gave her a slave named Dolius. Dolius became Penelope's gardener, serving her for a long time on the island of Ithaca, trimming the queen's trees and keeping her property in order. Dolius the slave was married to another slave—a woman from Sicily. The couple had seven sons and a daughter, and the whole family was enslaved to Odysseus, like many other families on the island.

After Odysseus left for Troy, the gardener Dolius, his wife, and six of his sons continued to work for the king's household. Yet months turned into years, and years into decades, and once two decades had passed, one of Dolius's sons, along with Dolius's daughter had relinquished their loyalty to Odysseus, choosing instead to serve the suitors. The disloyal son was a goatherd named Melanthius. The disloyal daughter was Melantho, a serving girl. And the story of Melanthius and Melantho is the most brutal and disturbing of all the *Odyssey*'s many inset tales.

The Slave Girl Melantho

Let's begin with Melantho, a pretty slave girl. She'd grown up under the care of Penelope. The queen gave her presents and treated the girl as her own child. Yet once suitors had invaded the royal residence on Ithaca, Melantho's devotion to Penelope faltered. She began a sexual relationship with the suitor Eurymachus. Melantho was likely the slave who betrayed Penelope's secret to the suitors, telling them about the queen's strategy for indefinitely delaying their courtship efforts by unweaving her shroud every night. Thus, although Penelope had been a kind mistress toward her slave Melantho, Melantho's loyalty toward Penelope, twenty years after Odysseus's departure, had run its course.

The Slave Boy Melanthius

Melantho's brother, Melanthius the goatherd, also shirked his family's obligations to the kingship and instead joined with the suitors. In the king's absence, he was supposed to take care of Odysseus's herds, assuring their safety and fecundity. Instead, Melanthius brought goats for the suitors' feasts and otherwise neglected his duties while attending banquets at the palace. When Odysseus returned to Ithaca and disguised himself as a beggar, he met Melanthius, and the traitorous goatherd's conduct toward him showed Odysseus how much Ithaca had changed while he'd been gone. (Melanthius the goatherd, by the way, should not be confused with Eumaeus the swineherd, who was loyal to Odysseus.)

The clearing where the disguised king met the renegade goatherd was a beautiful place. A clear spring watered a grove of poplars, and a fountain and an altar had long stood there. Melanthius, along with two other herdsmen, might have given the disguised Odysseus and the swineherd Eumaeus a polite nod, and nothing more. But instead, Melanthius was stunningly rude.

Melanthius called both men scum. He derogated Eumaeus for herding pigs and said that the old beggar accompanying Eumaeus was probably a pig. If the old beggar (Odysseus) were brought into the palace, Melanthius assured them, the drifter would wheedle and beg for scraps. Melanthius kicked Odysseus in the hip. Odysseus didn't move, and he considered beating the renegade goatherd to death right then and there.

The loyal swineherd Eumaeus spoke up for his humble companion, saying that he hoped Odysseus would come home presently so that the brash Melanthius would get what was coming to him. Melanthius scoffed, growling that Odysseus would never return home and that he wished Telemachus would die from an arrow from the gods. With this curse, off Melanthius went to join the suitors in feasting, and before long, the rude goatherd was chowing down with Penelope's aspiring husbands, having become a particular favorite of the suitor Eurymachus.

THE FATE OF MELANTHIUS AND MELANTHO

In subsequent scenes in the story, Melanthius and his sister Melantho have clearly gone all in with the suitors. Melanthius, seeing Odysseus in the palace on a later occasion, threatened to beat the king. Melantho upbraided Odysseus for daring to speak to the suitors, telling the hero-in-disguise to keep his mouth shut, or he'd be seriously hurt. The hero, who had arrived in disguise to evaluate the loyalty of those in his household, concluded that Melanthius and Melantho had utterly betrayed him. Additionally, the low-born brother and sister had disparaged Odysseus for seeking hospitality, and hospitality is one of the cardinal virtues of the Homeric epics.

And although the *Odyssey* clearly depicts Melanthius and Melantho as antagonists, what happens to them at the story's end is so horrific that when considered carefully, it changes the whole tenor of the second half of the epic.

The *Odyssey*'s climactic scene is a battle in the palace feasting hall. During this battle, the goatherd Melanthius betrayed Odysseus a final time. The herdsman slipped into a palace storeroom where weapons and armor had been hidden away, and Melanthius managed to get armaments to a dozen suitors just as the battle began. Odysseus dispatched two herdsmen to intercept him—the swineherd Eumaeus and another cowherd who is a minor character, and Odysseus's deputies managed to catch Melanthius and tie him up while the main battle in the feasting hall raged on.

When the fighting was over and Odysseus had massacred the suitors, the epic's protagonists set their sights on Melanthius and Melantho. Melanthius was tortured. They cut off his nose with bronze blades, and then they cut off the goatherd's ears. They ripped off his genitals and fed them to dogs. They chopped off Melanthius's hands and feet. Homer doesn't tell us who performed the torture, but it was definitely sanctioned by Odysseus, if not actually performed by him.

The slave girl Melantho's fate is not entirely certain. She was likely one of the serving girls Odysseus ordered to be traumatized and murdered. The hero, victorious after the battle, announced that every serving girl who'd taken a suitor for a lover must help clean the blood and mangled bodies out of the hall. Then, Odysseus said, the girls were to be taken outside and sliced to death with swords.

In a piercing and awful sequence, the girls wept together and clung to one another as Odysseus forced them to clean the carnage from the dining hall. Telemachus, unsatisfied with the idea of slicing them to death with swords, proposed something else. The girls would all be lined up in a row and hanged. Homer tells us that the mourning slave girls died like trapped doves, their feet twitching as they suffocated.

DOLIUS AND ODYSSEUS

But there's actually more to the story than this. The ill-fated brother and sister, once again, had a father named Dolius. Dolius, the queen's gardener, was still enslaved to Odysseus after the king came home and killed his children. In the final book of the epic, in a brief scene, Odysseus met Dolius, his wife, and Dolius's surviving six sons. The gardener ran to Odysseus, stunned to see that the king had returned. But, whatever Dolius thought or knew about the loss of his children, Odysseus soon presented more danger to the old gardener's family. Following the execution of the suitors, a large revolt had arisen on the island. The rebels were coming for Odysseus, and Odysseus needed Dolius and his six remaining sons to help defend him! Athena, fortunately, forestalled further violence at the epic's end. But even so, the *Odyssey*'s closing moments remind us that every single one of Odysseus's slaves lives and dies at the king's mercy.

To modern readers, the story of Dolius and his family is a sort of dark mirror of that of Odysseus and his family. The enslaved people have no rights or property. The suitors toss Melanthius scraps of meat, as though he's a dog. Ithaca's slaves are expected to be loyal to an absentee king who has been away for two decades. Melanthius and Melantho are not appealing characters, but as powerless domestics trying to adapt to a changing social order, their cozying up to the suitors is not illogical.

In an alternate timeline, Eurymachus might have become king of Ithaca, and Melanthius and Melantho might have had a leg up on the future. From the perspective of the lowborn brother and sister, a charming local lord was at least as good a boss to have as the terrifying killer responsible for the sack of Troy. Melanthius and Melantho, unlikable as they are, and cruel to the wandering poor to boot, still represent what Odysseus and his family might have looked like had they not been born into royalty—powerless servants vulnerable to the lusts and violence of their owners. The Homeric epics (and real ancient Greek history) are full of instances of men and women made slaves during wars, and every Homeric warrior is constantly one lost battle away from slavery.

To ancient Greek audiences, acculturated at birth to the idea of slavery, the executions of Melanthius and Melantho would have probably been a bit less shocking. Highborn listeners hearing the *Odyssey* sung at a glitzy party in 600 BCE might have even nodded in approval at the story of rude thralls being disciplined. But whatever ancient audiences made of it, the *Odyssey*, in 600 BCE as well as today, is a work of fiction, and the Homeric universe has its own ethical framework. In the *Iliad* and *Odyssey*, Odysseus is a hero, with approval from Zeus and thorough support from Athena. Within the internal logic of the poem, Odysseus is fated to come home and reestablish himself, albeit with considerable difficulty. Anything that gets in his way, or worse, anything that crosses him, is subject to the unstinting savagery of a man who is a warlord and enslaver, in addition to a Homeric protagonist.

NOW YOU KNOW

Part of the *Odyssey*'s climactic confrontation is a herdsman-on-herdsman battle, during which the goatherd Melanthius fights the swineherd Eumaeus and the cowherd Philoetius. Generally, the latter two herdsmen fight valiantly during the epic's climax. Eumaeus, in particular, must have been doing some push-ups and squats in his pigpen in between shoveling manure, because he fights right alongside Odysseus and Telemachus without a problem.

EURYCLEIA

WHAT'S THAT ON YOUR LEG?

PRONUNCIATION: yer-ICK-lee-uh

LIKES: Odysseus and His Family

DISLIKES: Traitorous Domestics

SPECIAL POWERS: Hard Work, Loyalty, Keeping Secrets

NARRATIVE ROLE: Eurycleia, Odysseus's elderly slave, offers what support she can to the hero's family throughout the *Odyssey*.

Most of the characters from Homer's first epic, the *Iliad*, are sweaty, muscle-bound warriors, aged roughly 20–50, stampeding around the battlefield on foot and in chariots and slaying each other. The slaying stretches on for more than fifteen thousand lines. It's a gorgeous, tragic, unremittingly violent tale of the powerlessness of humanity beneath the press of far greater forces. But the *Iliad*, being a war story, more or less stays on the battlefield. The *Odyssey*, on the other hand, is very different.

The ancient literary critic Longinus described the *Odyssey* as a κωμῳδία ἠθολογουμένη (*komoidia ethologoumene*), or "comedy of manners," intending it as a criticism, because he preferred the *Iliad*. Yet to modern readers, the *Odyssey*'s broader catalog of humanity and subtle portraiture of different echelons of society are actually some of its greatest strengths. In it, we meet slaves, herdsmen, servants, sailors, layabouts, and bards of various ages, from the youths who dance in Phaeacia all the way up to geriatric Nestor. And speaking of old-timers, among the epic's most prominent senior citizens is Eurycleia, Odysseus's childhood nurse, who's still working for his family in Ithaca when the epic begins. Eurycleia, in spite of all the malice in the palace, keeps a low profile and does what she can to help Telemachus and Penelope up until Odysseus gets home. Here's Eurycleia's story.

Eurycleia's Background

Eurycleia was a slave. She'd been purchased for the price of twenty oxen by Odysseus's father, King Laertes, at a very young age. Eurycleia enjoyed a privileged position in Laertes's court. The king treated her as an equal to his wife, although Laertes never slept with Eurycleia. When Odysseus was born, Eurycleia served as the hero's wet nurse and caretaker. She was present to see Odysseus's grandfather name the boy and watched the clever child grow up into a young man. Years later, Eurycleia served Penelope, as well as Odysseus, after the king and queen were married. Upon the birth of Telemachus, Eurycleia took care of the boy, just as she had his father. And when Odysseus vanished, and old Laertes lost himself to grief, and greedy suitors cornered the queen and her son in the palace, Eurycleia stayed with Penelope and Telemachus, even as many of the domestics around her began to serve the impudent newcomers. Thus, as we open the first book of the *Odyssey*, it's clear that Eurycleia has a track record of steadfast loyalty to the hero and his family.

Telemachus, planning his voyage over to Pylos at the bidding of the disguised Athena, asked Eurycleia to secure him some wine and grain for the journey, and to do so in secret. The old nurse, worried about his safety, reminded Telemachus that he was still basically a kid. She said the suitors would surely scheme against him during his absence. Telemachus told her that his journey had been sanctioned by a god, and he made the old woman swear not to tell his mother or anyone else. It would not be the last time Eurycleia vowed to keep a secret in the *Odyssey*.

Later, when Penelope found out about Telemachus's covert journey, Eurycleia admitted that she'd been in on it. The queen was understandably upset, but she also realized Eurycleia had kept a promise to Telemachus. When the young man returned safely from his mission, Eurycleia was the first to see him enter, and she greeted him with kisses and exclamations of joy.

Toward the end of the *Odyssey*, after the hero made it home, Eurycleia became more and more enmeshed in Odysseus's plans. First, she obeyed Telemachus's request to close the female servants in their rooms for a little while. Telemachus also needed to remove Odysseus's old weapons from the feasting hall, he said, to get them out of the grease and smoke of the room. While at the outset Eurycleia had no idea that Telemachus was helping his father plan an attack on the suitors, in one of the *Odyssey*'s most famous scenes, Eurycleia figured out what was going on all by herself.

THE SCAR ON ODYSSEUS'S LEG

Odysseus, disguised as he was throughout so much of the *Odyssey*, had a long and complicated conversation with Penelope, in which he predicted that Penelope's husband would be home very soon, though the queen did not appear to be convinced. Melancholy, Penelope said that at least they could get the respectful old beggar a bath and some comfortable bedding. Odysseus, however, playing the role of a vagabond to the hilt, said he'd be fine sleeping on any rough bedding they had lying around, and as far as baths, none of Penelope's servants probably wanted to touch him. If Penelope had an old serving woman, said Odysseus (perhaps having seen Eurycleia and having her in mind), he'd accept a footbath from her.

Eurycleia then approached the disguised Odysseus, full of emotion. In an unprompted soliloquy, the old woman spoke about how she missed the real Odysseus desperately and said that the hero had faced bad luck in spite of being pious toward all the gods. Eurycleia remarked that the old beggar in the palace sure bore a close resemblance to Odysseus, and then she began washing his feet. It wasn't long before the old woman's hand happened upon a large scar above Odysseus's knee. Eurycleia had seen and touched the exact same scar before.

Odysseus (Homer tells us in a flashback sequence) had been over on the mainland, visiting his grandparents and cousins. The family had been hunting, and a boar had sunk a tusk into Odysseus's thigh, although he'd managed to kill the animal. Eurycleia remembered when the hero had come home, telling stories about his perilous adventures. Thus, having noticed already that the disguised Odysseus looked like the real Odysseus, and having the added evidence of the very distinctive scar on the king's thigh, Eurycleia, shocked, dropped Odysseus's leg, and the bowl of water spilled all over the floor. She brushed her fingers through his beard with incredulity, and, misty-eyed, she said he was Odysseus! He was her child!

This moment is one of the *Odyssey*'s ἀναγνώρισις (*anagnorisis*), or "recognition," scenes, with a woman who was effectively a mother figure for

Odysseus ready to wrap him in a great big hug. Unfortunately for Eurycleia, Odysseus had other plans.

He grabbed the old woman by the throat with one hand, and with the other, he drew her in so that she could hear him whisper. Do *not* betray his secret, Odysseus hissed. If she told anyone, he would kill her along with all the disloyal slave women. Eurycleia chose her next words carefully. She whispered that she could be trusted and that, if Odysseus won, she would help him by directing him toward the slave women who had disrespected him. Odysseus said he could figure that out for himself and once again urged her to be quiet. And hearing this final directive, the poor old nurse retrieved a fresh basin of water, so as to complete the operation of washing Odysseus's feet. This is the nurse's last sustained appearance in the *Odyssey*, though she has a few more small parts.

The next morning, playing along with what she now understood was a ruse, Eurycleia assured Telemachus that the disguised Odysseus had been given a place to sleep. She ordered the slave girls to prepare the palace for what would end up being the suitors' last feast there. It was Eurycleia, acting on orders of Odysseus, who locked the doors to the feasting hall to trap the suitors inside. After the massacre, Odysseus summoned Eurycleia into the chamber where all the suitors lay dead, and she saw him standing there, splattered with blood. Odysseus, as he had before, told her not to talk, snarling that the suitors had got what was coming to them, and that he *did* want to know which slaves in the house had dishonored him. Eurycleia told him. Out of the fifty household slaves who worked in the palace, twelve of the women had been disloyal.

Following the execution of these domestics, the last we hear of Eurycleia in the *Odyssey* is that she helped Odysseus and Penelope reunite, and that she and one other servant prepared the royal couple's bed. And that's a synopsis of Eurycleia's role in the *Odyssey*. Like Athena, Nausicaa, Arete, and Circe, she's one of the women in the epic who helps get Odysseus where he needs to go. Unlike these other women, however, Eurycleia is a slave, and Odysseus treats her like one.

The scene of Eurycleia recognizing Odysseus's scar is one that people tend to remember from the *Odyssey*. On the one hand, it's a sweet moment. A matronly old servant recognizes her king, and she's overjoyed that he's finally come home. On the other hand, within forty-eight hours of Eurycleia being reunited with Odysseus, he's grabbed her by the throat and threatened to kill her; he's killed over a hundred people in the palace, many of whom begged for their lives; and he's grilled Eurycleia about which female slaves he should kill, and then murdered them too. Within the callous moral logic of the *Odyssey*, Odysseus is the protagonist, and divine will propels his vengeance, in addition to his personal vendetta. For readers today, however, the casual contempt with which Odysseus and Telemachus treat lowborn characters like Eurycleia is hard to ignore. As the *Odyssey* ratchets up to its violent conclusion in the final books, the hero's reunion with his childhood nurse demonstrates that a great many Ithacans would have been better off if the wrathful, jealous Odysseus had never made it home.

NOW YOU KNOW

Disguises and recognition scenes are a major part of the *Odyssey*'s narrative mechanics. Later in ancient literature, at the end of the 400s BCE, the tragedian Euripides wrote plays like *Ion* and *Helen* that also featured recognition scenes, in which long-lost relatives and friends reunite. During the 300s BCE and afterward, ancient Greek and Latin plays (of writers like Menander, Plautus, and Terence) used recognition scenes to create climactic narrative moments, as did ancient Greek novels like *Daphnis and Chloe* and the *Aethiopica*, which were popular in Europe during the early modern period. As famous as the island-hopping section of the *Odyssey* is, the Ithaca sequence of the epic *also* had an incredible influence on the stories that we're still telling today.

PENELOPE: THE TACTICIAN

SHE MAY KNOW EXACTLY WHAT'S GOING ON THE WHOLE TIME.

PRONUNCIATION: pe-NELL-uh-pee

LIKES: Puppeteering the Action, Noticing Everything

DISLIKES: Waiting While Her Husband Dillydallies

SPECIAL POWER: Throwing Out Clues and Hints

NARRATIVE ROLE: Many readers of the *Odyssey* have theorized that Penelope is a more perceptive participant in the epic's action than it seems at first glance.

Penelope, throughout the later books of the *Odyssey*, remains a puzzle. Everyone speaks very highly of her—in fact, the chief of the suitors says she has the finest mind in all of history. Homer calls her περίφρων Πηνελόπεια (*períphron Penelópeia*), or "wise Penelope." Even in Hades, Odysseus's old comrade Agamemnon compliments Penelope, emphasizing that Odysseus's wife is loyal and wise. In spite of her evidently considerable intelligence, however, Penelope isn't able to *do* very much during the *Odyssey*. The funeral-shroud gimmick worked for a surprisingly long time before the heroine was caught in the act of unweaving. In comparison to brawny Athena and wand-waving Circe, Penelope is not in a position to defend herself. Bullied by the suitors, belittled by her own son, and coddled and coaxed to sleep by Athena, Penelope spends Homer's *Odyssey* in a drowsy purgatory of baths, costume changes, and naps.

Or does she?

Late in the epic, in Books 19 and 23, the heroine finally gets a couple of prolonged appearances onstage. And during these appearances, there's some decent evidence that Mrs. Odysseus is far more than a meek, devoted housewife. Here's what happens with Penelope toward the end of the story, with an emphasis on Penelope's perspective.

Does Penelope Know Who the Disguised Odysseus Is?

One night, after Odysseus had come home to Ithaca, he stayed in his palace feasting hall after the suitors had left. It was late. Telemachus lit the room's torches and went to bed. Penelope came downstairs, looking around guardedly, and the slaves set her chair by the fireplace, where the queen liked to sit. One of the serving girls scolded the disguised Odysseus for lingering in the palace after hours. Both Odysseus as well as Penelope chastened the serving girl for insulting the old beggar, and the queen had Odysseus come and sit near her. She didn't get to speak to very many travelers, she said. She wondered if the old fellow might have news of her missing husband?

She told the disguised Odysseus her situation. Her husband had gone missing, which left her vulnerable to the courtships of a hundred nearby princelings. She told him about the shroud, and explained how her enemies had found out about it. She said she was out of ideas, and that her family wanted her to remarry. That was her life at the moment. Who was he, really?

Odysseus, who loved making up fake origin stories more than anything else in the world, then disgorged a tall tale about how he was from Crete and, in fact, how he had *met* her missing husband Odysseus when the hero was marooned there on the way to Troy. Odysseus and his comrades, Odysseus said, had stayed with him for twelve days!

Penelope had never known that Odysseus had got stuck in Crete, and this fresh piece of news about her husband, though two decades old, made her cry, the tears over her cheeks like melting snow. Then (her natural wariness overcoming her emotions), she asked Odysseus to describe what Odysseus had looked like two decades before. The hero then gave Penelope a very detailed account of Odysseus's garb, down to a specific golden brooch that Odysseus had been wearing. The description of Odysseus's bygone wardrobe saddened the queen further, and she admitted that she had sent the king off with the very same accoutrements.

Odysseus, seeing Penelope's renewed grief, took it upon himself to comfort her with another lie. He said he'd *heard* that Odysseus was alive and well, and just a few clicks north over on the mainland. Then the disguised Odysseus offered a weirdly detailed and honest account of what he'd "heard" about Odysseus. Odysseus, the disguised Odysseus said, had lost his men after a storm near the island of Thrinacia. They'd eaten the forbidden cattle of the sun. Then Odysseus had washed up on the island of the Phaeacians. The Phaeacians were going to send Odysseus home, but rather than going home, Odysseus had decided to dash off elsewhere and acquire a great deal of wealth. Why, Odysseus was *great* at gathering wealth, said the disguised Odysseus. Odysseus was coming home with enough treasure to feed his family for ten generations! Also, Odysseus had gone up to Dodona, on the mainland, to consult an oracle about whether to come home as himself, or *in disguise*. Also, Odysseus really was very close by, and he was safe, said Odysseus. He'd be home within a month!

Now, let's pause for a moment and consider what Penelope was thinking while the blathering beggar sitting by her fireside spewed all this information at her. We know that even in his beggar's disguise, Odysseus *looked* like himself, because his old nurse Eurycleia says so, in this very same scene. We also know that Penelope is as sharp as a tack, because the epic has told us this numerous times. Odysseus is almost *laughably* fond of lying, a characteristic with which his wife would surely have been acquainted. Thus, as Penelope watched the motormouthed bum tell her all about what her husband *wore* on the way to the Trojan War, and then how *awesome* Odysseus was at making money, and then that Odysseus *might just* come home in disguise, it seems very likely that Penelope could have realized that the voluble vagrant was, in fact, her husband.

Their subsequent conversation in the same book makes sense either way. Penelope, after hearing from Odysseus that the *amazing* Odysseus was nearby and possibly in disguise, remained guarded. She said she *hoped* the stranger was right but that she had no other evidence to suggest she'd see Odysseus anytime soon. She said they needed to get him cleaned up and oiled so that he could sit beside Telemachus in the feasting hall the next day. Later, after Eurycleia washed Odysseus's feet and recognized him, Penelope and Odysseus continued to speak for some time.

Penelope told Odysseus she was really running out of options, and not doing well. It would soon be time to marry whichever of the suitors was wealthiest. Additionally, Penelope said, she'd had a dream. She'd dreamt that twenty geese were waddling around her house. Then an eagle had come and killed them, telling her that the suitors were the geese and that the eagle was her husband. What did he make of this dream?

Odysseus, perhaps taking the bait, said that the eagle was Odysseus! He'd come home and kill all the suitors! Hell, yeah! *He* was the dream eagle! Penelope said she wasn't convinced. Then she had an idea. Back in the old days, Odysseus used to line up twelve axes and shoot an arrow through them. It was a very difficult shot, and even more so because he did it with a massive, stiff bow that only he could string. Penelope said that whoever strung the enormous bow and made the difficult shot through the twelve axes all lined up would be her husband.

Odysseus, still in disguise, was excited. He said the bow-stringing and archery contest was a *great* idea, and that she should hold the contest sooner rather than later. They would all screw up with the bow, and then masterful Odysseus would appear! Penelope said nothing else about the contest. She told the old beggar that she was tired and that it was time for her to turn in for the night, and Book 19 comes to an end.

This is Penelope's longest scene in the epic. Now, it's possible that Penelope has no idea of who the disguised beggar is. And yet, it may also be that Penelope, who knows her husband's appearance, his quirks, and how to goad him, has not only figured out that the Homeric hobo is Odysseus, but is *also* prompting him to get his act together and *do* something about all the schmucks still freeloading in their house. Understanding that her husband is overfond of scheming for its own sake, *maybe* she suggests the archery trial to lure her competitive husband out of his dawdling and get him to help. Read this way, in the long conversation between Penelope and Odysseus in Book 19, she appears absolutely in control of the situation, nudging her gullible husband to stop delaying and act. Odysseus, by contrast, seems like a doofus, utterly outwitted by his wife.

Why Does Penelope Grill Him with Questions at the End?

There's just one problem with the "Penelope is a secret mastermind" interpretation of the *Odyssey*'s second half. In Book 19, as we just noticed, Penelope may know full well who Odysseus is. Later, however, in Book 23, Penelope doesn't exactly fly into her husband's arms after the battle in the dining hall. Rather, Penelope continues to proceed with caution. The reunion between husband and wife that the whole epic has been building toward begins as a game of cat and mouse, with Penelope only begrudgingly accepting Odysseus as himself. It happens as follows.

After Odysseus dispatched the suitors, the nurse Eurycleia hurried upstairs to tell Penelope that the king had returned. Penelope, just waking up from a deep slumber (evidently not having heard the noise of a Homeric battle downstairs), told Eurycleia to cut it out. Eventually, the old nurse convinced the queen that she was telling the truth, or at least that some great turn of fortune had taken place. Still, Penelope had questions. There had been a *lot* of suitors. Indeed there had! said Eurycleia. And Odysseus had killed all of them.

Penelope, cagey and perhaps still half asleep, was eventually persuaded to go downstairs. She saw Odysseus there but kept her distance. She considered going to him, but caution and prudence made her restrained. Telemachus chided her, telling her to go to her husband, and Penelope, for once, did not let her son talk down to her. She said, "My child . . . If this is really him, / if my Odysseus has come back home, / we have our ways to recognize each other, / through secret signs known only to us two" (Wilson translation, 23.105–9). Odysseus, seeming to agree, shooed Telemachus and several others off.

As he was dirty from his beggar's disguise as well as bloody from the great battle, Odysseus had a bath, and Athena made the hero look strong, tall, and handsome. Then, the estranged husband and wife sat down in chairs opposite one another. The disguises were off. The crisis was over. But Penelope had one more move to play. She asked the old nurse Eurycleia to move Odysseus's bed outside their bedroom so that he could sleep there.

The request sent the hero into a sudden gush of emotion. Move his bed! he exclaimed. One of their marriage bed's posts was the trunk of an olive tree, and it couldn't be moved. She hadn't destroyed their marriage bed, had she? Was their bed, at least, still safe?

Penelope was finally convinced that Odysseus was Odysseus when she heard her husband's response to her remark about the bed. And although their marriage in the greater epic tradition is not sunshine and rainbows forever after, the tree-bed exchange is the moment in the *Odyssey* when Odysseus and Penelope, after twenty years apart, finally become husband and wife again.

If we interpret Penelope as a tactician akin to her husband, and one who pretty quickly intuits that the burly bum from Book 19 is her husband, then *why would Penelope keep her distance from Odysseus later, after the crisis has passed*? There could be a couple of answers to this question. One of them is simply that Penelope is angry at him. He's been gone for two decades, strutting around in a useless war, and after returning, he's treated her with cunning and mistrust. Her climactic question to him about the bed is perhaps not a coincidence. Does Odysseus, off dallying with other women for so long, remember his marriage bed?

Whether or not Penelope knows exactly what's happening in the epic's second half, and whether she conducts her own test of Odysseus out of anger, it's easy to imagine that the heroine knows more than she lets on. The conversations between the leading couple have the feel of two very cunning people talking in code to one another. She tells artless young Telemachus that she and Odysseus have ways of communicating that no one else understands, and some shell game or secret signs surely are exchanged during their long interactions in the later parts of the *Odyssey*. And ultimately, she is one of a number of women in the *Odyssey* who determine the hero's fate, from frisky Calypso to noble Arete to otherworldly Circe to mighty Athena.

NOW YOU KNOW

In 2005, Canadian author Margaret Atwood published *The Penelopiad*, a tremendous novella retelling the events of the *Odyssey* through Penelope's perspective. With a chorus made up of the twelve maids whom Odysseus and Telemachus execute at the *Odyssey*'s end, Atwood's *Penelopiad* gives an account of Penelope's life from her early years in Sparta onward. A rich, literary, learned work, the *Penelopiad* is a great companion book for the Homeric epics.

A HOMERIC BATTLE

IT'S ALL FUN AND GAMES UNTIL AN EPIC HERO GOES BERSERK.

LIKES: Blood and Guts, Glory and Doom

DISLIKES: Handshakes, Hugs, Peace Talks

SPECIAL POWER: Extremely High Body Counts

NARRATIVE ROLE: Book 22 of the *Odyssey* tells of one of the most violent battles in the Homeric epics.

The Homeric epics are astonishingly violent. At the *Iliad*'s gory crescendo, when the hero Achilles is on the warpath after his friend's death, he becomes a threshing machine on the battlefield. Severed limbs are flying everywhere. Men screech in agony and bite the earth as they die. Achilles knifes a man so hard that the man's liver pops out. He decapitates a man so forcefully that his victim's bone marrow flies all over the place. Achilles' entire chariot is drenched with blood. The *Iliad*'s main theme, as Homer describes it in the first line of the poem, is "the rage of Achilles," and once that rage goes into full effect on the battlefield, heads begin to roll in stunning quantities.

The Greek and Latin epics of antiquity often involve building toward what's called an ἀριστεία (*aristeia*), or "moment of excellence." In the *Iliad*, many prominent warriors have an *aristeia*, or scene of battle glory, during which they carry their team forward through blood and fire, dispatching many foes against all odds. A warrior's *aristeia* is his spotlight, beast-mode moment in an ancient epic. Prompted by vengeance, the defense of comrades, pride, or sheer desperation, Homeric warriors abruptly rise above themselves and become untouchable for a few pages, and the battle glory that they achieve, though transient, can never be taken away afterward.

BATTLE IN THE HOMERIC EPICS

Homeric battle scenes can be absolutely exhilarating. A truce breaks down into renewed fighting in the *Iliad*, and the Greek hero Diomedes fights with such sudden ferocity that he wounds the goddess Aphrodite and drives a spear into the god of war Ares. Later in the epic, the Greek king Agamemnon personally leads a defense of the Greek fortifications, and as unlikable as he is, for a time, the entire war hangs on his sudden and explosive display of skill. The Trojan champion Hector has an *aristeia*, and then the Greek warrior Patroclus, and in all cases, each warrior's moment of battle glory testifies to a core truth about humanity: Sometimes, whether due to intrinsic personal merits or something from beyond, we do extraordinary, surpassing things as individuals.

As mesmerizing as the *Iliad*'s moments of battle glory are, they are punctuation points within the epic's more prosaic carnage. Homer's first epic tells us, untiringly, that *this warrior* we've never heard of killed *this other warrior* we've never heard of, and *this guy* took out *this other guy*, and *this* guy killed *that* guy and *this* guy killed *that* guy, page after page and book after book, until it's hard to imagine there are very many Greeks or Trojans left. With hundreds of proper names and dozens of subdivisions within each of the two main armies, to all but the most scholarly readers, the *Iliad* sometimes degenerates into wearisome lists of murders.

Homer is also fond of a core set of colorful, but very predictable, similes related to battle. Achilles, he writes, was like a bloodied lion, standing over his prey. Agamemnon was like a lion. Diomedes was like an eagle. Diomedes was like a lion. Achilles was like an eagle. Patroclus was like a wolf. Patroclus was like a lion. Ajax was like a wolf. Ajax was like a lion. Menelaus was like a wolf. Menelaus was like a lion. Homer's longer similes can be earth-shatteringly beautiful. But in the more workaday battle narratives of the *Iliad*, the formulaic similes about lions and wolves and eagles start to blur together pretty quickly. Rather than making warriors seem uncommonly strong and fierce, the *Iliad*'s combat similes sometimes make war itself seem monotonous and mechanistic.

Sometimes, the way that the *Iliad* describes war is absolutely riveting. Scenes during which Achilles and Diomedes and Hector grip their swords and spears and fight with and against the gods have drawn readers to the edges of their seats for thousands of years. At other times, due to the sheer

quantity of battles, casualty lists, and rote animal similes, the horror and finality of war in the *Iliad* can become dreary and colorless, and this may have been part of the way the epic worked in antiquity as well. Readers of any generation can surely grow numb reading page after page about who killed whom.

The *Odyssey*, on the other hand, is not a war story. The *Odyssey* concerns itself mostly with civilian life during peacetime. When Book 22 comes around, and the latent violence that has crackled around Odysseus throughout the epic surges to the surface, the wolves and eagles and lions all come out. The bloodshed at the epic's climax is so sudden, so complete, and so extreme that for five hundred lines, in a sequence classicists call the "Mnesterophonia," or "slaughter of the suitors," the *Odyssey* becomes the *Iliad*. Homer's martial swan song begins as follows.

THE *ODYSSEY'S* CLIMACTIC BATTLE

The *Odyssey*'s final showdown begins with an archery contest. Penelope suggested that the suitors line up twelve axes, and fire an arrow through them using Odysseus's bow. Whoever could make this challenging shot with the absent king's weapon could marry her. Many suitors tried, but not a single one of them could even string the bow. Telemachus almost accomplished it, but Odysseus shook his head, indicating that the king wanted to be the victor in the contest. And so Odysseus strung his bow. The suitors watched in disbelief as the shabby old drifter bent it effortlessly and then held it aloft, plucking its string, which, the poet tells us, sounded like a swallow's song. (Original bardic performances must have involved a carefully timed twang of the singer's lyre string at just this juncture!) Odysseus shot through all the axe heads. Then, Odysseus pulled off his beggar's disguise, standing naked in his palace feasting hall. And he shot Antinous, the chief of the suitors, through the throat, with no warning. Blood gushed from the young man's nose and all over the food on the table.

The suitors were shocked and bewildered. They said the old beggar was in big trouble and fumbled around for the weapons that had until recently hung in the hall. They found nothing. Odysseus told them that the king had returned, and that they were all going to die. The intruders realized they were in a room with one of the most dangerous executioners from the Trojan War. The clever suitor Eurymachus protested. It had all been Antinous's idea, he said, and now that Odysseus was back, the suitors would compensate him for all the food and drink they'd consumed. Odysseus said no amount of money would suffice. He was going to kill every last one of them.

Eurymachus began trying to rally the men. They were sitting ducks, he said, and he drew his sword. But a moment later, Odysseus shot Eurymachus in the chest. The third-most prominent of the suitors, Amphinomus, driven by desperation, then attacked, and Telemachus killed him. Telemachus then dashed toward the storeroom for armaments as Odysseus held the pack of suitors back with arrows. Telemachus returned with the two herdsmen who'd been helping the heroes, and the men armed themselves. When Odysseus was out of arrows, he strapped on a shield, put on a big helmet with a horsehair crest, and gripped a spear in each hand.

The suitors and their allies tried a few more sneaky maneuvers to secure weapons and armor for themselves, but they failed. Soon, Odysseus, his son, and two herdsmen faced off against about a hundred enemies. Athena appeared beside Odysseus and taunted him, telling the hero he'd once been a terror during the Trojan War. Did Odysseus still have his old courage? Was he too scared to defend his old home? With these provocations voiced, Athena hid up in the rafters of the room.

Six suitors hurled spears at Odysseus, but Athena caused them to miss. The room exploded into violence. A return volley of spears from Odysseus's quartet killed four suitors, and though more suitors managed to tear the thrown spears from the bodies of their fallen comrades and hurl them back at Odysseus, they missed again. The warring groups grew closer until Odysseus and Telemachus were stabbing suitors directly. Overhead, Athena hefted her giant shield, and the ranks of the suitors dissolved into a fearful throng. The chamber filled with screams and the sounds of cracking skulls, and blood streamed over the floor. Odysseus and his men were eagles, and the hapless suitors were their prey.

A suitor begged Odysseus for his life, but the hero decapitated him as he pleaded. But Odysseus wasn't entirely merciless. When a bard named Phemius pleaded to be spared, Telemachus vouched for him. Phemius was cool, said Telemachus, and Telemachus also made sure that they spared a young attendant named Medon. It would have been an occupational hazard for a bard, singing the *Odyssey*, to tell of the death of a bard!

The battle, which had begun with volleys of arrows and spears, and then quickened into close-quarters combat, was abruptly over. The horror of the scene and the way that Odysseus trapped the suitors in his palace hall have prompted comparisons between Odysseus and Polyphemus the Cyclops, both of whom ensnare and methodically slaughter their prey. With his foes all exterminated, Odysseus looked around the room and observed the suitors lying piled on top of each other. He told Telemachus to fetch Eurycleia, and when the old nurse came in, as Homer tells it:

She found Odysseus in the thick of slaughtered corpses,

splattered with bloody filth like a lion that's devoured

some ox of the field and lopes home, covered with blood,

his chest streaked, both jaws glistening, dripping red—

a sight to strike terror. So Odysseus looked now,

splattered with gore, his thighs, his fighting hands.

—Eurycleia sees Odysseus after the battle, *Odyssey*
(Fagles translation, 22.426–31)

Odysseus, baptized by the blood of his victims, is reborn here as the Odysseus of the *Iliad*, and he looks, of course, like a lion, as just about every Homeric hero does during their moments of battle glory in Homer's first epic. As Eurycleia sees him standing there, the genteel charmer who endeared himself to the Phaeacians is gone. The melancholy prisoner of Calypso who dreamt of home is no more. The poor supplicant who apologized to the wind god Aeolus for his men's error has vanished. Instead, we see Odysseus the warmonger, who, after killing a hundred people, is still looking for more.

The battle at the end of the *Odyssey* is ultimately a jolting reminder of who Odysseus is, and where he's been. He had been an Ithacan, once, a whiz kid loved by his parents and wet nurse. He grew up in a palace, but he knew the island's domestics and laborers and herdsmen, and some of them loved him. He'd married a woman he adored who was also appropriate to his station. But just as his wife became pregnant with their first son, Odysseus had been dragged into the Trojan War. And in that war, year after year, a generation of people slowly lost their humanity, becoming Greeks and Trojans, besiegers and besieged, wolves, eagles, and lions.

NOW YOU KNOW

Generally, the epic poets of antiquity imitated the extreme violence of Homer's war scenes in their own. However, from ancient times onward, some readers have found the war sequences of the *Iliad* a bit excessive. A poem called the *Batrachomyomachia*, or the *Battle of the Frogs and Mice*, is the first surviving example of what we call the "mock heroic." Mock-heroic works, from the final few centuries BCE onward, made fun of the various conventions of classical epics, drawing attention to the ways that the *Iliad* can be a bit "sillyad." In the *Batrachomyomachia* and other mock epics, Homeric language and similes are applied to zany battles between animals and fairy-tale creatures, all for the purposes of eliciting laughter. The greatest critics of ancient Greek epics were, without a doubt, ancient Greeks themselves.

THE KING & QUEEN

HAPPILY (?) TOGETHER AGAIN IN
THEIR WEIRD TREE BED.

LIKE: Mind Games, Hustling, Reconnaissance

DISLIKE: Honesty, Simplicity

SPECIAL POWERS: Swindling, Stalling for Time

NARRATIVE ROLE: Odysseus and Penelope finally reunite in Book 23 of the *Odyssey*, but it looks like things will probably go sideways for the couple pretty quickly.

Odysseus and Penelope—two people notorious for their brainpower and their duplicity, after a twenty-year separation, numerous affairs, and considerable dangers—finally get together again at the end of the *Odyssey*. By Book 23, we know they're both high-grade con artists and accomplished liars and that fraud and bamboozlement come as easily to them as putting on their sandals every morning. As the couple turns down their bedding after the previous book's bloodletting, it's a little hard to imagine that Odysseus and Penelope, as a couple, are going to live happily ever after.

Their reunion is, of course, a sweet moment in the epic. Homer compares the pair to swimmers in a storm-tossed sea, finding land after their ships have gone down as they finally fly into each other's arms. At the same time, though, their reunion is a manufactured thing, having taken place, more than anything, due to Athena sneaking around and telling people what to do. It proceeds like this.

Penelope and Odysseus's Last Scene Together

Athena carefully prepared Odysseus for his reunion with his wife. First, a slave woman bathed Odysseus, slicked him with olive oil, and adorned him with a new tunic and a fresh cloak. Then Athena showered handsomeness all over the hero. He grew more muscular. He became taller. His hair became as profuse and curly as hyacinth flowers. The hero sat down across from his wife, perhaps expecting her to melt with desire, and called her δαιμονίη, which, in context, means something like "strange woman" or "extraordinary woman." Hearing her husband's admonishment, Penelope replied back by calling her husband δαιμόνιε, or "strange man" or "extraordinary man." Facing each other, the husband and wife began by acknowledging that however well they had aged, and however much Athena had given them magical makeovers to make them appear young again, they were, to some extent, strangers with one another.

Once Odysseus correctly passed Penelope's stumper test about their tree bed, the guardedness of the couple broke down, and they embraced each other. Penelope then said something characteristically perceptive. The gods, she said, had ravaged their lives and taken years together from them. The gods had started the Trojan War. It really wasn't his fault. The couple embraced once more and cried, and Athena, evidently still creeping around and watching them, made the night longer so that the couple could catch up before the break of dawn.

They needed the extra time to chat too. Because Odysseus, following their reunion as a couple, had some news. He would soon leave again, he said. The ghost of Tiresias had told Odysseus in Hades that the hero would, once more, embark on a long, perilous journey. But anyway, said Odysseus, it was time for them to go to bed. Penelope, listening cautiously, agreed that they could certainly go to bed, but first, she said, how about letting her know more about this upcoming trip he'd just mentioned?

Odysseus grumbled but then passed on what old Tiresias had told him in Hades. Odysseus was going to have to go on a long journey through many towns of people, carrying an oar with him. He was supposed to go so far inland with the oar that he came to a place where people knew neither the taste of sea salt nor the sight of the ocean, up until someone mistook his oar as a fan used to winnow grain. Then, Odysseus explained, he was supposed to sacrifice a bunch of animals to Poseidon. Finally, he could come home, make more sacrifices, and die peacefully of old age, far from the sea, surrounded by loved ones. The prophecy was vague. It's ending was odd, considering that Odysseus's home, Ithaca, was a small island, and *not in any way* "far from the sea."

Whatever she was actually thinking, Penelope said that the gods willed what they willed, and that one could only hope for the best. She concluded that if the gods had promised him more contented years as a senior citizen, then they had to place their faith in that promise.

As the night drew onward, they talked. Penelope told him about how she'd been stuck in the palace and oppressed by all the suitors, who'd gobbled food and guzzled wine without ever seeming to grow tired of it. Then Odysseus offered her his story, not omitting the parts about Circe and Calypso but, in the case of the latter, emphasizing that the sexually voracious nymph had never won his heart.

The next morning, Odysseus awoke early, and he told Penelope that he would soon head out on some raids in order to replenish all the flocks of livestock the suitors had eaten, adding that their subjects on Ithaca would hand over the rest of the sheep and goats. First things first, though, Odysseus said—he was off to see his father. Also, Odysseus added, the Ithacans that they ruled over? They were probably going to be a little upset that he had needlessly butchered a hundred plus local men who had begged for their lives. In the Fagles translation, Odysseus's very last words to Penelope in the *Odyssey* are "So climb to your lofty chamber with your women. / Sit tight there. See no one. Question no one" (23.413–14).

Incredibly (and infuriatingly, if you like Penelope as a character), her husband tells her *exactly what the suitors have been telling her*, and precisely what Telemachus tells her during his several snippy, misogynistic dismissals of his mother in earlier books. This is Penelope's last appearance in Homer's *Odyssey*. Having endured eight hundred pages of baths, naps, clothing changes, and masculine malarkey, the heroine ends her story where it began: confined and isolated in her upstairs chambers, because a man told her to go there.

The reunion between Odysseus and Penelope is the happy ending that the *Odyssey* has been sailing toward. At the same time, though, it is a morally murky and brisk conclusion for a couple who have longed to see one another for so long, and when it's over, Odysseus is still lumbering around, armed, dangerous, and unhinged; the clown car of the Olympian gods is still blaring circus music; and poor Penelope is still shut in her room.

NOW YOU KNOW

The later ancient Greek scholars Aristophanes of Byzantium and Aristarchus of Samothrace (at work around 200 BCE) *both* claimed that the *Odyssey* should have ended with the words that "Finally, at last, / with joy the husband and the wife arrived / back in the rites of their old marriage bed" (Wilson translation, 23.293–5). Ending the story here would have put the leading couple happily back together again, and done away with the narrative about the families of the suitors. It makes sense that these later ancient Greek scholars wanted the *Odyssey* to conclude with this happy reunion. By the 200s and 100s BCE, ancient Greek and Latin plays commonly wrapped up with joyous marriages and reunions, just as our romantic comedies do today. The *Odyssey*, however, was written prior to our millennia-long preoccupation with happy endings.

LAERTES

"I'M NOT DEAD YET! I'M GETTING BETTER! I FEEL HAPPY!"

PRONUNCIATION: lie-AIR-tees

LIKES: Retirement, Horticulture, Moping

DISLIKES: Confrontations, Current Events

SPECIAL POWERS: Grafting Fruit Trees, Keeping a Low Profile

NARRATIVE ROLE: Odysseus's father, Laertes, has a very short role in the final book of the *Odyssey*.

Laertes, former king of Ithaca, onetime Argonaut, father of Odysseus, and grandfather of Telemachus, spends the *Odyssey* putzing around in an orchard. As gluttonous suitors eat the royal family's flocks and swig their wine, old Laertes has been put out to pasture, growing pear trees in the hinterlands of Ithaca and bemoaning his son's prolonged absence. He is a sad, strange, and moderately ridiculous character in the *Odyssey*. One might imagine that the old codger could slap on his former crown for a week or two and tell the suitors to skedaddle. But instead, Laertes spends twenty-three books sniveling, pruning, and shoveling, even as Penelope weaves him a funeral shroud for three years. (It is never made clear why Laertes, who is not actually dead, requires a funeral shroud.) Peculiar as Laertes's role is in the *Odyssey*, he's still important to the story's ending.

Odysseus first heard about what had happened to his father in Hades. The hero's dead mother, Anticleia, told Odysseus that his father had been spending a lot of time in the country. Old Laertes refused to come to the palace. He slept by the fire in his cottage, lying in the ashes next to his slaves. In the warmer months, Laertes slumbered in piles of fallen leaves.

His existence was bleak and sorrowful, and all he thought of was his son's return.

Much later in the epic, after Odysseus reached the island of Ithaca, buddied up with the swineherd Eumaeus, went to visit the suitors, reunited with his son, allied with another herdsman, did more reconnaissance work among the suitors, played mind games with Penelope, won an archery contest, went on a large-scale murderous rampage, tortured and executed some people, revealed his identity to his wife and spent the night with her, and resolved to replenish his herds of livestock, Odysseus *finally* went to check on his dad.

Laertes, when Odysseus saw him for the first time after twenty years, was working among rows of fruit trees. The old man had on a filthy tunic with patched legs and was adorned in a goatskin hat. The sight of slumping, mournful old Laertes brought tears to Odysseus's eyes. Then, Odysseus made a questionable decision.

> *The veteran, Odysseus,*
>
> *seeing his father worn by age and burdened*
>
> *by desperate, heartfelt sorrow, stopped beneath*
>
> *a towering pear tree, weeping. Then he wondered*
>
> *whether to kiss his father, twine around him,*
>
> *and tell him that he had come home again,*
>
> *and everything that happened on the way—*
>
> *or question him. He thought it best to start*
>
> *by testing him with teasing and abuse.*
>
> **—Odysseus decides to question his father, *Odyssey***
> **(Wilson translation, 24.233–41)**

It's one of those moments during which you realize there is something deeply wrong with Odysseus. The conflict is over. The ghost of his mother has told him that his father's isolation and grief are genuine. Everyone's cards are on the table, but Odysseus wants to keep playing games.

Odysseus remarked that Laertes had the look of a nobleman, not a peasant. Was this the land of Odysseus? Why, Odysseus said, he had once met Odysseus, and given the hero fine gifts. Hearing the name of his long-lost son, Laertes brightened. The old man asked Odysseus about how he'd met Odysseus. The hero then began spewing one of his characteristic stories. He was from Italy, he said, and he had met and hosted Odysseus just five years prior. When Odysseus left Italy, there had been good signs, and he'd hoped the hero would soon return. And then—

Here, Odysseus stopped. His father was standing in front of him and crying. Old Laertes dumped handfuls of ashes over his stooped gray head. Odysseus did something he'd never done before. Abruptly, unprompted by gods or personal advantage, he stopped telling his tall tale and ran to hug his dad, telling Laertes it was him, Odysseus! He was home!

It was Laertes's turn to be skeptical now. He wanted proof that the liar waltzing around his orchard really was Odysseus. The hero showed his father a distinctive scar on his thigh. Then Odysseus went deeper into their reservoir of shared memories. When he was a boy, said Odysseus, he'd follow his dad around, asking Laertes to tell him the name of every tree, the apple trees, the pear trees, the fig trees, and all the grapevines that ripened in different ways from season to season. Then Laertes knew. Odysseus had come home.

Happy as their reunion was, there was also a dark cloud over it. Both men knew that trouble was brewing. The massacred suitors had families, and those families would soon be coming for Odysseus, and Odysseus Senior. And so, like Telemachus and Penelope in the epic, Laertes soon found himself swept up into Odysseus's dangerous typhoon. The hero ushered his father to the orchard's farmhouse. Laertes received a bath and change of clothing, and Athena magically made him look younger and more handsome. Then the old man, along with an elderly family slave, was furnished with armor and armaments. Telemachus promised to fight his hardest. And Laertes (who, peculiarly, has had no relationship with his grandson in the epic, even though Ithaca is about four miles wide and eighteen miles from north to south) then expressed pride to be fighting alongside his son and grandson.

The families of the suitors were arrayed around the farmhouse when Odysseus and his motley team of combatants clattered outside. Though we are not told that the bereaved islanders attacked Odysseus, Laertes himself began the fighting, hurling a spear that went through a man's helmet and into his head. The man in question was the father of the suitor Antinous, and as he fell, Odysseus and Telemachus flew into violent action once again, preparing to further depopulate Ithaca until, perhaps, they had no one left to rule over at all.

The slaying of Antinous's father is the last we hear of Laertes. As with so many other Ithacans in the story, the return of Odysseus is a mixed blessing for the old man. His son, upon coming home, lies to Laertes and then drags him into a civil war that threatens to destroy the Ionian Islands. Sad as Laertes allegedly is among his fruit trees over the course of the epic, it's easy to imagine that the retired king of Ithaca might miss being a simple orchardist, following the return of his volatile, unpredictable son.

NOW YOU KNOW

Odysseus's unnecessary tall tale to his father, Laertes, is the fifth of five such stories he spouts on Ithaca. He tells Athena he's a Cretan who killed a Cretan prince. He alleges to Eumaeus that he's a Cretan who fought at Troy, though he's fallen in fortune, and he offers the suitor Antinous a similar story about going from riches to rags. Odysseus seems to like lying about being from Crete, because he also tells Penelope he's from Crete, although when he lies to his father in Book 24, he says he's from Italy. Reading all of Odysseus's tall tales carefully (except the final one to Laertes), scholars have observed that Odysseus tailors content to impress and charm specific listeners.

THE BEREAVED OF ITHACA

AS IT TURNS OUT, THE SUITORS HAD FAMILIES WHO LOVED THEM.

LIKE: Changing with the Times, Moving On to New Leadership

DISLIKE: Tyranny, Mass Executions

SPECIAL POWER: Banding Together Against Murderous Dictators

NARRATIVE ROLE: In the final book of the *Odyssey*, the families of Penelope's suitors come after the hero, in search of revenge.

The ending of the *Odyssey*, by many standards, is an unmitigated disaster. An absentee king comes home after twenty years, lies to everyone, kills a hundred plus young men, and is about to kill their families, as well, before the gods intervene. Odysseus has been many things in the *Odyssey*, but in its final few books, he is a bloodthirsty tyrant, a pathological liar, and an enemy of the people. But as ugly as things get at the *Odyssey*'s end, what happens in Ithaca just before the curtains close is still congruent with the story as a whole. To understand why Homer would chronicle the blowback that followed Odysseus's murder of the suitors, we need to reconsider the epic's principal antagonists.

THE SUITORS ENTER HADES

The suitors have a gloomy coda in the *Odyssey*. Book 24 opens with the deity Hermes leading the suitors down into the underworld. Fearful, the spirits of the suitors clustered close together during the descent, until they came to the meadow where the dead resided, which the ancient Greeks called Asphodel. Some of Odysseus's old military comrades from the Trojan War approached the arriving suitors, but did not immediately address the newcomers. Instead, the Greek king Agamemnon spoke with the Greek champion Achilles.

Agamemnon had met a bad death, murdered by his wife and her lover when he'd come home. Achilles told Agamemnon he wished the Greek king had died in battle, so that Agamemnon could have lived with glory up until the very end. Agamemnon agreed, telling Achilles that the champion had perished universally admired. Achilles then learned that his fellow soldiers had given him a lavish funeral and buried him on a promontory overlooking a busy waterway so that Achilles would be admired forever.

As the old warhorses finished comforting one another, they addressed the suitors who had descended into Hades all together. Agamemnon was shocked at how many young men were all coming down at once. He asked them what had happened. Had it been a shipwreck? Had the young men been troublemakers, caught during a livestock raid? Or had they been attacking a city?

One of the suitors told of how he and so many other young men had converged in Odysseus's palace to court his grieving wife, and how Penelope had tricked them with the shroud. He described how Odysseus had come home in disguise and, with divine aid, had killed all the suitors. Their bodies were still unburied, and lying in Odysseus's house. Compared to the illustrious Achilles, then, the poor suitors had died ignominiously in an awkward domestic skirmish, and no one would remember their names.

EUPEITHES LEADS A REVOLT

Meanwhile, as Odysseus finally went off to meet his father, many fathers of Ithaca and the surrounding islands were mourning their dead sons. The bodies of the suitors were collected from the palace in Ithaca, and ships brought them home for burial. A convocation of mourners gathered in the town square. The mood was bleak among the parents and families of Odysseus's victims, and one man gave voice to the general sentiment. His name was Eupeithes, and he was the father of the suitor Antinous.

Odysseus, Eupeithes said, was a plague! The hero had taken many young Ithacans off to fight in a fruitless war. Not a single one had returned. Odysseus had taken all of Ithaca's ships. None had come back. Now he had killed the flower of the kingdom's youth. They couldn't let Odysseus get away with this. He'd killed their sons and brothers, and it would be better to join the dead men than let such a villain get away with what he'd done.

But another man in the crowd expressed his reservations. His name was Medon. He was a young attendant, and he'd been there during the slaying. The attendant Medon said that it had been very clear that Odysseus had divine help. Then, an old warrior in the crowd, following Medon's counsel, threw in his two cents. The suitors had been foolish, he said. They'd treated Odysseus's wife dishonorably and squandered the hero's wealth. The lusty young men had reaped what they'd sowed. Their families, however bereaved, shouldn't opt for revenge.

This is an interesting scene, historically speaking—a public assembly in which a community deliberates on collective action. The Homeric epics date from a time when archaeology begins to suggest the proliferation of the *polis*, or "city-state," becoming a widespread feature of ancient Greek civilization, and so the tableau of angry commoners on Ithaca may be a snapshot of something happening in Archaic period Greek history.

The grieving families in the town square wavered, deciding what to do. Many, concluding that enough blood had been shed, opted for peace. But more than half followed the counsel of Eupeithes. In desperate rage over their dead family members, they armed themselves and went to search for the man who had killed their loved ones.

With the Ionian Islands about to explode into war, Athena went to speak with Zeus. She asked Zeus if he'd let the incident on Ithaca flare up into a greater regional conflict. Zeus said it was really up to Athena. Athena, after all, had been the one who wanted to get Odysseus home and have him kill all the suitors. Zeus's advice was to make peace. This, evidently, was what Athena wanted to hear.

The goddess took her time getting back down to earth. The families of the suitors converged on the farm where the hero was hunkered down. Odysseus, his father, his son, and a ragtag band of workmen had already begun killing more Ithacans when Athena finally arrived and roared that it was time to stop the rebellion. She told Odysseus he'd better find a way to stop the fighting, or else he'd incur the wrath of Zeus. And the final lines of the epic, in the Lombardo translation, are "The goddess made both sides swear binding oaths– / Pallas Athena, daughter of the Storm Cloud, / Who looked like Mentor and spoke with his voice" (24.570–2).

SIMONE WEIL AND FORCE IN THE HOMERIC EPICS

In a classic *deus ex machina*, then, a deity descends from the machine of Olympus and curtails the complex action of the story with all the subtlety of a meat cleaver. There will be no penalty for Odysseus's massacre, because Athena sees all of humanity as her diorama to play with, and she, and any other god, can smite whomever they choose with minimal consequences.

Today, the ending of the *Odyssey* leaves a sour taste in the mouths of many readers. Even more Ithacans are dead, and from the perspective of the islanders who went to fight Odysseus, Darth Vader has defeated the Rebels, and the Death Star will rule over all. It's just that in ancient Greece, there were neither Jedis and Sith Lords, nor good guys and bad guys. There was only, as the French philosopher Simone Weil observed in 1939, *force*, and it had neither a light side nor a dark side. In ancient Greek mythology, the gods are a force that acts upon humankind, and some humans have more force at their disposal than others. Nature, as well, has a vast cyclonic force to it, and regular people, their backs bowed underneath all the powers acting on them, do what they can beneath the compound pressures of gods, civilization, and nature. The Homeric universe is not an orderly system, administered by a single divine intelligence. It is a conflux of forces of varying magnitudes in which the only constant is change.

The suitors die grisly, unavenged deaths because Athena thinks Odysseus should win. Their deaths are tragic, and are intended to be seen as such. Throughout the *Odyssey*, though many readers miss it, the suitors are depicted as *young* men. Penelope calls them young on multiple occasions. Agamemnon, seeing the cavalcade of suitors shuffling bleakly into Hades in the epic's final book, notes that they're all *youthful*–a procession of similarly aged petitioners ultimately interested in the fortune that Penelope promises but, in the shorter term, happy to lounge and play games and live off the fat of an absent king. When we consider their youth and inexperience, the suitors appear as oafish and callow as they do evil.

Like Odysseus's crewmates, who dash off like puppies and get into trouble time and again in the *Odyssey*, the suitors are hotheaded and hasty, obeying hormones and mob mentality. Odysseus himself, we learn late in the epic, was once overeager in his pursuit of a giant boar, and it took a chunk out of his leg. But unlike his crewmen, and unlike the suitors, Odysseus survives, thanks to the combined forces of gods and nature that favor him again and again.

Reactions to the *Odyssey*'s ending have been mixed. A goddess skydives down and magically puts an end to the fighting. Scores of grieving family members throw up their hands and presumably go home. A battle-scarred hero yawps in victory and then, perhaps, checks to see if he has a ship ready to take him on his next morally sketchy adventure. It seems that the world will continue to be messy, dangerous, and unjust.

And yet within the moral murk of the *Odyssey*'s ending, there is also a haunting realism. Had the story ended with Odysseus and Penelope's reunion, as some readers have wished, the Homeric world would have been smaller, and more trite—suspiciously, insidiously tidy. By showing us the ramifications of Odysseus's homecoming, and not simply sweeping the suitors' families under the rug, the *Odyssey* shows us that human actions have uncountable ripples, and that heroes are, as often as not, also villains.

NOW YOU KNOW

Eupeithes, the father of the suitor Antinous, gets a spear through the head in Book 24 of the *Odyssey*. His name (Εὐπείθης) means "obedient" or "compliant." Once a docile subject of the king, to whom Odysseus had showed kindness, when Eupeithes went his own way, he forfeited his safety on the island of Ithaca, just as Odysseus's renegade slaves had—at least, according to the logic of the epic.

ODYSSEUS: THE VILLAIN

THE *ODYSSEY'S* PROTAGONIST HAS AN EXTREMELY DARK SIDE.

PRONUNCIATION: oh-DISS-ee-us

LIKES: Totalitarianism, Mass Graves, War Crimes, Power

DISLIKES: Democracy, Mercy

SPECIAL POWERS: Malice, Vindictiveness

NARRATIVE ROLE: Odysseus's dark side occasionally comes through in the *Odyssey*, although it is more frequently evident elsewhere in ancient Greek mythology.

Ancient audiences had different moral expectations of heroes than we do today. The protagonists of ancient Near Eastern epics, like Gilgamesh, Marduk, and Baal, are marauders out to win fame and fortune and survive at any cost. The biblical David makes sure Bathsheba's husband is killed so that he can marry her after he has sex with her, and the child that they have, Solomon, has vast carnal appetites. Odysseus was a hero cut from the same cloth. Like other leading men from Bronze and Iron Age narratives, Odysseus murders and sleeps with anyone he wants to. He is not a moral exemplar. He's a coalescence of meteoric forces, divine and human, and anything that exerts pressure against him is going to be overwhelmed.

As we've learned in earlier sections of this book, Odysseus is at some moments an everyman figure trying to make it home. At other moments, he's an ingenious tactician, wielding violence as well as diplomacy to move through very dangerous waters. In the end, though, he is a despot. Having

reasserted control of his small bailiwick in the Ionian Sea, he makes it clear that he will tolerate no further agitation against his tyranny.

Punishing dissenters was something with which Odysseus already had extensive experience. In fact, the *Iliad* begins with a scene in which Odysseus puts down a rebellion in the ranks of the Greek army. Odysseus's first appearance in the Homeric epics is as follows.

ODYSSEUS THE LACKEY

The Greek king Agamemnon was the western leader of the Trojan War. An autocrat and a slave driver, Agamemnon was also a selfish, arrogant person. At the beginning of the *Iliad*, the Greek king did something entirely unexpected. He called all his troops together and made an announcement. Everyone could go home! Nine years of war had passed, Agamemnon grumbled. Their ships were rotting on the Trojan beach, and their loved ones had been waiting for them at home for many long seasons. They were not going to take Troy. It was time to cut their losses.

The Greek men cried out in jubilation and began loosening their ships from the sand. So instantaneous was the response from the exhausted Greek army that a sudden dust swirled around their siege camp as they hurried to depart. The gods, however, were displeased. Hera told Athena that the war needed to continue, and so Athena dove down to speak with Odysseus. She told him the Greeks couldn't possibly make peace after so much fighting, so Odysseus had to intervene and keep the Greeks on the beach at all costs.

Odysseus burst into action. He ran through the ranks of the departing westerners, telling them that they were abandoning the war effort too quickly. Agamemnon had more words for them, Odysseus insisted. Agamemnon didn't actually want them to go home. The Greek king was testing them! Odysseus then did more than chastise the Greek soldiers. Odysseus smashed and beat dissenters with a scepter, telling them that they were cowards and that they must wait for further orders. To one man, he barked, "Heed the word of others / who are your betters . . . the rule of many is not a good thing; let there be one ruler, / one king" (Alexander translation, 2.200–5). Slowly and obediently, the Greeks shuffled back into their ranks and prepared to listen to Agamemnon's further instructions.

One Greek man, however, spoke out. His name was Thersites, and he said what many westerners were thinking. Agamemnon's camp tent was full of treasure and beautiful women. Did Agamemnon now want even *more* gold and *more* beautiful women to sleep with? The Greeks were foolish to serve Agamemnon. He was a greedy oppressor, and he had very foolishly alienated his greatest warrior, Achilles. (This had just happened in the previous book of the *Iliad*.) In conclusion, Thersites raged, it was time for the Greeks to leave Agamemnon to lord himself over the war camp alone. The king had enough treasures.

It was a very dangerous moment of dissent for the Greek army. Agamemnon *had* been greedy. He *had* just lost the support of the greatest Greek warrior. He had also not managed to lead them to success, even though they outnumbered the Trojans. But rather than Agamemnon, it was Odysseus who sprang into action.

Odysseus broadsided Thersites with insults. Thersites was a low-ranking man, said Odysseus. Thersites had no business speaking about kings! Thersites shouldn't criticize Agamemnon for hoarding treasures his forces had won. They would win the Trojan War, Odysseus proclaimed. And if Thersites spoke out again, Odysseus would rip off the protester's clothing and whip him. As if to prove it, Odysseus began beating Thersites with a gold-spangled scepter. Bloodied and in tears, the dissenter sat down, forced into silence.

To be clear, this is Odysseus's first appearance in the Homeric epics. He is the loyal lackey of a dictator, and the minion of an egomaniacal strongman. He is an opponent of free speech among the Greeks. He clubs and insults his comrades in order to force them to submit. The Odysseus of the *Iliad*'s beginning is the same as the Odysseus of the *Odyssey*'s ending. He's a callous authoritarian, more than willing to wield violence against dissent. But in fact, this was not Odysseus's most fiendish role in ancient Greek mythology. Not by a long shot.

Beyond Homer: Odysseus's Darkest Moments

The sack of Troy happens off camera in the Homeric epics. Though other writers, most prominently Virgil, wrote about it in more detail, in the Homeric poems, the war's end is a shadowy thing, understood but never narrated; terrible but buried deep by Greek soldiers who were there to see it happen. Odysseus, the engineer of the Trojan Horse, brought about the end of the war. But Odysseus was also, beyond the Homeric epics, associated with several prominent atrocities.

The worst of them is also the murkiest. During the Trojan War, the Trojan champion Hector had a baby son named Astyanax (pronounced as-TEE-ann-axe). Astyanax has only a short cameo in the *Iliad*. After the youngster's parents had a troubled conversation about the war, Hector leaned in to embrace Astyanax, but the baby was terrified at his father's horsehair crest. Hector then removed his helmet and gave his boy a hug before reluctantly going off to fight. It's one of the *Iliad*'s precious few scenes of family life, and reminds us that all the macho men down on the battlefield were once toddlers, and that they have wives and families of their own.

According to several different traditions, baby Astyanax met an awful end, and Odysseus was involved in the boy's killing. The later author Proclus, our main source on the original Epic Cycle, wrote that in one of the lost works of this cycle, Odysseus murdered Astyanax during the sack of Troy. The fifth century BCE tragedian Euripides also implicates Odysseus in the toddler's death, and various sources and surviving visual art concur that Astyanax was thrown to his death from a tower as Troy burned. Sometimes in ancient traditions, the child killer is a different Greek hero. But the point is that it's possible that the *Odyssey*'s original audiences may well have associated Odysseus with infanticide as well as, more broadly, authoritarianism.

Hurling little Astyanax from a tower wasn't the only transgression linked with Odysseus in antiquity. In two Sophocles plays, Odysseus is effectively an antagonist. The first of these is *Ajax*, staged in Athens in roughly the 440s BCE. Ajax was Odysseus's friend and comrade during the Trojan War. Ajax was also a cousin of the Greek warrior Achilles. When Achilles died, the Greeks had to decide who would receive his armor. Their king, Agamemnon, held a contest of speeches to decide who got to keep Achilles' gear. The giant warrior Ajax made a case for himself, emphasizing that next to his cousin Achilles, he'd done the most for the Greek war effort (he wasn't exaggerating). But then, Odysseus slithered in and made a different speech, one that explained his own eligibility and at the same time praised Agamemnon's tenure as a ruler. Agamemnon, who liked flattery, picked Odysseus, and Odysseus got to keep Achilles' stuff. Ajax, absolutely devastated that Odysseus would seize his rights as next of kin, killed himself by falling on his sword. Ancient Greeks remembered this story, because the suicide of Ajax is a very common subject in Greek art from antiquity.

Other Greek plays from the 400s BCE also depicted Odysseus as an unlovely, malicious person. In Sophocles's *Philoctetes*, Odysseus is once again an enforcer for Agamemnon's brutal regime, heading to an island to recruit a skilled archer by any means necessary. In Euripides's *Hecuba*, Odysseus is lockstep with Agamemnon, marching a helpless Trojan princess to an altar after the war ended, where she would be sacrificed to honor the Greek dead.

In *all these cases*, whether the *Iliad*'s beginning, the lost work of the Epic Cycle, the writings of Greek tragedians in the 400s BCE, or the works of the Roman playwright Seneca in the first century CE, Odysseus is Agamemnon's most dangerous and effective acolyte. The monarch of a small cluster of islands off the west coast of Greece, Odysseus understood that bootlicking was his likeliest route to further power and wealth, and of all his many betrayals and deceits, the king of Ithaca always maintained his loyalty to Agamemnon. Today, we imagine Odysseus as a hero heading home on a boat. But in antiquity, Odysseus was also understood as a cruelly ambitious deputy, and one with little conscience or moral fiber.

ODYSSEUS IN HINDSIGHT

Homeric similes commonly compare Greek warriors to eagles, lions, and wolves. Odysseus, more than any of these, is a chameleon. He is sometimes as malevolent as Shakespeare's Richard III, gleefully gliding from scene to scene and notching up victories with each murder he commits and each lie he tells. He is sometimes as simple as Tolkien's Frodo, who just wants to complete his awful quest and go home. In a world of bronze and iron, Odysseus is plastic, capable of infinite transformations, and for a council of gods who also enjoy toying with the mortal world, the hero is the perfect vessel for divine chicanery.

Though often reprehensible, and perhaps *because* he is so often involved with shadiness and delinquency, Odysseus has invited three thousand years of readers into voyeuristic participation in his adventures. With him, we get to trespass, swindle, bamboozle, explore, and kick ass. He is a gateway to forbidden pastures, to sketchy eroticism, to the wholesome countryside and tricky city, to terror, and to triumph. Ultimately, he moves, like all tricksters do, through scores of strange places, instilling wanderlust in audiences across time. In his adventures and in his restless transformations, he is ultimately an emblem of what literature does. Because while reading and hearing stories, we become new things, just like Odysseus does, and we travel to faraway worlds, even if it's only for a little while.

NOW YOU KNOW

Of all the art inspired by the *Odyssey* in modern times, Greek author Nikos Kazantzakis's *The Odyssey: A Modern Sequel* (1938) is striking in its ambition. A full-scale epic poem in twenty-four books (just like the *Odyssey*), Kazantzakis's sequel tells of Odysseus's further adventures after the *Odyssey*. During these adventures, the hero travels to Sparta, and then Crete, Egypt, and down the Nile into Africa, where Odysseus establishes a new religion. Traveling south to proselytize, Kazantzakis's Odysseus eventually winds up in Antarctica!

EPILOGUE: THE *TELEGONY*

THE *ODYSSEY* WAS NOT THE END OF THE ORIGINAL STORY.

Long ago, the *Odyssey* was the seventh part of an eight-book-long cycle of epic poems. Our sources on the eighth and final installment are sparse. A certain writer named Proclus, who was either a philosopher from the 400s CE or a tutor from the 100s CE, set down a full summary of what used to be in the Epic Cycle, including the final book in the series. This final book was called the *Telegony* (pronounced tell-EGG-oh-nee).

THE EVENTS OF THE LOST *TELEGONY*

The *Telegony*, a cuckoo tale of adventure, war, illegitimate children, incest, and high-calorie feasting, invites us to remember that some ancient literature just wasn't very good. It sounds a bit like a low-budget sequel, filmed by an ambitious but inexperienced director who was on at least three different kinds of drugs. Here's Proclus's summary of the *Telegony*, which, though it might not be accurate across the board, should at least serve as a memorable reminder that Odysseus did not stay in Ithaca for long.

The families of the suitors buried their dead. Odysseus, tactfully, left town during the funerals, heading over to the territory of Elis on the west coast of the Peloponnese. There, he inspected some of his herds and enjoyed the hospitality of a king named Polyxenus. Polyxenus offered Odysseus a nice mixing bowl and told him a long story about a pair of tricky brothers who were architects. Following Odysseus's stayover on the Peloponnese, the hero sailed back to Ithaca, where he performed the sacrifices to the gods that Tiresias had told him to make back during Book 11 of the *Odyssey*. After making these sacrifices, Odysseus, obeying the mandates of Tiresias's foreboding prophecy, set out from Ithaca once more.

The hero sailed north for about fifty miles, disembarking in a land called Thesprotia. There, Odysseus married a woman named Callidice. (Yes, you heard that correctly. After twenty-four books of whimpering about Penelope and paddling to get back to Ithaca, Odysseus *immediately* left, dropped anchor in the closest mainland kingdom, and married a second wife.) Odysseus impregnated his new wife and then became involved in a war with an inland tribe. The gods lined up variously behind Odysseus's Thesprotian forces and the forces of his enemies. Athena and Ares, in particular, snarled and barked at one another. Eventually, Apollo stopped the war. Callidice and Odysseus had a son named Polypoetes, who became king. Later, Callidice died. Odysseus, evidently believing that his work in Thesprotia was complete, dusted off his hands, abandoned his young son on the throne, and headed back to Ithaca.

Ithaca, at that point, was under attack by a volatile young man named Telegonus (the *Telegony* is named after him). Telegonus was the son of Odysseus and the witch Circe. Telegonus was searching for his father, as Odysseus had ditched Circe back in Book 12 of the *Odyssey*, not knowing she was pregnant with his baby.

When Odysseus returned to Ithaca after abandoning his second family on the mainland, he saw that trouble was brewing there. Seeing his ancestral island under attack, Odysseus took up arms in order to defend it. Telegonus, not knowing who his father was, killed Odysseus. (So much for Tiresias's prophecy about Odysseus taking an oar inland to a place where the sea was unknown, and Odysseus dying peacefully of old age on his island.) Realizing that he had massacred the very baby daddy for whom he'd been searching, Telegonus opted to make amends.

Telegonus prepared Odysseus's body and brought it to his boat. Then, joined by Penelope and his half brother Telemachus, Telegonus sailed to the island of Aeaea, the home of his mother, Circe. On Circe's island, as always, things quickly got weird. Telegonus married his father's wife Penelope. And Telemachus married his father's lover Circe. And then, the witch Circe made all of them immortal. And that (according to Proclus, whoever he was) was the end of the *Telegony*, and the ancient Epic Cycle as a whole.

The *Telegony*, at first glance, sounds like subpar fan fiction, dashed out by a bargain-bin poet who didn't actually read the *Odyssey* very carefully. In it, the great hero is killed by a belligerent illegitimate son and then buried, of all places, on a remote island where he'd once had an ill-advised fling for a year with a witch. The Epic Cycle's ending, as it's come down to us, sounds random and unsuitable to the symmetry and relative consistency otherwise present in the Homeric epics.

And yet Proclus's summary of the *Telegony* is still worth taking seriously. The story of *two half brothers marrying each other's mothers* sounds *exactly* like the kind of folkloric nugget that ancient Greeks would have curated and adapted in poetry and plays. Sophocles's *Oedipus the King* chronicles a poor chump who kills his father and marries his mother, and the *Telegony*, along the same lines, tells of a man who kills his father and marries his *step*mother. The Olympian pantheon and their affiliates were a horde of inbred nymphomaniacs (pun intended), and so the deification of Odysseus's wife, lover, and sons in a zany erotic quadrangle would have fit right in with other stories that ancient Greeks told about the divine.

Beginnings and Endings in Ancient Greek Literature

We have different expectations about endings than ancient Greeks did. Before monotheism and the notion of Judgment Day, people in the polytheistic Mediterranean basin wrote stories that concluded where they concluded, with little concern for justice and loose ends. The *Iliad* breaks off with the Trojan War still broiling ominously. The *Odyssey* draws to a close by rather randomly telling us that Athena was still disguised as an old man named Mentor when she stopped the uprising on Ithaca. (Good to know, but again, an odd detail on which to end a twelve-thousand-line poem.) Seven hundred years after the *Odyssey*, Virgil ended the *Aeneid* with the protagonist stabbing the antagonist in the heart, with no denouement whatsoever. (Imagine Harry Potter climactically knifing Voldemort, and the credits rolling *just* as Voldemort screams with pain. It's *that* weird.) These endings are, again, out of accordance with what we expect when long sagas come to an end. But in the jolting suddenness with which ancient

Greece's and Rome's most famous stories end, there are important lessons for us about the past.

Modern audiences like clear beginnings, and we like endings with moral tidiness to them. In the Common Era, humanity became fond of deities that rewarded the good and punished the wicked, and singular gods that began and ended life on earth. The Homeric epics, however, were products of a world older than even the Old Testament, and they had a different way of looking at humanity's place in the cosmos. The god Apollo says it best in the *Iliad*. He describes humans as "pitiful creatures who like leaves on a tree / Flame briefly to life, eat the fruit of the fields, / Then wither and die" (Lombardo translation, 21.477–9). In the same epic and translation, a Trojan fighter observes that "human generations are like leaves in their seasons. / The wind blows them to the ground, but the tree / Sprouts new ones when spring comes again. / Men too. Their generations come and go" (6.149–52). The Homeric epics do not see human beings as precious souls, observed and cradled by an omnipresent deity, but instead as beautiful ephemera, present for a time and then gone for good. In the Homeric epics, humanity is a thing of tragic contradictions. We are magnificent, but fragile; brave, but bumbling; hopeful, but doomed. Like leaves, our generations come and go, and there is no systemic beginning nor ending to any of it, but instead a gorgeous and merciless continuity.

Greek mythology didn't bother much with beginnings and endings, then, because pagan antiquity saw time itself as a cyclical, continually unfolding thing that would never end. Odysseus was a multidimensional, crowd-pleasing dreadnought of a character, but he was also just a mortal, and whether he bit the dust peacefully or he was abruptly executed by an estranged bastard son, the ending would have been ordinary within the context of the literature of ancient Greece.

We Are Homer

The *Telegony* is worth knowing about, and it's good for a laugh. Next to Homer's *Odyssey*, though, the *Telegony* is an obscure, lost book alongside a colossus. And as big as that colossus is today, it's important to remember the roots of ancient Greece's most famous book. The *Odyssey*, as we learned in this guide's Introduction, was once a very long song. Its purpose was to be wondrous and entertaining—to bring audiences away from the routines of their everyday lives and into dazzling worlds of gods and wars, adventures and monsters. Homeric audiences have always been part of Homeric epics.

When bards like the Homeric Demodocus tuned up their lyres and began to sing, their listeners weren't watching performances in church-like silence, but instead laughing, crying, toasting, singing, and dancing according to the performance at hand. A performance in Archaic Greece, like a performance today, was an organism made up of both performers and audience members. From tens of thousands of unrecorded matinees and soirees in the ancient Mediterranean basin, the raw materials of the Homeric epics were alive and well and living in oral tradition by the year 800 BCE. A century or two later, they were set down in writing. A bard or bards got together with a scribe or scribes, or perhaps a bard who was also a scribe did the whole thing, but however it happened, the Homeric epics as we now know them were born from eons of talented singers plucking strings and telling tales, and audiences grinning, growing misty-eyed, and tossing tips.

Today, we have a romantic idea of artistry. We imagine poets as lonely individualists, dashing out stanzas, inspired by the muse of personal genius. We imagine artists as fraught figures, somehow slightly separated from society and thus in a position to comment upon it. We value originality, and artworks that endeavor to do what has never been done before. Ancient Greeks were different and, in many ways, wiser. They understood that cultural history is a long river, in which what seems new is more likely deft recycling. They understood that literature is created by civilizations as well as individuals. They understood that poets can be divas and show-men as well as introverted savants. They understood that audiences, foot-tapping and smiling and exchanging spellbound glances as a poet's breath brought tales to life and fire burned in braziers, were parts of poetry too. And, above all, they understood that literature, like all of humanity's great-est achievements, is a collective endeavor. To the age-old question of who wrote the Homeric epics, then, called the *quaestio Homerica* by specialists, there is an answer that is as simple as it is incontestable. We did. All of us. We are Homer. And we will keep telling stories about Odysseus and the gang until the lights go out.

FURTHER RESOURCES

Translations

Homer. *The Odyssey*. Translated and with an Introduction and Notes by Emily Wilson. W. W. Norton & Company, 2018.

> Emily Wilson's recent translation is already a classic. Known for its economy and clarity, the Wilson translation does away with some of the more convoluted aspects of Homeric language, using a lucid iambic pentameter to tell Odysseus's story. The Introduction, Notes, and Glossary, together with her accessible style, make this book not only an ideal introduction to Homer but also to classics more generally.

Homer. *The Odyssey*. Translated by Robert Fagles and with an Introduction and Notes by Bernard Knox. Penguin Classics, 1996.

> Robert Fagles (1933–2008) is one of the all-time great translators of classical literature. His rendition of the *Odyssey*, while in vibrant, readable modern English, also stays close to the strangeness and literary devices endemic to Homeric Greek. His collaborations with fellow classicist Bernard Knox (who writes the Introduction and Notes for this edition) have taught Homer to generations of readers.

Homer. *The Iliad*. Translated by Richard Lattimore and with an Introduction and Notes by Richard Martin. University of Chicago Press, 2011.

> The *Iliad* is where ancient Greek literature all begins. Richard Lattimore is known for faithfulness to Homer's original language and rhythm, and this rendition of the ancient Mediterranean's most blockbuster, action-packed war story gives you the closest thing you can get to reading the *Iliad* in Homeric Greek.

Virgil. *The Aeneid*. Translated by Frederick Ahl and with an Introduction by Elaine Fantham. Oxford University Press, 2007.

> The epic poem of Rome, Virgil's *Aeneid* begins with an *Odyssey*, or travel sequence, and concludes with an *Iliad*, or war story, carefully imitating Homer and the greater epic tradition. Sweeping, tragic, and gorgeously written, the *Aeneid* is a book everyone should read at least once.

Ovid. *Metamorphoses*. Translated by Charles Martin and with an Introduction by Bernard Knox. W. W. Norton & Company, 2005.

> When people talk about "ancient Greek myths," at least half of the time, what they're really talking about is Ovid's *Metamorphoses*, a Latin poem completed around 8 CE. With over 250 stories linked by the theme of transformation, the *Metamorphoses* was the most influential work of classical antiquity on the European Renaissance, and remains a delight to read in modern translations like Martin's.

Hesiod. *Theogony and Works and Days*. Translated by Kimberly Johnson. Northwestern World Classics, 2017.

> Hesiod was roughly a contemporary of Homer. His *Theogony* is the longest creation story to survive from ancient Greece. His *Works and Days* is a collection of myths and folk wisdom, showcasing a wry sense of humor and pragmatism that Homer's Eumaeus might have appreciated. Translator Kimberly Johnson is also a terrific poet, and her rendering of Hesiod's works brings his language to life in nuanced, beautiful English.

OTHER BOOKS

Mary Lefkowitz and James Romm, eds. *The Greek Plays: Sixteen Plays by Aeschylus, Sophocles, and Euripides*. Modern Library, 2017.

> After you finish the *Odyssey* and *Iliad*, it's time for ancient Greek theater! This anthology contains translations of the most celebrated Greek tragedies, including Aeschylus's *Oresteia*, Sophocles's three Theban plays, and Euripides's *Bacchae* and *Medea*. With excellent translations, Notes, and Introductions, this is the best single volume available on ancient Greek tragedy.

B.P. Reardon, ed. *Collected Ancient Greek Novels*. University of California Press, 2019.

> This book contains seven complete ancient Greek novels, all produced between about 50 and 350 CE, the most famous of which, today, are *Daphnis and Chloe* and the *Aethiopica*. While the *Odyssey* influenced later epics, it *also* influenced ancient Greek prose fiction, a genre of literature that is slowly becoming better known.

Robin Waterfield. *Creators, Conquerors, and Citizens: A History of Ancient Greece.* Oxford University Press, 2020.

> This single-volume overview of ancient Greek history and culture is a terrific gateway to the bygone Aegean world. Beginning around the time of Homer (750 BCE), the eminent classicist Robin Waterfield moves through the major phases and events of Greek civilization up until the end of the Hellenistic period in 31 BCE.

Sarah B. Pomeroy. *Goddesses, Whores, Wives, and Slaves: Women in Classical Antiquity.* Schocken Books, 1975.

> For all of us interested in the often-untold story of women in classical antiquity, Sarah Pomeroy's book is a classic. Focusing on women in the ancient Mediterranean, from pantheons of goddesses down to everyday life, Pomeroy explores how antiquity's second class lived and worked.

Thomas R. Martin. *Ancient Greece: From Prehistoric to Hellenistic Times.* Yale University Press, 1996.

> This short, illustrated volume is a fantastic introduction to ancient Greek history, going back a bit further in time than Waterfield's to discuss the Mycenaean world of the late Bronze Age, from whence the stories of the Homeric epics originally came.

OTHER RESOURCES

Literature and History Podcast

Doug Metzger, PhD, LiteratureandHistory.com

Literature and History is this book's author's podcast. The show covers Homer's *Odyssey* in detail, together with every work mentioned in this Further Resources section, and more. With an integrative approach to cultural history, the podcast begins with Sumerian cuneiform and then moves chronologically forward through ancient Mesopotamia, ancient Egypt, the Old Testament, Classical and Hellenistic Greece, ancient Rome, the New Testament, late antiquity, and early Islamic history, with literature of the Middle Ages soon to come. It's free, soundtracked, and peer-reviewed.

Ancient Greece Declassified Podcast

Dr. Lantern Jack, GreecePodcast.com

Ancient Greece Declassified is an interview-based program, hosted by a Princeton PhD in classics. Covering many aspects of ancient Greek and Roman history and culture, *AGD* has particularly strong content on ancient philosophy. Through engaging, accessible interviews with specialists in various fields, the host offers a fantastic window into the world of antiquity. The show also offers YouTube versions of many of its interviews.

Trojan War: The Podcast

Jeff Wright, TrojanWarPodcast.com

Storyteller Jeff Wright retells the tales of the *Iliad* and the *Odyssey* in two multi-part podcast sequences. A modern-day Homeric bard, Wright has a style that is fun and engaging but, at the same time, thorough and faithful to the material. Both of Wright's podcast sequences are terrific educational offerings for all ages.

In Our Time

BBC, BBC.co.uk/programmes/b006qykl

In Our Time is an educational interview series with more than one thousand episodes and is a long-standing pillar of educational audio. The program features panel interviews of experts on a variety of subjects, including many having to do with the ancient world. There are numerous offerings on ancient Greek culture and history.

Additional Citations

Aeschylus. *The Oresteia*. Translated by Robert Fagles. Penguin Books, 1979.

Homer. *The Iliad*. Translated by Caroline Alexander. HarperCollins, 2016.

Homer. *The Iliad*. Translated by Robert Fagles and with an Introduction and Notes by Bernard Knox. Penguin Books, 1990.

Homer. *Iliad*. Translated by Stanley Lombardo and with an Introduction by Sheila Murnaghan. Hackett Publishing Company, 1997.

Homer. *The Odyssey*. Translated by E.V. Rieu. Penguin Books, 1946.

Homer. *Odyssey*. Translated by Stanley Lombardo and with an Introduction by Sheila Murnaghan. Hackett Publishing Company, 2000.

INDEX